History Teaches Us to Resist

History Teaches Us to Resist

*How
Progressive
Movements
Have Succeeded
in
Challenging Times*

Mary Frances Berry

BEACON PRESS
BOSTON

BEACON PRESS
Boston, Massachusetts
www.beacon.org

Beacon Press books
are published under the auspices of
the Unitarian Universalist Association of Congregations.

21 20 19 18   8 7 6 5 4 3 2 1

This book is printed on acid-free paper that meets the uncoated paper
ANSI/NISO specifications for permanence as revised in 1992.

Text design and compostion by Kim Arney

In this work of nonfiction, which spans decades, the events are
portrayed to the best of the author's memory and records. Any factual
errors are the responsibility of the author.

Library of Congress Cataloging-in-Publication Data

Names: Berry, Mary Frances, author.
Title: History teaches us to resist : how progressive movements have
succeeded in challenging times / Mary Frances Berry.
Description: Boston : Beacon Press, [2018] | Includes bibliographical
references and index.
Identifiers: LCCN 2017030034 (print) | LCCN 2017053057 (ebook) |
ISBN 9780807005705 (e-book) | ISBN 9780807005460 (hardcover : alk. paper)
Subjects: LCSH: Protest movements—United States—History. | Government,
Resistance to—United States—History. | Political participation—United
States—History. | United States—Politics and government.
Classification: LCC HN57 (ebook) | LCC HN57 .B465 2018 (print) |
DDC 303.48/40973—dc23
LC record available at https://lccn.loc.gov/2017030034

In memory of Roger Wilkins

CONTENTS

History Lessons

WHEN HUNDREDS OF THOUSANDS of women, men, and children converged on Washington, DC, on January 21, 2017, the day after the inauguration of Donald Trump as president of the United States, they became part of a long protest tradition in the nation's capital. The tradition includes Coxey's Army demanding jobs for the unemployed during the economic crisis of 1894 to the Bonus Army of 1932 demanding payment of World War I pensions due to unemployed veterans. It also extends to the Poor People's Campaign and encampment on the National Mall in Washington, DC, after the 1968 assassination of Martin Luther King Jr. to the prochoice and antiabortion rallies of the late twentieth and early twenty-first centuries. Marches and other forms of protest, including street theater, and sharing complaints and organizing on social media have become a way to focus national attention on major social and political issues. And even when protests have resulted in uneven immediate success, they have raised important issues that often reverberated beyond the tactics utilized. However, the ease of communications and of organizing protest through social media can obscure the persistence and face-to-face contact necessary for staying organized and achieving policy change.[1]

History teaches us the value of resistance and protest. Women have fought for suffrage since at least 1848. But the 1913 march, marred by efforts to keep black women segregated at the rear, kicked off a series of protests, including hunger strikes, leading finally to the Nineteenth Amendment to the Constitution in 1920, which prohibited the denial of the vote because of sex. The Bonus marches got hustled away by troops led by General Douglas MacArthur, but in 1936, Congress overrode President Franklin D. Roosevelt's veto and paid the veterans the bonus they had sought nine years earlier.[2]

The despair, mourning, and fear that arise after the election of a president who promises devastation to causes supported by large numbers of people are painful and real. But it is also part of the push-pull of American politics. This is true whether the cause is gun rights on the one hand and gun control on the other. Trump's election has generated elation from his supporters and fear and loathing from those who believe that progressive change, whether on immigration, health care, or abortion rights, is at risk. But they should remember that resistance to presidential administrations has led to positive change and defeat of outrageous proposals even in perilous times. It is also worth noting that presidents considered progressive can require massive protest to induce policy decisions; Obama and the Indigenous peoples' protests against the Dakota Access Pipeline is one modern example of resistance built on earlier actions on specific issues.

It's crucial to recognize that resistance works even if it does not achieve all the movement's goals, and that movements are always necessary, because major change will engender resistance, which must be addressed.

In this book, I will examine several examples of resistance during presidential administrations, beginning with President Franklin Roosevelt, who refused to prevent race discrimination in the defense industry in World War II, despite massive unemployment. We will see how people involved in the protest used what they learned in later movements for progressive change.

The second example is Lyndon B. Johnson, another president who is often considered progressive; yet, while he responded to civil rights protests positively, he persisted in continuing the war in Vietnam. The antiwar protest movement was so effective that it influenced his decision not to seek another term. Richard Nixon (1968–1974) responded to the momentum generated by the continuing protests by concluding the war, which also ended the need for a draft.

Ronald Reagan's two terms offer more recent stories of courageous opposition to reactionary policies, such as ignoring the AIDS crisis and retreating on racial progress, and show how resistance can succeed. The pro-choice protests during the George H. W. Bush administration offer another example. There are other instructive stories of partial success and failure, such as opposition to Bill Clinton's "Don't Ask, Don't Tell" policy and his budget cuts and welfare reform and the protests against the war in Iraq and the Patriot Act during George W. Bush's presidency. The movement for

LGBTQ rights and the Dreamers (undocumented immigrants who came to the United States as small children) and other immigration protests are built on the style and methods of earlier efforts.

I was actively involved in some of these movements. I started as an antiwar protester as a student at the University of Michigan and then became an overseas correspondent, working as a "reporter" for local papers in order to go to Vietnam, where I saw the horrors of the war. My friend Joe Wildberger and I stood outside the White House after the Saturday Night Massacre, on October 20, 1973, yelling, "Resign! Resign!" as others who wanted to protest Nixon joined us. (The so-called massacre refers to Nixon's purge of the top leadership of the Justice Department to appoint an acting attorney general who would fire the special prosecutor, who was pursuing the release of the president's secret recordings.) I was later a member of the US Commission on Civil Rights and fired by President Reagan on October 25, 1983, for opposing his anti–civil rights policies. I won a lawsuit against him and continued until I was later appointed by President Clinton as chair of the commission. I was one of three antiapartheid protesters who started the Free South Africa movement in December 1984 and inspired nationwide protests. Two years later, US sanctions against the apartheid regime were enacted by Congress. My experiences confirm historical research—protest is an essential ingredient of politics and can effect change.

While researching the history of the movements described in this book, I have noticed some problems they have in common. Protesters sometimes have difficulty keeping to a simple goal, and complicated messaging inhibits growth. The March on Washington movement wanted FDR to order jobs for blacks in the defense industry. The Free South Africa movement wanted Congress to pass sanctions to end US business dealings with South Africa to help end apartheid: freedom, yes; apartheid, no. The anti–Vietnam War movement wanted to stop the war and end the draft.

If the goal is to educate the public about an issue, then idealism is its own reward. One example is Occupy Wall Street's effort in 2011 to elevate the income-inequality issue, while the press kept asking, What are the goals and who are your leaders? The more complicated the initiative, even a legislative one, the harder the work and the longer it takes to achieve success. The Civil Rights Act of 1991, remedying negative Supreme Court employment decisions, was too technical to easily explain on a poster and difficult to pass. It failed in 1990 and had to be restarted. Asking for jobs, while difficult, probably is simpler than obtaining real "freedom" or making "Black Lives Matter," which are both complicated and hard but necessary. Sometimes failure has reverberations. The confirmation fight over Clarence Thomas's nomination to the US Supreme Court helped achieve the Civil Rights Act of 1991, which was challenging to pass but vitally needed. Sometimes a movement must try what looks like desperate, last-minute protest to prevail, as when disability rights protesters in wheelchairs propelled the Americans with Disabilities Act across the congressional finish line by abandoning their chairs and crawling up the Capitol steps.

This book also shows that every growing movement uneasily incorporates newcomers who are attracted by some part of the message but don't agree with or understand the goal, or may feel they have a better idea. Sometimes they get bored and leave, other times they choose to either assimilate or be gently left behind. They may form their own movement. Thinking you've failed and becoming exhausted can lead to a radical spin-off, such as the Weathermen, a violent offshoot that arose after the seeming failure of the anti–Vietnam War movement, or the Black Power turn when the gains of the Southern civil rights movement didn't solve police brutality, economic inequity, and other problems of black people.

Also, the study of these movements shows some jealousy from established organizations that have not solved the problem but resent being what they regard as usurped by other organizations taking up their charge. Movement leaders should know that working with other organizations in coalitions toward overall goals has worked, once the fervor dies down. Figuring out the group dynamics is not always easy. The Free South Africa movement, for example, helped to end apartheid, but South Africa is still beset with economic inequality and corruption. Students for a Democratic Society (SDS) led the fight to end the Vietnam War, but when the organization dissolved, the people and groups it inspired carried on until the war ended. Then, there is the problem of seeking celebrity. Some people will join the movement and present themselves to the press as leaders for selfish reasons, including media coverage and speaker fees. They have to be politely denounced instead of embraced, because they may confuse the message and retard the movement's objectives. The surveillance problem is closely related, because sometimes celebrity seekers can give misleading information to official agencies that fear the changes proposed and make it appear that movement is engaged in suspicious activity. The Free South

Africa movement for the most part avoided this problem by having a small group of people who trusted each other make the day-to-day decisions about tactics and strategy. For complicated goals and longer time periods, exhaustion and other aspects of daily life may make this small-group approach impossible. But some way of keeping decisions close must be developed while not offending coalition members when coalitions are embraced.

Of course, no time period or issue is exactly like what has come before; other factors will have significance. Still, I do believe that history teaches us to resist, and I hope this analysis of several US resistance movements may provide useful information and guidance for our time.

CHAPTER 1

Franklin D. Roosevelt and the March on Washington Movement

Justice is never given; it is exacted. Freedom and justice must be struggled for by the oppressed of all lands and races, and the struggle must be continuous, for freedom is never a final fact, but a continuing evolving process.

—A. Philip Randolph[1]

THE 1941–1946 MARCH ON Washington movement (MOWM) was the first mass protest to force a civil rights change by the US government. A. Philip Randolph, whose experience as a labor leader inclined him toward the power of mass protest instead of individual action, envisioned this movement, which made possible the employment of blacks, who regardless of their qualifications had been totally excluded because of their race in the World War II defense industry.[2]

Franklin Roosevelt seemed like a sympathetic target. His amicability had helped him gain votes from blacks who had largely remained staunch Republicans since post–Civil War Reconstruction. Roosevelt, who made sure a few black reporters and delegates were conspicuously visible at the 1936 Democratic Convention, received 71 percent of the black vote in the general election.[3] After his 1936 reelection, FDR named the first black federal judge, William Hastie, to the Virgin Islands district. The president also officially denounced lynching and appeared publicly as comfortable with blacks as with everyone else. In addition, he appointed Mary McLeod Bethune as the highest black in his administration as the National Youth Administration's director of Negro affairs. She gathered a black cabinet, or brain trust, of people from inside and outside government who met weekly at her house to discuss how to address discrimination and opportunities for blacks. Eleanor Roosevelt listened to Bethune and to Walter White of the NAACP, and the First Lady had the president's ear. All this, with lukewarm black support for the war because of discrimination, led Randolph to believe that a positive response from the administration was possible.

Randolph's belief that FDR could be pushed to respond positively and would agree to the MOWM demand to issue an order ending defense-industry employment exclusion. But how and why Randolph and his cohorts prevailed has enduring significance and is instructive for those who wonder how to make politicians respond, whether "friends" or not. The March on Washington movement is a major example of how resistance to authority can achieve positive social change and lead to even more progress in the fullness of time. In fact, the entirety of their demands set the agenda for civil rights accomplishments over the next twenty-five years: from desegregation of the armed forces, in which Randolph played a major role, to the Civil Rights Act of 1957, the first enacted by the federal government since Reconstruction, through the Civil Rights Act of 1964 and beyond.

After issuing the call for the MOWM in 1941, Randolph was continuously engaged in activism and was a leader of the 1963 March on Washington. At a White House commemoration of the twenty-fifth anniversary of *Brown v. Board of Education* on May 17, 1979, at which I spoke as head of the federal education division, President Jimmy Carter publicly acknowledged news of Randolph's death the day before. The audience of civil rights advocates and government civil rights appointees knew he was not in good health and some had heard of his passing. But contemplating Randolph's legacy and how such an essential figure had almost disappeared from history already by that time was sobering. The president asked for a moment of silence and then summed up Randolph's accomplishments saying, "But what he gave us most of all was the power of his example, his great personal dignity, his absolute integrity, his eloquence, his unshakable commitment to justice and equal rights, combined with a remarkable gentleness and humanity and commitment to nonviolence. His values and his ideals have been the guiding spirit of the modern civil rights movement."[4]

Media and technology and other important developments have eased communication and some forms of movement organizing since the 1941 MOWM. And these advances also have made government surveillance, bent on stopping a movement, easier. Yet, as each new generation has taken up the antiracism cause, their protest activities have included similar demands, tactics, and rhetoric reminiscent of the 1941 movement. That is not surprising, because race discrimination continues, and ending it remains a clearly defined, overarching goal for many.

In addition to the employment demand, the 1941 march demanded the inclusion of African Americans in the benefits of the New Deal by ending discrimination in the military. The 1940 Selective Training and Service Act, which mandated a peacetime draft, prohibited excluding blacks from enlistment in the army but they would serve only in segregated units. Colonel Benjamin Davis, who had first served in the Spanish American War, his son, a lieutenant, and three chaplains were the only black officers in the entire US Army; there were no black pilots in the Army Air Corps and none in flying cadet programs. In the US Navy, blacks had long served only as messmen, and those men wore waiters' uniforms on the job.

As the March on Washington movement got underway, generally the work was done mainly by local people and "followers," especially women. This had also been true in earlier African American social movements such as the "Don't Buy Where You Can't Work" campaigns in major Northern US cities, and it was true later in the Southern civil rights movement of the 1950s and '60s. While the importance of women in these movements has gained some recognition, more work is needed to better appreciate their crucial role.[5]

Ella Baker, the NAACP and Southern Christian Leadership Conference stalwart and midwife to the Student Nonviolent Coordinating Committee protesters, has correctly insisted that for any movement to be effective leadership must be built among the masses. As she put it, "Instead of 'the leader' as . . . a 'magic man,' you could develop individuals who were bound together by a concept that benefitted larger numbers of individuals and provided an opportunity for them to grow into being responsible for carrying on the program."[6] Notably, Baker spent her time organizing, counseling, and inspiring and hardly ever appeared in the media.

Though Baker was correct, the MOWM reinforced another essential truth. While certainly followers, grassroots, structure, and administrative work are necessary as ingredients of struggle, charismatic leadership is also necessary to ignite and sustain movements. For the MOWM, the charismatic leader was A. Philip Randolph. He could inspire by his very bearing and oratory, as he had done in using arguments and charisma to persuade initially reluctant railroad porters to do what they needed to do to improve their working conditions and pay by forming a union. Randolph's committed base, the Brotherhood of Sleeping Car Porters and Maids (BSCP), a predominantly African American labor union founded in 1925, was in 1937 the first independent union organized and led by African Americans to force a multinational corporation, the Pullman Palace Car Company, to negotiate a labor contract. The union members' struggle was long and hard, and in the end, Roosevelt's legislation permitting workers to unionize, the National Labor Relations Act, was upheld by the Supreme Court in 1937. It meant that Pullman's strategy of ignoring the union became illegal. In recognition, the BSCP was admitted as a full member to the American Federation of Labor, and Randolph became the first African American union president in the AFL. The BSCP, which once boasted a membership of eighteen thousand passenger railway workers from Canada to Mexico, declined in the 1960s; in 1978, its remaining one thousand members merged with its former adversary, the Brotherhood of Airline and Railway Clerks, which had a long history of discrimination before the passage of the 1964 Civil Rights Act.

From the beginning, in 1867, Pullman's luxurious "hotels on wheels" employed African American men, primarily formerly enslaved house servants from the South, to serve its white sleeping-car passengers. By 1900, Pullman was the largest single employer of African Americans in North America, claiming itself as a benevolent father. Pullman porters were called the "aristocrats" of black labor, because they wore blue uniforms and ties rather than the denims and bandanas of packinghouse workers and agricultural peons. But behind the minstrel mask of the "Porters' Blues" was industrialized racial servitude: omnipresent supervision, four-hundred-hour work months, lives dependent on tips from passengers, and jobs deemed "fit" only for black people. The contract and union recognition made all the difference to the porters.

Now Randolph was conceiving how those lessons and successes could have a broad future impact. The reaction of FDR and his administration to the grievances blacks were expressing about continued joblessness and race discrimination led Randolph to ultimately conclude that his concerns required a march on Washington. Raised hopes followed by deceptive and dismissive treatment by the president left Randolph questioning whether polite entreaties would be effective. In what happened we can see patterns that appear when political officeholders perceive that resistance is palpable and publicized widely.

After NAACP head Walter White had been put off in his attempts to schedule a meeting with the president, Eleanor Roosevelt put a meeting on FDR's schedule for September 27, five weeks before the November 1940 election. Mary McLeod Bethune had told her for months about black discontent with continued segregation in the military. When she accepted an invitation to speak at a BSCP meeting, the First Lady listened as Walter White and Randolph spoke about the subject to wide applause. Republican Wendell Willkie was a formidable challenger, and the president needed black votes.

White had met with the president before, but this was Randolph's first exposure to the president's charm and ability to evade unpleasant discussion. They brought a discussion memorandum focusing on an order to desegregate the military. They didn't know that the president was secretly recording them through a system that had been installed in August after he was misquoted in a press conference. At the time of their meeting, he had just had a press conference and the system, perhaps deliberately, had not been turned off. After a warm discussion, Randolph assumed the president would make a positive announcement about an expanded role for blacks in the services. The delegation went away and kept quiet about the meeting while waiting for the president to say something clearly supportive. Nothing happened—and after realizing FDR also needed white segregationist votes to win reelection in November, they understood why. On October 9, the White House issued a statement rejecting their demands and reinforcing the policy "not to intermingle colored and white enlisted personnel in the same regimental organizations."[7]

The black press's reaction to FDR's rejection of the group's demands was swift and visceral. The *Baltimore Afro-American* denounced the black leaders as appearing to condone segregation. Roosevelt deflected Wendell Willkie's attempt to take advantage of his predicament with black voters by showcasing an endorsement by heavyweight champion Joe Louis, making campaign promises to include blacks in his administration, and appointing sixty-two-year-old Colonel Benjamin Davis a brigadier general in the segregated army. The president also announced that Judge Hastie would serve as a civilian aide to Secretary of War Stimson, and in addition named a black assistant to the Selective Service director. President Roosevelt received two-thirds of the black vote in winning reelection.[8]

Stung by Roosevelt's rejection and the press's reaction, Randolph pondered measures that might motivate the president to act. In December 1940, on a train ride through the South during which he stopped to visit Brotherhood chapters, he told Milton Webster, the first vice president of the Brotherhood and his right-hand man, that he had an idea. A march with a broad civil rights agenda, including jobs in the defense industry and desegregation of the military, would give the despondent masses something to work toward and might make FDR respond.

Randolph thought that a march of, say, ten thousand blacks "would wake up and shock official Washington as it had never been shocked before."[9] He announced the strategy publicly at a stop in Savannah, Georgia, on January 25, 1941. In his wake, longtime BSCP organizer and soon-to-be St. Louis MOWM chair T. D. McNeal stayed in each city after Randolph left to "work up Negroes to come to Washington on July 1" for the nascent demonstration. Chapters quickly developed in northern and midwestern cities. In Harlem, according to Milton Webster, African Americans openly wore MOWM buttons, distributed by supporters through local organizations, and African Americans nationwide talked up the planned protest. The movement had southern branches in Norfolk, Virginia; Jacksonville, Florida; Montgomery, Alabama; and other sites where BSCP had a strong presence. As organizers focusing on other issues, including antilynching campaigns and the ex-slave pension movement, had discovered, violence and intimidation made it hard to organize in much of the South.

Randolph's message was simple: "The future of the Negro depends entirely upon his own action, and the individual cannot act alone."[10] Group organization and protest could defeat racial inequality. They should organize blacks to carry the fight alone in their own interests. Randolph laid the groundwork for grassroots activists to use the MOWM to fight local battles in their towns and cities.

Benjamin McLaurin, a St. Louis porter and international union vice president who shared the podium with Randolph when the idea was publicly announced, recalled that he and others who heard it were initially "scared," but the audiences responded enthusiastically, and the idea caught on as a way to end Jim Crow at a time of worldwide instability. Walter White and others had described World War II as a rationale for positive change toward racial inclusion, but they remained mainly inside players who were slow to act while Randolph, in contrast, seized the opportunity.

The times were auspicious and the equation logical for the threat of a march to work. Not only did the defense industry have worker shortages because of war mobilization, but black unemployment was also horrific. In addition to economic considerations, politically, the New Deal's domestic policies were supposedly about relieving inequality, and the president's "Four Freedoms" speech on January 6, 1941, included freedom from want.

Randolph's Brotherhood had available an initial structure and workers when he issued the 1941 call for the march and designated July 1, 1941, as the day for thousands of blacks to come to the Lincoln Memorial on the National Mall. He had six months to make good on his threat. And he had not only the sleeping car porters but also their wives in the Ladies Auxiliary and their other friends and relations who would get the work started. He grew the movement by traveling widely to raise money, gain publicity, inspire the masses, conveying an undaunted assurance that the march would happen and succeed in its goals.

The logistical planning was complicated by racial segregation in accommodations and transportation. Chartering buses and restaurant arrangements that became familiar twenty years later in the 1963 March on Washington for Jobs and Freedom, and are routine today, presented entrenched and difficult challenges nearly two decades before the modern civil rights movement. Rosina Tucker, international secretary-treasurer of the Ladies Auxiliary of the Brotherhood, and other union wives canvassed Washington, DC, churches for volunteers, food, and facilities for the marchers when they arrived in Washington. White House staff were as cognizant, or more, as the MOWM organizers of the difficulty of crowd control if thousands of blacks showed up in the city to protest. The organizers wanted to avoid an encampment like the earlier Bonus Army protesters, who in 1932 were run off by the army, by having a one-day show of commitment and strength with thousands of black people there on the mall.

Randolph and his Brotherhood base received indispensable help planning the march from the NAACP, the Urban League, and other organizations. The leaders of these groups worried that Randolph's insistence that blacks must fight for themselves and constitute the body of protesters would alienate white donors and supporters, but they also didn't want to be on the wrong side of the black masses. Walter White's endorsement gave Randolph access to NAACP chapters and members nationwide. Official NAACP involvement was helped by Randolph's making clear this was just one event and not the development of a competing organization. Washington, DC, MOWM member Thurman Dodson gave central logistical support, producing a block plan with each block captain responsible for recruiting ten or more protesters. This process alone could increase the numbers to at least five thousand.

Randolph focused on maintaining a clean public image for the march and preventing violence. The admonitions he issued are familiar ones in marches and protests since. He asked for pointed but not defamatory signs and banners, a ban on drinking alcoholic beverages, and enlisting deputy inspectors from MOWM to control the crowd. The detailed instructions reinforced the seriousness of purpose and the real intention to march. He and the other organizers wanted to make sure the protest was dignified and respectable.

The Roosevelt administration, like administrations before and after when protests are afoot, was vaguely aware of the planned MOWM for months but only seriously tracked it as its occurrence seemed increasingly likely. My history professor at Howard University, Rayford Logan, was one of the "Negro brain trust" of advisers organized by Bethune. He told us years later about going to the White House for an increased number of meetings as the time for the march neared.

In June 1941, as it became clear that blacks widely supported coming to Washington, the administration attempted a standard administration ploy of suggesting a governmental body to investigate and make recommendations concerning the demands. The administration wanted to find a way to employ blacks to expand defense production, mollify protesters, and achieve it all without having to enforce desegregation, in order to avoid offending the racists and segregationists in Congress. The way forward for the administration seemed to be taking the least amount of action against racial segregation necessary to remove interference with the war mobilization.

What occurred next was what the legal scholar Derrick Bell would have called a convergence of interests. The administration believed that addressing the MOWM employment demand would be an effective resolution for both sides. So, in June 1941, Joseph Rauh, a young New Deal attorney, was called in to draft a fair employment executive order. His boss, Wayne Coy, in the Lend-Lease program, was politically close to the president and told him the order would stop the threat of a march on Washington. Over the next eighteen hours, Rauh worked on successive drafts of what became the Executive Order 8802. He didn't know much about Randolph or the MOWM at that point, but he understood that the threat of a march "had scared the government half to death." Rauh later became Randolph's lawyer. Thereafter, when he was in a storytelling mood, Rauh concluded that FDR issued the order for "pragmatic" reasons, to maintain order and not because he had any genuine interest in the plight of black workers.[11]

Since FDR only used the taping system from August to November 1940, there is no record of the June 18, 1941, afternoon meeting at which Walter White, Randolph, and other black leaders met to review and ultimately agree to Rauh's work. It became Executive Order 8802. Years later, Rayford Logan told his students, including me, that other important persons, including Lester Granger, who had taken over the Urban League in 1941, were at the meeting. In a later speech, Randolph named administration officials who were there, including Secretary of War Henry Stimson, Secretary of the Navy Frank Knox, William Knudson and Sidney Hillman of the Office of Production Management, Aubrey Williams from the National Youth Administration, and Anna Rosenberg from the Social Security Board—all of whom supported Roosevelt in urging Randolph to cancel the march. Mary Bethune, who officially worked for Williams, was not noted as present.

Before the meeting, Eleanor Roosevelt warned Randolph that following through with the demonstration could precipitate a reactionary rollback of unspecified civil rights gains that she attributed to her husband's administration. FDR thought a march threatened national security and the Democratic Party's balance between Southerners and Northerners, segregationists and antiracists. He was prepared to do something, minimally, to stop it.

New York mayor Fiorello La Guardia agreed with Eleanor Roosevelt that the march should not take place and that the president should take some public action to defuse it. He began conversations with black leaders in New York to stop it.

In January 1941, Walter White had already used his access to ask the president to support legislation assigning eight senators to investigate the participation of black citizens in all industrial and other phases of the national defense program with no enforcement mechanism. White knew

the Southern-controlled Senate wouldn't pass it, but it would send a pow-
erful signal and could be justified as a war measure. In fact, the Barbour
Resolution (S. Res. 75) formed the basis for the Fair Employment Practices Committee (FEPC) created by the executive order that Joe Rauh
had frantically written to stop the march, with civilians instead of senators composing the committee.

Randolph and his threat did in fact shape policy. Joe Rauh's impression—
that the government moved pragmatically out of fear of disorder—was reality. Aubrey Williams of the National Youth Administration telegraphed
Eleanor Roosevelt at Campobello, Maine, to inform her of Randolph's acceptance of Executive Order 8802, saying simply, "Executive order concerning the Randolph situation was signed today." When the order was signed,
Mary McLeod Bethune and others in the administration praised the president's action and Randolph's work at the rallies Randolph had organized to
implement the order.

The NAACP was conducting a campaign to educate the public and
the president about the impact of racial discrimination on African American support for the war. The combination of ongoing pressure from Randolph and White had an effect, but clearly it was not until the March on
Washington grew more likely that the executive order came to fruition.

The forty-five-minute meeting at which the executive order was agreed
to was preceded by at least one meeting in which Mayor La Guardia discussed his efforts to prime Randolph to accept the order. At the meeting on
June 18, 1941, Randolph had to weigh whether he could produce enough
protesters and if the logistics would work, on the one hand, over against
calling off the march and accepting the order on the other. What he agreed
to left some demands unmet: a prohibition of discrimination in industrial
training courses, an end to segregation in all aspects of the civilian federal
government and armed forces, and amending the National Labor Relations
Act to bar union exclusion of blacks by practice or by constitution. A provision requiring employers to hire workers in order of their draft registration number, thus obviating racial discrimination in hiring, was deferred
after the discussion at the meeting. Indeed, calling off the march with only
one major issue addressed, left MOWM branches and Randolph and the
Brotherhood with much work left to do.

Randolph's experience with proposing the march and FDR's response
taught several lessons. One was how smart it was to minimize logistical

problems by calling the march for a single day. Another was the importance of timing. The war, the "Four Freedoms" speech, and the political situation of the president in the 1940 presidential election all played a role.

Some critics thought Randolph should have gone ahead with the march; others used the chapters to work on issues in their community, with varying degrees of success. Randolph and the national MOWM worked to implement the executive order, and Randolph started a movement to desegregate the military. He believed that segregated job categories in the military only reinforced segregation in civilian occupations. Not until Harry Truman's Civil Rights Committee recommendations were accepted by that president did those efforts gain a degree of success. With the Korean War, enforcement of desegregation finally began.

In the meantime, Randolph interpreted Executive Order 8802 as a step toward the larger mission of eradicating racism in federal hiring practices. At his public explanation for canceling the march, Randolph closed with a call for local branches to "remain intact in order to watch and check how industries are observing the executive order."[12] This was salient advice, because even with the executive order, enforcement was lax and inclusion in employment was slow and uneven. However, the number of African American civil servants tripled during the war and the number of African Americans in defense industries rose from 8.4 percent to 12.5 percent. Randolph and others recognized that what they achieved wouldn't end racial inequality, but it was the best response they could get at the time. Historian Melinda Chateauvert concluded that "to African Americans, the Executive Order symbolized the president's willingness to act on issues of racial justice."[13]

After the march was cancelled, Randolph was no longer front-page news in the black press. But the 1943 riots in Chicago and Harlem showed the relevancy of Randolph's new campaign, "We ARE Americans Too." Using the civil disobedience work of the Fellowship of Reconciliation (FOR), a pacifist organization founded in 1915 to which many Christian reformers belonged, Randolph decided on a massive civil disobedience campaign attacking racial segregation and inequality generally. E. Pauline Myers, short-term executive director of the MOWM, planned "nonviolent goodwill direct action," a trademark protest technique developed and implemented alongside FOR. They held major rallies in New York, Chicago, and St. Louis attended by large numbers of people. The organizers put

Randolph last on the program, which was a waste, because everyone else spoke too long and after five hours audience enthusiasm had waned.

The rallies and conferences led the NAACP to wonder if Randolph was trying to make MOWM a permanent organization, which Walter White feared would be a competitor. Though he stopped working with Randolph, some local chapters continued to do so, and some individuals were members of the MOWM and the NAACP.

Between 1941 and 1945, local affiliates of MOWM continued to function in Harlem and other cities, most notably Chicago, Detroit, and St. Louis. These were sites of long-standing Brotherhood of Sleeping Car Porters chapters. Some local affiliates—for example, St. Louis—did great work monitoring and insisting on employers' enforcement of the executive order. They had protests, held meetings and marches, and applied constant pressure. MOWM put the pressure on to gain an FEPC office in St. Louis and then marched on arms manufacturing plants to open the defense industry. They also worked on local issues: picketing utility companies and conducting lunch counter sit-ins in the downtown business section to look for economic opportunity even beyond the end of the war.

After Randolph called off the March on Washington, he worked to inspire support for the admittedly weak FEPC, as it began hearings in 1942, and to push for enforcement of the executive order. The MOWM chapters scheduled summertime rallies in major cities to lift the spirit of the grassroots. The rallies focused on patriotism and included militant songs, theatrical performances, and religious speeches. In St. Louis, on a rainy Sunday in October, nine thousand advocates rallied, and about two thousand demonstrators showed up for a mass prayer protest held in the city's downtown.[14]

Randolph organized a meeting in New York along the same lines, with an additional focus on the lynching of two fourteen-year-old boys from Shubuta, Mississippi, which had nearly coincided with the St. Louis prayer meeting. His relationship with local ministers and highlighting the religious aspects of the struggle stood him in good stead in later work with Martin Luther King Jr. and the Southern Christian Leadership Conference (SCLC).[15]

Randolph also planned to hold a national MOWM convention in Chicago in May of 1943. He began to work with the Congress of Racial Equality (CORE) and FOR and to clearly advocate nonviolent direct action in his speeches, though the country was still at war. By the time the Montgomery bus boycott and subsequent civil rights protests, rooted in nonviolence, came to the fore, he was already experienced with the approach.[16]

Despite Randolph's efforts, calling off the 1941 march meant that the MOWM still lagged, except in places where the branches were strong, as in St. Louis. In 1943, Randolph tried another revival strategy. He hired Anna Arnold Hedgeman as executive secretary of a racially integrated National Council for a Permanent FEPC to work toward strengthening the wartime FEPC through a fair employment practices law. Hedgeman chaired the membership committee of the New York MOWM while being employed in the New York Area Office of Civil Defense. With five adult male staff, and one male starting in 1944 as the youth representative, the National Council for a Permanent FEPC sought to implement Randolph's plans and make sure local branches followed through.[17]

The subordinate role assigned to Hedgeman and to regional leaders, most of whom were women, perpetuated on a national scale the gender-based conflicts experienced in other MOWM work. Nonetheless, Randolph delegated an increasing amount of work to Hedgeman without giving her executive authority or financial resources. By January 1946, she told him it was impossible to meet all his demands, though she had recruited volunteer clerks from the Women's Army Corps to help with the work.

Eventually Hedgeman threatened to resign and terminate the entire Washington staff. Instead of accepting the blame for the difficulties, Randolph and the council's executive committee replaced Hedgeman and her white female assistant, Sidney Wilkerson, with two men, with higher annual salaries (and job titles) than any of the women had. Hedgeman and her staff formally resigned.

To compound the problem, before they received their back wages, the women had to go public in the press and announce a picket at a mass protest Randolph was planning to promote the FEPC. Randolph never acknowledged the problems and that the men were not able to gain the enactment of a permanent FEPC either. A federal Equal Employment Opportunity Commission did not become a reality until the Civil Rights Act of 1964, after the 1963 March on Washington.

Randolph had left desegregation of the armed forces on the table when he called off the 1941 march, when Roosevelt agreed to Executive Order 8802. He had raised the issue in a September 1940 meeting, and subsequently American Civil Liberties Union attorney Arthur Garfield Hays, but not the organization, represented Winfred Lynn, a New York landscape gardener in opposition to a segregated draft. The NAACP had refused to take the case, not willing to stir controversy in wartime. Lynn lost in the federal district court in December 1942 and in the court of appeals in February 1944.

Meanwhile blacks were drafted into the war, but like my cousins Joe Willie, John Charlie, Henry, and Wesley, they served as cooks and other support troops for the white soldiers and not in combat alongside them. This didn't mean they couldn't get fired upon like navy messman Dorie Miller, who killed Japanese with antiaircraft fire from the deck of the battleship *West Virginia* at Pearl Harbor, or my cousin Joe Willie, who came home severely wounded from service in the Pacific. Despite the segregation policy, when allied soldiers needed help fending off the Germans in the December 1944 Battle of the Bulge, the US Army blacks responded in great numbers to a request that they volunteer for combat. They joined in stopping the German offensive. The public relations effect of their bravery helped Randolph's continuous effort to find a way to end segregation in the military.[18]

In December 1946 President Harry S. Truman appointed the President's Committee on Civil Rights, which Randolph hoped would address the military service issue. As the committee worked on their report, in the summer of 1947, Truman asked Congress to pass a Universal Military Training proposal. It would require every male between the ages of eighteen and twenty to receive reserve force training for one year, subject to active duty thereafter, if necessary. In response, Randolph and black New York Republican Grant Reynolds formed the Committee Against Jim Crow in Military Service and Training.

In October 1947, when the president's committee report was announced, it included a recommendation to end racial separation in the armed forces. Randolph, fearful because despite the recommendation, the Universal Military Training bill in Congress still included segregation, asked the president for a meeting to discuss the bill. After his first request for a meeting was turned down, Randolph wrote again a month later. This time, Truman's administrative assistant, David Niles, suggested the president should hold the meeting since "Phil Randolph, the signer of this letter, is an important Negro. He is the head of the Negro Pullman Porters

Union, and is not a left-winger."[19] President Truman agreed, but only after his message on civil rights was sent to the Congress, so that the Committee to End Jim Crow couldn't claim credit.[20]

In February 1948, when Truman sent the civil rights message to Congress, he supported the other recommendations of the committee, but not military service desegregation. Instead, he simply instructed the defense secretary to make inquiries about discrimination in the military. The president met with Randolph and other black leaders on March 22. After some pleasantries, Randolph blasted Truman for leaving desegregation of the armed forces out of his message. The group then asked the president to issue an executive order ending segregation in the armed forces. As abruptly as FDR had ended the meeting on the March on Washington threat, Truman ended his meeting. Randolph left Truman a memorandum asking for an antisegregation amendment and civil rights safeguards in any Universal Military Training bill or Selective Service bill, to end segregation by executive order and to end the abuse and unequal treatment of black soldiers.

Instead of repeating his mistake after the first meeting with FDR—when he remained quiet, said nothing publicly, and waited for what he hoped was a presidential announcement, which when it came was negative—this time Randolph kept applying pressure. A few days later, as he and Grant Reynolds testified before the Senate Armed Services Committee, Randolph asserted that blacks would "choose imprisonment in preference to permanent military slavery." Unless race discrimination was outlawed in the proposed Universal Military Training bill, he personally pledged to help anyone evade a Jim Crow draft. Asked if he understood there might be indictments for treason, Randolph answered, "We would be willing . . . to face the music and to take whatever comes, and we, as a matter of fact, consider that we are more loyal to our country than the people who perpetrate segregation and discrimination upon Negroes because of color or race."[21]

In April, Secretary of Defense James V. Forrestal tried to co-opt and defuse the issue by calling a meeting of black leaders on how blacks could be used by the armed forces. The black leaders did not feel it was useful to talk about how to best use the services of blacks in the armed forces if the military was still segregated and would not denounce Randolph and Reynolds, who were not at the meeting. On May 7, 1948, Randolph marched with eight other protesters at the White House, carrying a sign saying "If we must die for our country let us die as free men—not as Jim Crow slaves."

When the debate over the draft bill continued without progress, Randolph gained reassurance in continuing his protest when the Youth Division of the NAACP poll of draft-age college men reported that 50 percent said they would serve their country in an emergency only if segregation was ended. When the draft act became law in June 1948 without prohibiting discrimination, Randolph organized protests in Harlem and major cities around the country.

He wrote the president that he was "morally obligated" to issue a desegregation executive order. Otherwise, "unless this is done, Negro youth will have no alternative but to resist a law, the inevitable consequences of which would be to expose them to the un-American brutality so familiar during the last war."[22]

Randolph wrote again to the president asking for action and then led a picket line outside the Democratic National Convention in Philadelphia, carrying a sign saying "Prison Is Better Than Jim Crow Service." In his acceptance speech on July 15, 1948, Truman announced he was calling Congress back into session on July 26 to pass laws on economic matters and civil rights legislation.

Randolph kept up the pressure. He wrote to the president that day, saying he was pleased but wanted to make sure the laws addressed antilynching and other protections for black draftees, and that those who refused to be drafted would not face imprisonment. He also still wanted that executive order.

On July 26, 1948, the president signed Executive Order 9981. It provided "that there shall be equality of treatment without regard to race, color, religion, or national origin" in the military. The policy would be put into place as quickly as possible, "without impairing efficiency or morale."[23]

After years of seeing how the details in political and labor agreements matter, Randolph sought assurances about the language to be used and steps to be taken going forward. He used what he had learned in years of activism and the labor movement. Satisfied, on August 18, 1948, A. Philip Randolph and Grant Reynolds called off their nonviolent civil disobedience. The Korean War accelerated the desegregation process. Randolph had worked successfully with other groups, had kept up the pressure, had stood firm despite criticism, had used media and direct action, had taken risks, had negotiated terms, and in the end had helped to achieve what African Americans wanted: desegregation of the armed forces.

In October 1949, the NAACP's National Emergency Rights Committee invited sixty civil rights, labor, religious, and civil liberties advocacy organizations to form a National Emergency Civil Rights Mobilization that would lobby for the issues the different groups wanted Congress to legislate. The list included Randolph's Permanent Fair Employment Practices Committee. About four thousand representatives showed up and spent three days in January lobbying Congress. They also agreed to form a coalition called the Leadership Conference on Civil Rights (LCCR) to lobby for civil rights laws, monitor compliance, and coordinate national legislative strategies for the entire civil and human rights community. Randolph, Roy Wilkins, who was executive director of the NAACP, and Arnold Aronson, program director of the National Jewish Community Relations Advisory Council, a coalition of major Jewish organizations, were the founders and coleaders of the LCCR. The coalition from then on coordinated legislative strategies on every civil rights bill that passed Congress from 1957 to the present.[24]

When the newly organized SCLC made its first national appearance at the May 17, 1957, Prayer Pilgrimage to Washington, which was the third anniversary of the *Brown v. Board of Education* decision, Randolph was a key organizer. Its purpose was to protest massive violent opposition to desegregation in the South and to expose racial injustice. The tensions in organizing the march arose from NAACP fears that King and the SCLC might undermine their leadership position on civil rights. Randolph, the elder statesman respected by almost everyone, acted as conciliator. He had learned that coalitions were the way to move forward. He got King and Wilkins to cochair with him, with Ella Baker and Bayard Rustin handling logistics and coordination.

The march, like the rallies Randolph had organized for MOWM and the Permanent FEPC campaign, were carefully patriotic to avoid red-baiting. When challenged about communist influence, they cited the call for the march they had issued in answer to media inquiries, noting, "No Communists have or will be invited to participate in the program either as a speaker singer, prayer leader, or scripture leader."[25] The event was a success. About twenty-five thousand people marched and rallied. Soon thereafter, President Eisenhower met with the civil rights leaders and introduced the Civil Rights Act of 1957, which, though weak, was the first civil rights act passed since Reconstruction.

The sit-ins and marches led by SCLC and the Student Nonviolent Coordinating Committee (SNCC) took center stage in the late 1950s and early 1960s, while Randolph remained a respected elder statesmen and functioning member of the LCCR coalition. He regularly called out discrimination in the labor movement, even though he was heckled and shouted down when he spoke at meetings. When the 1963 March on Washington needed executing, he was the only leader whom the other leaders uniformly trusted.

In 1959, disgusted with continued discrimination in the labor movement, Randolph organized the Negro American Labor Council to take on the AFL-CIO. Founded in 1960, the council joined with the SCLC in the late 1960s to organize workers in Baltimore and Memphis. It had some success until, in the late 1960s, it was overtaken by black nationalist movements and organizations like the League of Revolutionary Black Workers and the Dodge Revolutionary Union Movement (DRUM). In 1972, the Negro American Labor Council was entirely superseded by the founding of the Coalition of Black Trade Unionists.

Randolph had learned to use talented people to advance a cause whether they disagreed or had misunderstandings. Despite the Permanent FEPC experience, Anna Hedgeman kept close ties with Randolph and other black leaders as she remained a successful activist in New York. Randolph asked her to join the administrative committee to work with Bayard Rustin for the 1963 March on Washington for Jobs and Freedom. She took responsibility for making sure whites participated, and she is credited with bringing in forty thousand participants, consisting mostly of white marchers.[26]

Hedgeman tried to persuade Randolph and the men to permit a woman to speak at the march. She sent Randolph a memo pointing out the central role women played in the struggle, noting that a woman should be included in the march leadership, but that request went unacknowledged. Though Whitney Young, the new head of the Urban League, was included in the "Big Six," a group of six national civil rights leaders, the League was not instrumental in the Southern Freedom movement. Dorothy Height and the National Council of Negro Women had started several programs, given financial support to ten educational and recreational centers for African American children in Prince Edward County, Virginia, where all the public schools had been closed to prevent desegregation. Though Height was sometimes the only woman included among the most prominent civil rights leaders, the council was not listed in the program.

Hedgeman asked Randolph to let Medgar Evers's widow, Myrlie Evers, speak. He didn't answer her letter until she sent copies to the other civil rights leaders and raised $15,000 for the march. Randolph then agreed to let a woman give a "Tribute to Women" and introduce the female platform guests. The tribute was given by NAACP leader Daisy Bates, who shepherded the Little Rock Nine when Myrlie Evers could not attend. The tribute named Rosa Parks; Diane Nash, leader of the Nashville demonstrations and savior of the Freedom Rides; and others, but none of the women was permitted to speak. Lena Horne tried to interest television reporters in interviewing Rosa Parks, but the march leaders sent Parks back to her hotel in a taxi.[27]

The organizers in 1963 learned from Randolph and each other about how to implement a successful march on Washington. The threatened March on Washington in 1941 reinforced the effectiveness of a one-day march and keeping the logistics simple. The 1963 march would also have a simple goal and theme.

A. Philip Randolph's enduring significance is that he knew what to do at the right time, and did it.

CHAPTER 2

The Movement Against the Vietnam War

I saw the tiredness and anguish in the eyes of our "grunts" on the ground and some asked me why they were there. I saw the plight of the refugees who tried to climb in our helicopters or Caribou aircraft when we took off near villages. I saw the Viet Cong owned the night and sometimes the day. I saw the fruitlessness, casualties mounting in what could be called victory.

—Author's personal diary, August 1967 near Pleiku, Vietnam

BY THE SUMMER OF 1967, about a half million American military were in Vietnam; about twenty thousand US servicemen had been killed and even higher numbers wounded. Further, thousands of South Vietnamese had been killed and wounded, including noncombatants, and many others had been reduced to refugee status. The havoc wreaked was horrendous. But the protests against the war arose not because of the increasing number of casualties but from the sense that the Vietnam War was an unnecessary war. It was, for many, a mistake that irrevocably changed the lives of the young people who served and their families. The lives of the draft-eligible men changed too, even those who managed to obtain deferments by crowding into colleges and universities or who fled to Canada.

I had become increasingly concerned about the war, which disproportionately sent young blacks into battle and seemed to have no rationale except extending US imperialism. The antiwar movement on campus had heated up considerably since 1964 with the acceleration of American involvement. Martin Luther King Jr.'s Riverside Church speech, "Beyond Vietnam: A Time to Break Silence," on April 4, 1967, when he talked about the diversion of funds from fighting poverty to funding the Vietnam War, strengthened my resolve to participate in protests and help bring it to an end. I was a graduate student and antiwar protester at the University of Michigan and realized the only way to truly understand the conflict was to witness it firsthand, and so I went to Vietnam that summer to see the war for myself. I persuaded the campus paper, the *Michigan Daily*, and enough local newspapers to constitute the one hundred thousand subscribers I needed for Defense Department press credentials. By this time, protests against the war had increased exponentially and even Secretary of Defense Robert McNamara's son at Stanford University was an antiwar activist.

I saw no news reporters attached to a particular military unit, no "embeds," when I went throughout South Vietnam from the Mekong Delta to the demilitarized zone (DMZ) on the border with North Vietnam—from Can Tho and Buon me Thuot and Nha Trang to Pleiku, Da Nang, and Dong Ha—tagging along with men in every branch of the service. Wherever I could hitch a ride: in a truck convoy, an airplane, or walking with the troops, I just joined in as we all tried not to get killed. It was not only the danger but also the confusion about why we were there, expressed to me by the troops, that left me upset and further disillusioned. After that summer, I came home further disgusted by our foreign policy, by the harm done to the Vietnamese population, and the exploitation of our own young people—the troops on the ground.[1]

Like others in the student movement, I had assumed for years that the protests had failed because the war had continued until 1975. The feeling of failure gained reinforcement because much of the literature about the war focused on why we failed and internal divisions in the antiwar movement. Moreover, we knew these analyses held some truth: like the contemporaneous example of SNCC, as more volunteers joined and the antiwar movement grew, fissures among the "founders" and newcomers were among the reasons the movement collapsed in 1969.[2]

Those of us who protested the war before and after 1968 were stunned to find out decades later that candidate Nixon's intervention disrupted the peace process that our protests had helped to bring about. Free of the political pressure of a reelection bid, Johnson had decided in October 1968 to take a chance on ending the bombing of North Vietnam to make peace. But when Nixon, a presidential-candidate-in-waiting, learned that a deal was forthcoming, he used political supporters who had connections with the North Vietnamese to persuade them to stall talks so the Democrats wouldn't get credit for peace and presumably win the presidential election. There is no way to know what the outcome would have been if Nixon hadn't intervened. But the course of history was inexorably changed, and it's possible that the many lives lost and the continued suffering endured from 1968 to 1975 could have been avoided.[3]

Though Students for a Democratic Society (SDS) splintered in 1969, huge coalition protests played a role in pressuring Nixon to end the draft and agree to peace terms in 1973. The war ended when the North Vietnamese took over Saigon in 1975. The press, until the Tet Offensive on January 31, 1968, when the North Vietnamese made simultaneous attacks on cities and towns across Vietnam, was mostly negative about the antiwar movement. But with Tet, mainstream press coverage turned generally positive, since everyone could see North Vietnam's aggressiveness on their television screens. Reporters' wives and children had become protesters and the carnage and the persistence of the enemy could not be ignored.[4]

The origins of the Vietnam War before American involvement helped to determine the ultimate US military failure and the concomitant resistance movement. In summary, the conflict started during the peace arrangements after World War II: Nazi Germany had invaded France, and Japan occupied the French colonies of Vietnam, Laos, and Cambodia, gaining rice, rubber, and territory. At the war's conclusion, the Viet Minh, a communist-led group of Vietnamese and Ho Chi Minh's organization, gained national self-determination. After the war, the Viet Minh announced the independence of the Democratic Republic of Vietnam (DRV). France, helped by the United States, battled the DRV in the 1950s and lost. The Geneva peace agreement in July 1954 gave Laos, Vietnam, and Cambodia independence and divided Vietnam. The DRV kept the North and the French kept the South, pending specified elections to be conducted within two years to reunite the country. Although the anticommunist government of South Vietnam and the United States agreed to respect the agreement, they refused to sign it.[5]

It became obvious to US officials that the North Vietnamese would win any fair election; so in October 1955, a rigged election established a puppet South Vietnamese republic headed by Ngo Dinh Diem. The communist forces, the Viet Cong, supplied by the North on the paths and tunnels of the Ho Chi Minh trail, started to defeat Diem's forces. When

South Vietnamese Buddhists mounted protests to his rule, Diem ordered a violent response. On June 11, 1963, a monk responded to the government's shooting of Buddhists by immolating himself in a crowded Saigon street, an image that was captured on camera and circulated widely.

During this period, the Kennedy administration kept increasing the number of US military, calling them "advisers" and hoping active combat forces would not be used or acknowledged and hoping Diem could prevail. Implementing the US strategy of increasing forces to outnumber the Viet Cong, designed by Secretary of Defense McNamara, required more recruits. And so, in 1962, the Selective Service began plans to execute a military draft. The nation's young men anxiously wondered whether they would be drafted under the United States Universal Military Training and Service Act, passed in 1948, which required all male American citizens to register with a local draft board at age eighteen.

The Viet Cong continued to rout the South Vietnamese, and Diem was killed on November 2, 1963, twenty days before President John F. Kennedy was assassinated. Not wanting to "lose" Vietnam, which seemed imminent, President Johnson shifted the US military from acting as "advisers" to first a covert, and then to an overt, combat role. As the Viet Cong continued winning despite US military ramp-up, President Johnson in 1964, acting in desperation, supported another coup and elevated another general, Nguyen Khanh.

College campuses are ideal locations for finding people who have enough social and economic freedom to form a pool of available protesters. In the 1960s, some students joined the civil rights movement and others the antiwar movement or both. The University of Michigan became an epicenter through the founding there of the SDS in 1959. Founded before the Vietnam issue developed, SDS became the leading antiwar movement in the period before 1969 and inspired many of the protesters who contin-ued to demonstrate against the war until the 1973 peace accords and end of the draft, and even until the Viet Cong and North Vietnamese took Saigon in 1975 ending the war.

SDS originated in the student branch of the League for Industrial Democracy, founded in 1905, as the Intercollegiate Socialist Society by Democratic Socialist intellectuals to bring their message to campuses. In 1959, Robert Alan Haber, a graduate student, took over the league's stu-dent branch, then called the Student League for Industrial Democracy, and renamed it Students for a Democratic Society. He trolled Northern campus demonstrations supporting the Southern sit-ins for recruits who agreed with the need for a "silent generation" to become engaged about societal and university reform. Tom Hayden, the editor of the campus *Michigan Daily*, was one of his recruits.

Hayden went to the National Student Association (NSA) and met other students, including Casey Cason, a fellow activist from the University of Texas, Austin, whom he later married. Founded at a conference at the University of Wisconsin in 1947, the NSA was a confederation of college and university student governments that operated from 1947 to 1978. From 1950 to 1967, the Central Intelligence Agency (CIA) secretly infiltrated some of its programs.[6]

Haber and Hayden traveled to campuses looking for recruits. Hayden went to the South to cover Southern organizing, where he met SNCC activists. He and his fellow SDSers, inspired by SNCC, began to develop the idea of a movement based on participatory democracy. The idea arose from the American philosopher John Dewey's vision of extending the opportunity for human beings to have a voice in public decisions with democratic deliberation in every institutional structure, from the nation-state to the family. The SDSers decided to target racial separation, militarism, and middle class alienation as related problems. While on a "Freedom Ride" from Atlanta to Albany in 1962, twenty-three-year-old Hayden wrote a draft statement of their views. The group went to a labor camp at Port Huron, Michigan, where they revised the draft, and Hayden became the nation's most prominent voice of participatory democracy.[7]

The Port Huron statement reflected SDS's view that in a conservative and controlled campus environment they were "people of this generation, bred in at least modest comfort, housed now in universities, looking uncomfortably to the world we inherit."[8] The students felt hampered by conventional channels and wanted a new approach. They saw some "bridges to power" in an occasional election campaign, sit-ins, Freedom Rides, and voter registration activities; in some relatively large Northern demonstrations for peace and civil rights; and infrequently through the United States National Student Association, whose notable work had not focused on political change. But they wanted a "new left" of young people built from within the university with allies outside. They wanted student and faculty reform of courses and administrative structure in the university and, working with allies in labor, civil rights and other liberal allies outside to prepare to assault power and create a democratic society.

Consistent with their views, in 1963, some students began to act outside the university to promote interracial peace and justice in Northern cities instead of working only with SNCC and the Congress of Racial Equality (CORE) in the South. With a $5,000 grant from the United Auto Workers in September 1963 they launched ERAP, the Economic Research and Action Project, to organize poor whites in an alliance with blacks. They had problems gaining traction, primarily because the alliance didn't come to pass; the students didn't know the people or the communities on the ground. When they retreated from their own original vision of democracy and focused on the locals' goals, the students had some success. By 1965, SDS and the groups they organized won rent strikes in Newark and took over the local War on Poverty board, an extension of President Johnson's policy initiative. In Chicago, they gained concessions from the welfare office; in Cleveland, they became centers for organizing the National Welfare Rights Organization (NWRO). SDSers who had some experience and knew the communities where they worked had some success. But elsewhere the program failed.

Then the student movement changed direction, not yet to the war but to campus issues. In September 1964, University of California, Berkeley, students raising money for SNCC and CORE found they were violating the university's solicitation ban. A group of students, led by Mario Savio, resisted university efforts to prevent students from using the campus to rally support for off-campus political activities. Savio called his crusade the Free Speech movement, emphasizing the goal of criticizing university policies. Some eight hundred students occupied the university's central administration building on December 2, 1964. When they refused to leave, Governor Edmund Brown sent state police, who dragged out and arrested 732 protesters. Two months of a faculty strike ensued. To end the demonstrations, the university eventually announced free speech would be permitted on campus. The movement took hold at other universities, with students demanding a role in governance, including curriculum. Some SDS leaders saw in the growing protests the rationale for shifting their focus back to the campuses.[9]

Soon events would overtake plans for future anti-administration campus protests. The military expansion that took place with the Gulf of

Tonkin Resolution drew SDS's attention to the war and the draft. The Johnson administration announced that on August 2, 1964, three North Vietnamese patrol boats fired on the US destroyer *Maddox* in the Gulf of Tonkin. The *Maddox* returned fire and, with the aircraft carrier *Ticonderoga*, sank one of the patrol boats and damaged the other two. Johnson sent an official warning to North Vietnam and deployed another destroyer, the *C. Turner Joy*, to assist the *Maddox* in its patrols of the gulf. On August 4, 1964, came another announcement.[10] The United States suspected the North Vietnamese of another unprovoked attack. Johnson responded with a retaliatory strike against North Vietnam. On August 7, 1964, Congress gave President Johnson full authority to take any necessary measures against threats in Vietnam.

Congress gave Johnson this blanket authorization for war based on the president's contention that American warships had been attacked. But similar to the fake evidence of weapons of mass destruction that led to the war in Iraq, this contention was also false. There was no attack. A report declassified by the National Security Agency years later, in 2005, pointed out that the American ships had been firing at radar shadows on a dark night. Their agents, however, had told McNamara that the evidence of an attack was ironclad. McNamara gave the raw data to the president as evidence, and he immediately embraced it and decided to act. Ray Cline, then the CIA's deputy director of intelligence, observed, "It was just what Johnson was looking for." The escalation of the war now had popular approval. President Johnson could use any military force he wished to prevent North Vietnam and the Viet Cong from taking control of the South.[11]

At Michigan, antiwar fever surged, especially among the undergraduates. In December 1964, angered and disillusioned by the Gulf of Tonkin resolution and subsequent escalation of the US military presence, SDS began planning for a national demonstration in Washington, DC. "We were outraged" at the president's betrayal and by Cold War liberalism more generally, SDS president Todd Gitlin, a graduate student in political science at Michigan, recalled in his 1987 memoir. SDS first considered a resistance campaign against the draft but decided to first issue a resolution demanding "American withdrawal from South Vietnam."[12]

Concerned University of Michigan professors considered a work stoppage in protest, but decided against that idea when it provoked criticism that they were lazy and simply didn't want to work. They then organized the first teach-ins on the war and asked colleagues on other campuses around the country to follow suit. On March 2, 1965, about three thousand Michigan students and faculty participated in the teach-ins, crowding into classrooms after classes ended. Two days later Columbia University professors held an all-night teach-in attended by two thousand students. "The students of the universities are coming out of a long sleep," declared an economics professor who spoke at the event. They were no longer a "silent generation."[13]

At the University of California, Berkeley, after an overflow crowd attended the initial University of Michigan–inspired teach-in, the Vietnam Day Committee organized a second outdoor event in May that drew a crowd of thirty thousand. After the State Department declined an invitation to send a representative, the Vietnam Day Committee placed an empty chair on stage to mock the Johnson administration for being too cowardly to debate its foreign policy. By the end of the 1964 academic year, more than 120 colleges and universities had held teach-ins.

THE WAR AND THE RESISTANCE GROW

After Operation Rolling Thunder, the large-scale bombing of North Vietnam that began in March 1965 and an increase in ground troops, the resistance to US involvement in the war swelled to a national movement. In spite of this, President Johnson kept ratcheting up the number of troops deployed.

Michigan professors and students organized an ad hoc Faculty-Student Committee to Stop the War in Vietnam and agreed on April 6, 1965, to have a National Teach-In in May 1965. They also decided to send a delegation to lobby Secretary of Defense Robert McNamara and to support the SDS-led March on Washington scheduled for April 17.[14]

On that day, SDS and SNCC led the first of several antiwar marches on Washington, which drew about twenty-five thousand protesters. Many peace groups—National Committee for a Sane Nuclear Policy (SANE), Student Peace Union, Women's International League for Peace and Freedom, Turn Toward Peace, and several others—declined to join the march, arguing that SDS had proposed no alternative policies in Vietnam. Some groups also feared reprisals, because SDS allowed anyone to participate, including communist organizations even though the nation was still gripped in Cold War anticommunism scares and the domino theory of spreading communism generated support for the war.[15]

Signs at the march insisted "War on Poverty—Not on People," "Ballots Not Bombs in Vietnam," and "Freedom Now in Vietnam," linking the antiwar movement to the domestic civil rights and antipoverty campaigns. The protesters picketed outside the White House and listened to music from folk singers Joan Baez and others and speeches at the Washington Monument. Bob Moses, identified as a leader of the Mississippi Freedom Summer, spoke of how the federal government's neglect of civil rights enforcement and poverty were related to the goals and expenditures from the war. Paul Potter, a founding member and president of SDS, connected the war to the original SDS vision, saying the march was to end the war but also part of a "movement to build a better society." The system had to be changed, he insisted, to stop the "forces that create a war in Vietnam today or a murder in the South tomorrow or all the incalculable, innumerable more subtle atrocities."[16]

The White House displayed concern about the growing antiwar movement on college campuses. On April 7, ten days before the April 17 antiwar march on Washington, LBJ, in a major speech on Vietnam at Johns Hopkins University in Baltimore, used American Revolutionary War imagery to justify intervention in Southeast Asia. He said: "The principle for which our ancestors fought in the valleys of Pennsylvania . . . is the principle for which our sons fight tonight in the jungles of Viet-Nam."[17] On the day after the march, he dismissed the protest, regretting having to bomb North Vietnam but promising "there is no human power capable of forcing us from Vietnam. We will remain as long as necessary, with the might that is required, whatever the risk and whatever the cost."[18]

In the years after the Gulf of Tonkin, LBJ continued to increase the number of ground troops; the bombing and American and Vietnamese casualties also increased, fueling the growth of the antiwar movement. After the march, SDS grew from 29 chapters and 1,000 members in June 1964 to 80 chapters and 2,000 members in June 1965 and 124 chapters with 4,300 members by the end of 1965.[19] The new members were focused almost entirely on ending the war, not structural improvements in American government and society that still animated the SDS founders. Other groups continued to protest domestic non-war concerns with SDS's involvement increasingly episodic.

By the end of 1965, the administration's decision to use the draft elicited heated protests. There were 184,300 American troops stationed in

South Vietnam and the number was rising.[20] To increase the flow of needed manpower, in 1965, Congress amended the Selective Service Act to prohibit the willful destruction of draft cards or registration certificates. The small, white draft cards showed the registrant's identifying information, including the date and place of registration and his Selective Service number, which indicated his state of registration, local board, and birth year.[21]

The Selective Service Act had already required that all eligible men always carry the certificate and prohibited forgery or fraud. The 1965 amendment, however, made it a separate crime to "knowingly destroy" or "knowingly mutilate" the card.[22] In response to the amendment, protesters burned draft cards, which led to First Amendment freedom of expression court cases. Though protesters lost the cases, the growing antiwar movement alarmed the administration and became the nation's fixation.

On May 5, 1965, student activists at the University of California, Berkeley, marched on the Berkeley draft board and forty students staged the first public burning of a draft card.[23] Another nineteen cards were burned May 22 at a demonstration following the large Berkeley teach-in. The students protested the draft as a means of protesting what they regarded as immoral warfare.

In fact, only a fraction of all men of draft age were inducted. Draftees sent to fight were mostly poor and working class and not middle-class college students in prestigious institutions waging protests. And local draft boards had broad discretion in determining who to draft and who to exempt. In late July 1965, Johnson doubled the number of young men to be drafted per month from 17,000 to 35,000, and at the end of August, he signed a bill making it a crime to burn a draft card.[24]

By the fall of 1965, anti-draft protests were taking place in cities across the country. Draft cards were burned, Selective Service buildings were picketed, teach-ins and sit-ins were ubiquitous. The International Days of Protest, an idea from the University of Wisconsin, Madison, and the University of California, Berkeley, set the stage for draft protests to occur across the United States. They were staged after a period of quiescence when only a few marches and rallies were held. Meanwhile, the teach-ins served to increase radical views among the students.

Throughout May, there were several events where students at Berkeley participated in the burning of draft cards. Students marched to the local draft board to present a black coffin to the staff to protest the United

States, invasion of the Dominican Republic to prevent the restoration of Juan Bosch, a democratically elected president who had been ejected in a coup. President Johnson and many US business leaders opposed Bosch's reforms and his alleged closeness to Cuba's Fidel Castro. The largest teach-in at Berkeley, on May 21–23, 1965, concluded with students marching to the draft board once again to "hang" Lyndon Johnson and participate in the burning of more draft cards. In an event leading up to International Days of Protest planned by the Berkeley Vietnam Day Committee, several hundred students attempted to stop trains carrying troops to the Oakland terminal for embarkation to Vietnam. They were criticized by some faculty and government officials. According to Joseph Bort, an Alameda County Board of Supervisors member, "The manner in which these people protest is tantamount to treason."[25]

The Berkeley Vietnam Day Committee designated October 15 and 16 of 1965 as the International Days of Protest, inviting participants everywhere to protest the US military presence in Vietnam and the threat of a nuclear war. The group wanted an open forum because "silence is an overt form of consent."[26]

At the University of Michigan, as elsewhere, antiwar activists participated in the International Days of Protest on October 15 by holding a rally and vigil on campus and then sitting-in at the local draft board office. Thirty-nine students, professors, and activists were arrested. Thirty-six protesters were sentenced to ten days in jail and fined sixty-five dollars each. Local draft boards chose to reclassify protesters for defying the Selective Service Act; some thirteen students lost their deferments (upon reclassification by their local draft boards) for participating in the protests.

On October 15, 1965, in New York, the student-run National Coordinating Committee to End the War in Vietnam staged the first draft-card burning that resulted in a prison sentence under the new law. Holding his draft card, David Miller, a twenty-four-year-old pacifist and member of the Catholic Worker movement, talked of napalm, a mixture of naphthenic and palmitic acids added to gasoline. Napalm was spread by flamethrowers, causing severe burns all over the body. A tarlike substance, it created wounds too deep to heal and unbearable pain. Upon contact with humans, it would immediately stick to the skin and melt the flesh; the Americans followed the French in using it in Vietnam. From 1963 to 1973, 388,000 tons of napalm were dropped on Vietnam.[27] That is ten times the amount used in Korea and almost twenty times more than was used in the Pacific during World War II. Napalm was used by the US Army and the South Vietnamese forces to clear out bunkers, foxholes, and trenches. Then it was used to clear villages.

Miller told the crowd, "I believe the napalming of villages is an immoral act. I hope this will be a significant political act, so here goes."[28] After his statement, Miller burned his card at the rally held near an Armed Forces Induction Center in Manhattan. He was not trying to evade the draft but to stop the war. The pacifist and member of the Catholic Worker movement became the first man convicted under the 1965 amendment. He was sentenced to thirty months in prison. His conviction was affirmed in the court of appeals and not appealed to the US Supreme Court. He served his sentence.[29]

Right-wing media and politicians targeted SDS as the leader of the antiwar movement, which meant they had to expect smears undermining their work. The Johnson administration, following in the wake of the Right, argued that SDS was sabotaging the war. Attorney General Nicholas Katzenbach held a press conference on October 17 to make the sabotage accusation amid the days of protest and anti-draft actions. Though the national SDS rebutted allegations that communists had organized the Days, the news coverage reported they were in communication with the national Coordinating Committee to End the War in Vietnam in Madison, which had instigated the project.[30]

As the resistance continued, in addition to draft-card burnings, several American protesters, emulating the continuing Buddhist protests in Vietnam, immolated themselves. On November 2, 1965, a thirty-two-year-old Quaker, Norman Morrison, died by setting himself on fire forty feet from the Pentagon office window of Defense Secretary McNamara. Then, on November 9, Roger LaPorte, a twenty-two-year-old member of the Catholic Worker movement, burned himself to death in front of the United Nations building in New York City.

Shortly after the immolations, on November 27, the National Committee for a Sane Nuclear Policy (SANE), organized as a pacifist and no-first-use-of-nuclear-weapons group in 1957, brought thirty thousand protesters to Washington's National Mall. Organized by Sanford Gottlieb, the political director of SANE, this march called for protests not just against the Vietnam War but also against the denial of civil rights and the persistence of poverty. Benjamin Spock, physician and cochair of SANE, said a second protest was necessary because of the "absence of Congressional debate." SDS endorsed the march, though some moderates did not want them involved. SDS president Carl Oglesby followed up on Paul Potter's challenge to upend the system at the April march when he criticized protesters who did not agree with SDS's position that the system must be challenged not just the war as a discrete issue. The SANE organizers took care to avoid appearing radical, but the press talked up differences among the various groups present, focusing on signs and protesters, including SDS, who wanted US withdrawal from the war.[31]

The *New York Times* reported that "the sparsity of civil rights leaders indicated they were having second thoughts about involving their organizations in a foreign policy protest."[32] None of the civil rights leaders listed as sponsors—CORE's James Farmer, SNCC's John Lewis, and Bayard Rustin—attended. Neither did Martin Luther King Jr., who had, according to the *New York Times*, already "criticized the Vietnam policy."[33]

However, Coretta Scott King, long active in the women's Strike for Peace, attended and spoke, insisting that "freedom and destiny in America are bound together with freedom and justice in Vietnam. I am here as a mother who is concerned about all the children of the world."[34]

In December 1965, a group of students in Des Moines, Iowa, and opponents of the war, decided to wear black armbands throughout the holiday season and to fast on December 16 and New Year's Eve. The principals of the Des Moines school learned of the plan and announced a policy that any student wearing an armband would be asked to remove it, and refusing would result in suspension. On December 16, Mary Beth Tinker, a junior high school student, and Christopher Eckhardt, a high school student, wore their armbands to school and were sent home. The following day, John Tinker, Mary Beth's brother, did the same with the same result. The students did not return to their schools until after New Year's Day, when they planned to end the protest.

Through their parents, the students sued the school district for a violation of the First Amendment right of freedom of expression and asked for an order to stop the school from punishing the students. They lost in the district court and in the court of appeals. However, the Supreme Court, in an opinion by Justice Abe Fortas, held that the armbands represented pure speech that is entirely separate from the actions or conduct of those participating in it. Therefore, the students were protected by the First Amendment. The school had not proved the protest disrupted their educational mission.[35]

On December 25, 1965, as part of decreasing pressure and to show good intentions, President Johnson ordered a Christmastime bombing halt. The pause remained in effect until January 31, 1966. By that time, Senator William Fulbright (Democrat-Arkansas), chair of the Foreign Relations Committee had learned he was duped about the evidence for the Gulf of Tonkin Resolution, and after trying private persuasion, he wrote the president a memo on April 5, 1965, stating that the United States should get out of Vietnam. He told the president that since the United States tolerated communist nations such as Yugoslavia, having Vietnam unified as communist was not worth a war. Also, closed congressional hearings on the April 25, 1965, intervention by the United States after a coup in the Dominican Republic confirmed that the administration had lied about a threat to the United States when it dispatched the marines to the country, fearing the rise of another Fidel Castro–like communist. Senator Fulbright angered Johnson when, in a speech on September 15, 1965, he publicly announced his opposition to the war.

Senator Fulbright then decided to hold hearings beginning in January 1966. He sat throughout the proceedings hour by hour hearing testimony from respectable former government figures. He wanted to show that the antiwar cause extended beyond student protesters.[36]

In February 1966, Vietnam War veterans joined the protests. On February 5, one hundred veterans marched to the White House to return their service medals and discharge papers in disgust. On February 23, about four thousand demonstrators gathered outside the Waldorf Astoria Hotel where Johnson was being honored for working toward peace. A longtime pacifist, Jim Peck, shouted, "Mr. President, Peace in Vietnam," and pulled off his jacket to reveal a shirt with these words front and back, and was hustled outside as he repeated his plea. He served sixty days in jail for his actions.[37]

ANTI-DRAFT PROTESTS AND DRAFT-CARD BURNINGS
In March 1966, in Hue, Da Nang, and Saigon, protesters led by Buddhist monks demonstrated, demanding that the United States "get out of Vietnam." As protests continued and spread, more Americans began to question continuing the war, and the nation became more deeply divided. On

the morning of March 31, 1966, David Paul O'Brien and three companions burned their draft cards on the steps of the South Boston Courthouse in front of a crowd that happened to include several FBI agents. After fifty to seventy-five schoolboys beat and knocked the four to the ground while about two hundred spectators watched, an FBI agent took O'Brien inside the courthouse and advised him of his rights. O'Brien proudly confessed to the agent and produced the charred remains of his certificate.[38]

O'Brien represented himself at his trial and argued that the Draft Act was unconstitutional. He informed the jury that he burned the draft card "so that other people would reevaluate their positions with Selective Service, with the armed forces, and reevaluate their place in the culture of today, to hopefully consider my [O'Brien's] position." He was convicted and sentenced to the maximum of six years as a "youth offender" in the custody of the attorney general "for supervision and treatment." After his conviction was reversed in the circuit court, the government appealed to the US Supreme Court, where O'Brien lost. In an opinion with only Justice Douglas dissenting, Chief Justice Warren wrote, "The governmental interest and the scope of the 1965 Amendment are limited to preventing harm to the smooth and efficient functioning of the Selective Service System. When O'Brien deliberately rendered unavailable his registration certificate, he willfully frustrated this governmental interest."[39] Because of his conduct, and not his speech, the court said, it upheld his conviction.

Along with draft burnings, protests against the use of napalm increased. Students at the University of Wisconsin, Madison, started the demonstrations in 1966, calling for a boycott of the Dow Chemical Company that produced napalm for the US military. It spread to other universities. It was not until 1980 that the United Nations Convention on Certain Conventional Weapons (CCWC) declared the use of napalm against concentrations of civilians a war crime. A number of countries did not sign this protocol, which became international law in 1983. The United States signed the convention approximately twenty-five years after the General Assembly adopted it, on January 21, 2009: President Barack Obama's first full day in office.[40]

As the Johnson administration was confronted with a more emboldened antiwar movement along with an inability to win the war, many in the US government became increasingly alarmed. On August 16, 1966, the House Un-American Activities Committee (HUAC) began investigations of Americans who were suspected of aiding the Viet Cong, intending to make their activities illegal. Antiwar demonstrators disrupted a HUAC hearing in Washington, DC, resulting in the arrest of seventeen protesters for disorderly conduct.[41]

The year 1967 was another year of failure of US military strategy, and the protests continued to grow. In January 1967, President Johnson increased the ceiling on the number of troops to 525,000. In February 1967, the *New York Review of Books* published "The Responsibility of Intellectuals," an essay by MIT professor Noam Chomsky, who argued that much responsibility for the war lay with intellectuals and technical experts who were providing what he saw as misleading justifications for the administration's war policies. He proposed, "The question, 'What have I done?' is one that we may well ask ourselves, as we read each day of fresh atrocities in Vietnam—as we create, or mouth, or tolerate the deceptions that will be used to justify the next defense of freedom."[42]

Then on April 4, 1967, one year to the day before his assassination, Martin Luther King Jr. gave his antiwar speech, "Beyond Vietnam: A Time to Break Silence," at Riverside Church in New York City, binding the civil rights and antiwar causes tightly together. Speaking of the "fierce urgency of now," he denounced the war as immoral and consuming resources that could better be used for the poor. King's speech added to Johnson's misery over the Watts riot in 1964, the civil disorder occurring in inner cities each long, hot summer, and the antiwar movement; they all interfered with his domestic policy agenda as he sank lower in the polls.[43]

The National Mobilization Committee to End the War in Vietnam (the Mobe) then held successful rallies on April 15, 1967, in both New York City and San Francisco. The Mobe's goals included increasing public hostility to the war and support for the cause of ending racial inequality. Peace and other action groups joined in the marches. They planned to focus attention on the war during the run-up to the 1968 elections. At the April 15 rally in New York City, Martin Luther King Jr. joined the speakers as four hundred thousand protesters walked from Central Park to the United Nations, and on the other coast, seventy-five thousand antiwar protesters marched in San Francisco.[44]

On April 28, 1967, while the nation was deeply split and increasingly emotionally overwrought over the war in Vietnam, heavyweight champion Muhammad Ali became a protester. His persona embodied both the civil rights and antiwar movements, which student protesters had tried to link from the beginning and King's antiwar position had formally forged. Ali, years earlier a very public convert to Islam, refused to be inducted into the armed forces, saying "I ain't got no quarrel with those Vietcong."[45] Denied conscientious objector status, Ali was convicted of draft evasion on June 20, 1967, sentenced to five years in prison, and fined $10,000. He was stripped of his title and banned from boxing for three years. Three years later, in 1971, the Supreme Court overturned his sentence.[46]

In the summer of 1967, adding to LBJ's woes, including his political fears of being thought soft on crime, an episode of police brutality ignited violent disturbances dubbed "race riots" in Newark, New Jersey. In six days of disorder, sixteen civilians, eight suspects, one police officer, and one firefighter were killed. National Guard and state troopers were deployed to quell the disturbance. Given the role of police brutality that sparked the unrest, the nation's peaceful well-being was apparently increasingly imperiled. In Detroit, police raided a "blind pig," or speakeasy, in the early morning of July 23, 1967. As the officers waited to haul away the patrons for illegal activity, the community responded by harassing the police. The subsequent violence resulted in the deaths of forty-three people, thirty-three African Americans, and ten whites. Many other people were injured; more than seven thousand people were arrested; and more than one thousand buildings were burned in the uprising. Detroit became nicknamed "De-stroit," or "De-stroyt." The Vietnam War protests made Johnson wonder if with the deployment of federal troops in Detroit, he would be accused of not being content to kill Vietnamese but now women and children at home too. He established the Kerner Commission to report on the causes of the inner-city disturbances and how to prevent them. The disorder in the Watts neighborhood of Los Angeles in 1965, in Cleveland and Omaha in 1966, and then in Detroit and Newark in 1967 outraged Johnson. According to my friend Roger Wilkins, a holdover from the Kennedy administration who was head of Community Relations in the Justice Department, LBJ was furious. A political advocate for civil rights legislation, Johnson complained that after he'd done so much on civil rights and created antipoverty domestic programs, the domestic unrest seen as black rebellion was undermining his policies.

The president still had the moderate wing of the civil rights movement, consisting of the NAACP's Roy Wilkins and the Urban League's Whitney

Young, on his side after Martin Luther King Jr.'s antiwar speech at River-side. Wilkins and Young had long criticized the use of nonviolent direct action protest instead of negotiation, legislation, and litigation, which they believed were tried and true ways to make progress. The Urban League's employment and economic mission made it necessarily dependent on business and philanthropists, who didn't like disruption, for jobs and other programs. But King was more prominent than these organization leaders, and younger civil rights activists were rejecting older leaders; moreover, Johnson was still losing the war. In fact, Johnson was under so much pressure from the antiwar movement that he was anxious about traveling outside Washington.[47]

WHAT I SAW IN VIETNAM

I was in Vietnam during the summer of 1967 writing weekly reports for the University of Michigan *Daily* and beginning each article with the brutal fact "We're not winning the War." The military press briefings, called the Five O'Clock Follies by reporters, at the Rex Hotel in Saigon, where the United States was always winning the war, according to the military briefers, had practically nothing to do with the reality on the battlefield. I saw the tiredness and anguish in the eyes of our "grunts" on the ground and heard some ask me the heartbreaking question "Why are we here?"

I saw the plight of the Vietnamese refugees who literally tried to climb in our helicopters or already crowded Caribou aircraft as we flew away from their villages. I felt the fear of living in regions where the fighting Viet Cong owned the night and sometimes the day. I saw the fruitlessness of our military campaigns, even those dubbed successful. We walked in the hot sun in Operation Cochise in July 1967 as the marines attempted to clear the densely populated area around Da Nang Air Base. The US command reported 156 enemy killed and 13 captured, and only 10 marines killed and 93 wounded. The South Vietnamese reported 83 killed, 174 wounded, and 3 missing. The marines had expected a large operation with a definitive outcome, but it turned into mostly a bush-beating effort—some bloodshed, wounding, and killing with hand-to-hand fighting—which was clearly not a victory.[48]

We were not winning the war at Con Thien either, which the Marines, who saw heavy casualties and enemy fire, later called a little piece of hell. Two miles down from the DMZ, the base was a slight hill of red dirt with barbed wire encircling the artillery, trenches, and underground bunkers covered with sandbags. The incoming enemy artillery fire seemed continuous. The Viet Cong kept their guns hidden in caves, brought them out to fire at us, and then hid them again. As the marines fired back, the barrage continued.

Down below us at the base of the hill, marine engineers had been working since early 1967 to bulldoze a fence to at least five hundred meters wide on the border as part of the so-called McNamara Line, an electronic anti-infiltration barrier to block communist flow of arms and troops into South Vietnam. From our vantage point above, we could see the engineers working with heavy equipment in the heat and suffering higher casualties than the rifle companies on the hill where we stood. They well deserved the steak and potatoes dropped to them in jerry cans, while on the hill we ate C rations.

The marines hunkered down during the firing, and despite the death and destruction, everyone kept up their spirits by telling jokes, while running from bunkers to the latrine, skipping to evade the mortars we called Puff the magic dragon. Everyone, fatalistically, pretended to be unafraid in the face of unspeakable danger. I sought out Michiganders and wrote hometown news when I found one. I sent the story to the papers each week along with my regular dispatch, which began, "Today I am at Con Thien and we're not winning the war." I wrote that so many times: at Sa Dec in the south in the Mekong Delta, where I first encountered our Korean-soldier allies and learned to eat kimchi, or at Dong Ha, where my reporter friend from Swedish Broadcasting, Björn Ahlander, and a soldier from Hawaii who was lost from his unit, and I slept on a tarmac all night. Björn told us stories about a wonderful smorgasbord to ease our hunger pains while we waited for a ride north. And wherever I was, I realized and recorded the same fact: "We are not winning the war."

Once at Con Thien we sat exposed in the night air around a birthday cake in a C ration cup and sang "Happy Birthday" as loud as possible to a young Michigan marine. I came back to campus in fall 1967 with greater resolve and went around the state speaking about what I saw and how we were not winning the war.[49]

I still have the notebook, covered with dirt, documenting what the troops—the grunts all over South Vietnam—told me about their confusion over the purpose of war and how scared they were. One physically and emotionally drained black soldier said to me, "You write down what we say.

Other reporters talk to us, but they never write down what we say. How will anyone remember me?" I told him they probably had a lot more experience and knew better how to remember what they heard.

In 1967, as about forty thousand men were inducted each month, the draft issue increasingly became a focus of the resistance movement. The local, politically controlled draft boards let white, middle-class college-going men gain deferments while the poor and young African American men served. In 1967, 64 percent of eligible black men were drafted and only 31 percent of eligible white men. The black unemployment rate was 7.3 percent, while for whites it was 3 to 4 percent. Blacks were more likely to serve in the infantry and to volunteer for hazardous duty to receive more money and perhaps a promotion.

On October 16, 1967, countrywide draft-card burnings and turn-ins led to more than one thousand draft cards collected at the Justice Department. However, Attorney General Ramsey Clark only prosecuted leaders, including Benjamin Spock and Yale chaplain William Sloane Coffin. By the late 1960s, men accused of draft dodging and those seeking conscientious-objector status dominated federal court dockets. More than 210,000 were accused of draft-related offenses.

On October 21, 1967, one hundred fifty thousand protesters gathered in Washington, DC, to "Confront the Warmakers." They marched to the Pentagon while twenty-five hundred federal troops and marshals helped police maintain order. Some seven hundred protesters were arrested on allegations of violent behavior during the march. These events received nationwide press coverage, heightening awareness of the growing antiwar sentiment, and Vietnam veterans among others began organizing their own groups at the march.[50]

PEACE PRESSURE INSIDE THE JOHNSON ADMINISTRATION
By the end of 1967, the war seemed endless and the country was increasingly polarized over civil rights pressures and urban disorder. By November, Secretary of Defense McNamara, who had become increasingly troubled by the war, left office. He was either fired or resigned; the truth has remained unclear. President Kennedy had hired him away from Ford Motor Company, where as a master of systems analysis, he had been named president only ten weeks before. His first failures were the Bay of Pigs, a

plan inherited from the Eisenhower administration to overthrow Castro's government, and the Vietnam War.[51]

"Every quantitative measurement we have shows we're winning this war," McNamara announced after returning from his first trip to South Vietnam in April 1962.[52] After Kennedy was assassinated, on November 22, 1963, Johnson depended on McNamara to win the war Congress authorized in the August 7, 1964, Gulf of Tonkin Resolution, which was based on an enemy attack that didn't happen.

But nothing McNamara authorized—not the Operation Rolling Thunder bombing campaign starting in March 1965, not the sensors and walls of the McNamara Line—stopped the unending supply of soldiers and weapons from the north into South Vietnam. By February 1966, McNamara said with conviction, "No amount of bombing can end the war."[53] When he became convinced gradually that the war would not be won, he had his aides compile a top-secret history of the war—later known as the Pentagon Papers. Later, he took to heart the growing antiwar movement that his son had joined and acknowledged failure.

LBJ announced on November 29, 1967, that McNamara would leave to run the World Bank. He ignored the conclusions of McNamara and other advisers who were increasingly discomfited. In December 1967, Johnson increased US troops to a total of 485,000 and the United States was still not winning the war, though General William C. Westmoreland told the president there was "light at the end of the tunnel."[54]

Then came the lunar new year Tet Offensive on January 31, 1968, when about seventy thousand North Vietnamese and Viet Cong forces concentrated attacks on cities and towns in South Vietnam, giving more credibility to the antiwar movement. Though US and South Vietnamese forces defeated the North Vietnamese and Viet Cong, the extensive firepower and casualties the enemy could inflict, after four years of war, increased media criticism of the administration and public opinion against the war. Many people had accepted the optimistic reports they had seen previously from the president and his administration and discounted the protesters. When General Westmoreland asked for some two hundred thousand more troops for the war, skepticism about victories and the costs of the war deepened. On February 27, 1968, Walter Cronkite in a special report made the consensus mainstream media judgment and affirmed my reporting: we were not winning the war. The most respected name in broadcasting told America the war was "mired in stalemate."[55]

Eugene McCarthy, a senator from Minnesota, began campaigning against Johnson for the Democratic presidential nomination. Then, on March 16, 1968, Robert Kennedy, then a senator from New York, announced his own campaign for the presidency. On March 31, 1968, LBJ announced he would not seek reelection. His chief of staff, James Jones, recalled that Johnson pursued the war, though he had "questioned" it as a senator and "brooded" about it as president, because he felt "compelled . . . to pursue the commitments made by Presidents Dwight D. Eisenhower and John F. Kennedy."[56]

Jones concluded that it was not the fear of losing the election that drove Johnson to announce he would not seek reelection but the war. For LBJ, the anxiety grew daily. Johnson knew for months that peace talks were possible, but he didn't want to be blamed for Vietnam becoming a communist nation. As early as January 3, 1968, a North Vietnamese official told Bernard S. Redmont, a reporter for Westinghouse Broadcasting in Paris, that they were willing to start peace talks if Johnson stopped bombing and called a pause to other acts of war. Redmont's story was picked up and highlighted by press around the world.[57]

But LBJ was still hoping for positive news and for reelection. The stress mounted, as did the awareness that victory was not in sight. The casualties did not end, and then the president became aware that his son-in-law, Charles Robb, a marine captain, was in harm's way. LBJ had been a teacher, and now students had organized an antiwar movement with people outside the White House yelling, "Hey, hey, LBJ, how many kids did you kill today?" In addition to his awareness of the protesters outside the White House was Johnson's sense that if he traveled outside of town, protests would arise wherever he ventured.[58]

So, in his speech announcing his withdrawal from the presidential race, Johnson announced a unilateral halt to bombing in the top half of North Vietnam and deployment of only a fraction of the troops General Westmoreland had asked for. In October, he was presented with a decision for a major bombing halt that could lead to a peace settlement. Free of politics, he decided to take the chance. Henry A. Kissinger, then an outside Republican adviser, had called to alert Richard Nixon, the Republican nominee for president, that a deal was in the works: if Johnson would halt all bombing of North Vietnam, the Soviets pledged to have Hanoi engage in construc-tive talks to end a war that had already claimed thirty thousand American lives. On October 22, 1968, fearful that Hubert Humphrey might catch up to him in the polls and win the presidential race, Nixon ordered H. R. Haldeman, his campaign aide and later chief of staff, to "monkey wrench" Johnson's initiative.[59]

Haldeman did so, enlisting several operatives with a pipeline to the president of South Vietnam to get him to stall. But Nixon himself had a pipeline to Saigon, where the South Vietnamese president, Nguyen Van Thieu, feared that Johnson would not protect his government's con-tinuation. If Thieu would delay the talks, Nixon could declare Johnson was not serious about peace and was just playing a political game. Anna Chennault, a Republican doyenne and Nixon fund-raiser and a member of the pronationalist China lobby with connections across Asia, acted as go-between. Nixon also had CIA director Richard Helms pressured to pro-vide the "right" intelligence to Johnson if Helms wanted to stay in the next administration. We will never know whether a peace deal would have been reached without the interference of Nixon, the next president. But we do know that the antiwar movement was a major factor in Johnson's giving up on the war and wanting to come to the peace table. In addition, failure to find a way to win the war and the antiwar-movement pressure drove him from office.[60]

The antiwar protests persisted as the war seemed endless. One group of protesters targeted Dow Chemical in a bid to get the company to stop manufacturing napalm. This later morphed into a demand for universities to rid campuses of Dow recruiters and connections to the military industrial complex in general. In February 1967, Mark Rudd, who had been an SDS member since 1963 and later became chair of Columbia's SDS chapter, was chastised by the Columbia College dean for sitting in during a navy ROTC class and attempting to disrupt it. On February 24, he helped stage a sit-in blocking a Dow Chemical recruiter from the building where he was to conduct interviews. In early March 1967, another SDSer at Columbia University, Bob Feldman, found materials in a campus library describing Columbia's involvement with a weapons analysis research group in the De-fense Department. When Feldman wrote about his discovery, the FBI put him under surveillance. In March, a draft official speaking on Columbia's campus was hit by a lemon pie, another act of defiance to protest the draft and the weapons research group connection with the university.

Mark Rudd started a Columbia SDS campaign from April 1967 to April 1968, demanding the university administration dissociate from the Defense Department research group. The Columbia administration had placed Rudd and six protesters on probation after a protest on March 27, 1968, for violating a rule against indoor demonstrations.[61]

Martin Luther King Jr.'s assassination on April 4, 1968, and the civil disturbances in major cities that followed, brought out federal troops and the National Guard to help police. New York City avoided the major street disturbances experienced in other cities. The city's mayor, John Lindsay, got some credit for maintaining strong relationships with gangs, black leaders, and politicians. But the assassination gave more energy to the Columbia University antiwar protesters, whose mission now coalesced with reactions to King's assassination. As elsewhere, Columbia students were divided between more militant undergraduate and graduate students and the graduate students enrolled in professional schools who worried about interference with their academic work toward graduation. The high percentage of black men sent to Vietnam left black students very concerned about the draft, even though they were themselves exempted. T. J. Davis, a history PhD student, remembers living in a building next to a family with three sons. The middle son got drafted and was the sole survivor from his unit. Everyone in the building said he "was a mess." The consensus was if you go, if you come back, you'll never be the same. They are still on our streets today, homeless and troubled veterans of Vietnam and subsequent wars for which they volunteered but who are a "mess."[62]

On campus, undergrads disrupted a memorial service for King to protest Columbia's plans to build a gymnasium on public park land that offered only limited use for residents of nearby Harlem. On April 23, SDS and the Student Afro-American Society held a protest against the war and the gym project. They broke through a fence around the construction site, fought police, and then marched. Some went to Morningside Park, where they tore down a fence around the gymnasium construction site and battled with police; then black students took over a classroom building. Another group of students, mostly white, occupied President Grayson Kirk's office and others took over other buildings. The occupation lasted six days, during which faculty tried to mediate. On April 30, Kirk called in the city police, who arrested more than seven hundred people; police were accused of beating the demonstrators. After that, thousands of students and faculty, many radicalized by the police action, went on strike, effectively shutting down the university for the rest of the semester. The university decided not to build the gym at the selected location and ended the weapons association. Some alumni stopped giving for a while and students like those at other campuses—Michigan, for example, where there had been sustained protests—gained greater participation in the policymaking and administration of the university.[63]

Protests continued elsewhere. On April 26, 1968, one million college and high school students boycotted class to show opposition to the war. In May, the Poor People's Campaign to address the issues of unemployment, housing shortages for the poor, and the impact of poverty on the lives of millions of Americans settled in on the National Mall. Many students and other reformers took part, but without Martin Luther King Jr. and with the unceasing rain that turned the mall into a mud pit and the hostility of the FBI and federal agencies, the campaign got no traction. On June 6, 1968, Robert Kennedy, whose candidacy for the presidency was the hope of many reformers, was assassinated right after he won the California primary.[64]

The antiwar movement continued, however. The National Mobilization Committee to End the War in Vietnam and the Youth International Party (Yippies) planned a youth festival in Chicago during the August 26–29, Democratic National Convention. Rennie Davis, who had done a great job with SDS's Economic Research and Action Project, and Tom Hayden organized protests throughout the convention. Thousands of Vietnam War protesters battled police in the streets on August 28, while inside, the party debated internal disagreement concerning its stance on Vietnam. Chicago mayor Richard Daley, from his seat at the convention, dispatched twenty-three thousand police and National Guardsmen to control the protesters outside. Police used tear gas, mace, and beatings—all captured for seventeen minutes on prime-time television. Protesters, being dragged and beaten, chanted, "The whole world is watching." Daley gave the police pay raises, and when he ran for reelection, he won overwhelmingly.[65]

Eight leading antiwar activists were prosecuted for conspiracy to riot: Tom Hayden, Abbie Hoffman, David Dellinger, Jerry Rubin, Lee Weiner,

Rennie Davis, John Froines, and Bobby Seale. The convictions of the
Chicago Seven (Bobby Seale was tried separately), including Davis and
Hayden, were subsequently overturned on appeal. The police actions on
the evening of August 28 became a widely disseminated image of the
demonstrations.[66]

When the war continued after the early protests and through 1968,
SDS gradually came apart, but not the movement it had inspired. Some
SDS founders assumed they were losing, not knowing about Nixon's perfidy. Others who achieved the spotlight became celebrities burnishing their
own images and making a living thereby. The media usually develops a
storyline based on one individual. Flamboyance helps focus government
and media attention. In the antiwar movement, Jerry Rubin and Abbie
Hoffman embraced their celebrity images as outrageous white radicals.

Another problem emerged from the additional volunteers who joined
because it was popular and because they were against the war. They didn't
embrace the original SDS vision of social change and the views of these
protesters were difficult to accommodate. Also, the media kept wanting
something new to report. Beyond the Chicago protests, the media needed
continuous shows of conflict to follow the many fiery suicides and draft-card
burnings. When a demonstration was not on the front page or on television, the issue seemed to disappear from public consciousness. An additional problem for SDS was that student protesters, while the most likely
to organize a movement, are also the most fragile and easily bored. And
they graduate.[67]

SDS broke into factions in 1969. National office leaders such as Bernar-
dine Dohrn came to the fore. In June 1969, her group, the Weather Underground, cofounded by Bill Ayers, took control of the SDS national office at
the convention, arguing that confrontational militancy was needed, since
the nonviolent actions had not brought an end to the war. They distributed
a position paper calling for a "white fighting force," allied with the black
liberation movement and other radical movements, to replace imperialism
with communism. The group was also called the Weathermen, named after
Bob Dylan's lyric from "Subterranean Homesick Blues" (1965): "You don't
need a weatherman to know which way the wind blows."[68]

The Weathermen conducted bombing campaigns through the mid-
1970s, targeting government buildings and banks. Because they issued evac-
uation warnings along with the rationale for each protest, property was

destroyed but the only people killed were participants. Three members of the group died in a Greenwich Village townhouse explosion.

After Nixon and the North Vietnamese made peace in 1973, and the arrests of some Weathermen, with others on the run, the organization was no longer viable. Congressional investigations into counterintelligence and surveillance by the government, COINTELPRO, disclosed due-process violations that in 1973 led the government to drop most charges against members.[69]

But despite the split in SDS, the antiwar movement grew and remained strong. Nixon said he had a "secret plan" for winning the war before he won, but as president he rejected calls from the antiwar movement to order an immediate withdrawal of US troops.[70] Following the election of Nixon, the National Mobilization Committee, the Mobe, organized a "counter-inaugural" to take place in Washington, DC, on Inauguration Day. This demonstration also attracted about ten thousand people, but some street violence broke out. With the disintegration of SDS and the decline in attendance, the Mobe disbanded but that didn't end the peace movement.

The similarly named and inspired New Mobilization Committee to End the War in Vietnam (New Mobe) was founded in July 1969 at a conference at Case Western Reserve University in Cleveland. That group and the Vietnam Moratorium Committee and Student Mobilization Committee (SMC), organized an October 15, 1969, moratorium to end the war. Thousands took part in demonstrations across the United States. Many workers called in sick from their jobs and teenagers skipped school.

On November 12, 1969, Seymour Hersh reported the mass killing of about 109 unarmed civilians in South Vietnam on March 16, 1968, by US soldiers under the leadership of Lieutenant William Calley. Later figures determined that more than four hundred civilians were massacred.[71]

The Mobe held another large demonstration in Washington, DC, on November 15, 1969, by which time John Lennon's "Give Peace a Chance" had become a universal chant at anti–Vietnam War demonstrations. During the protest rally, folk singer Pete Seeger led nearly half a million demonstrators at the Washington Monument in singing "Give Peace a Chance." President Nixon commented on the protest that he understood there were opponents to the war, "however, under no circumstances will I be affected whatever by it."[72] The civil rights activist Dick Gregory responded that if Nixon thought he wouldn't be affected by anything the protesters did, he should "make one long distance phone call to the LBJ ranch and ask that boy how much effect you can have."[73]

Resistance did not end as the war continued under President Nixon, just as it had during the Johnson presidency. In the end, over a third of Americans who were killed died during Nixon's presidency. But Nixon worked more strenuously than Johnson to deflate the protesters. Dow Chemical lost its napalm contract in June 1969. And according to staff memoirs and White House documents, the administration gave the media talking points and bogus information in order to define the protesters as radicals. Despite the administration's efforts, some press reported, for example, the difference between the peaceful marchers and a small group who damaged property at the Justice Department until the police teargassed them away.[74]

Nixon's strategy, called Vietnamization of the war by his secretary of defense, Melvin Laird, was a precursor to the strategy that subsequent presidents have used to avoid American casualties in unpopular wars. It relied on having South Vietnamese soldiers do the ground fighting while the United States supplied an increased number of weapons and training and staged the withdrawal of its military. It required the bombing of cities and harbors and Soviet and Chinese pressure on North Vietnam to seek peace, extending the Paris peace talks started by Johnson in October 1968. Cutting off supplies led Nixon to begin secretly bombing and invading Cambodia and Laos, inciting a civil war in Cambodia. On April 30, 1970, he announced the invasion of Cambodia, though the bombing had been proceeding secretly for over a year.

On May 2, 1970, in the aftermath of the United States and South Vietnam invasion of Cambodia, students burned down the ROTC building at Kent State University. The mayor of Kent, Leroy Satrom, declared a state of emergency the same day. He requested that Governor James A. Rhodes send the Ohio National Guard to Kent to help maintain order. On May 4, the guardsmen killed four students during a large protest demonstration on the campus. On May 8, ten days after Nixon announced the Cambodian invasion and four days after the Kent State shootings, one hundred thousand protesters gathered in Washington and another one hundred fifty thousand in San Francisco. More than four hundred fifty university, college, and high school campuses across the country were shut down by student strikes and both violent and nonviolent protests that involved more than four million students.[75]

After becoming spokespersons for Mexican American high school students protesting against unequal education in Los Angeles in 1968, the local Chicano movement organized demonstrations against the war in 1970. For several days, thousands of students had participated in walkouts, which they called "blowouts," demanding more Latino teachers and administrators, smaller class sizes, better facilities, and the revision of textbooks to include Chicano history.[76] The Chicano leaders, emphasizing the high casualty rate of Mexican Americans, successfully attracted twenty thousand to thirty thousand people to an antiwar protest, a National Chicano Moratorium, on August 29, 1970. The police ended up attacking the demonstrators, and several people were killed, including a *Los Angeles Times* reporter, Ruben Salazar, who was covering the event. He was an experienced and respected journalist who had been brought back from heading the *Times* Mexico bureau to cover the Vietnam protests and the Chicano movement. He was sitting in a bar, taking cover from violence outside, when a sheriff's deputy fired a tear-gas canister inside, which killed him. Salazar's writing documenting the period is celebrated with murals, exhibits, a film, and a US postage stamp. The Chicano movement organized a short-lived independent party and then shifted its emphasis to immigration reform.[77]

Richard Nixon's accomplishments as president have been rightly overshadowed by his near impeachment. But he did oversee the creation of the Environmental Protection Agency, made reasonable proposals for welfare reform and national health insurance, and reestablished US diplomatic relations with China that endure today. On Vietnam, for most of the Nixon administration, the president benefitted from a media story that he was trying to end the war. Not much attention was paid to whatever interfered with the story, though the antiwar movement was treated positively by the news media. In 1971, excerpts from the Pentagon Papers, which McNamara and his staff had started compiling, had been leaked by Daniel Ellsberg. They were published by the *New York Times* and *Washington Post*. When he first became aware of the leak, Nixon dismissed it as not about his administration. Later, he attempted to stop publication on Kissinger's advice that they were more harmful than Nixon thought. The newspapers won a Supreme Court ruling, and excerpts from the Pentagon Papers continued to be published.[78]

At Ellsberg's request, *Washington Post* journalist Ben Bagdikian gave a copy of the papers to Senator Maurice "Mike" Gravel (Democrat-Alaska).

Gravel read from the Pentagon Papers during a subcommittee meeting, which brought them to official notice. Gravel wanted to make the papers, and not just excerpts, publicly available and unsuccessfully sought a publisher for them. Publishers worried about political retribution and unreimbursed costs. However, Gravel, one of just two Unitarian Universalists in the Senate, asked Beacon Press, a department of the Unitarian Universalist Association, and Beacon agreed to publish the papers despite the risks.

President Nixon personally attacked Beacon Press; the director of the press, Gobin Stair, was subpoenaed to appear at Daniel Ellsberg's trial; and J. Edgar Hoover approved an FBI subpoena of the entire denomination's bank records. Beacon Press and Senator Gravel lost their Supreme Court case, leaving the press vulnerable to prosecution. Not until after the disclosure of the Watergate break-in in June 1972 did the government harassment relent. The Pentagon Papers showed the racist, imperialist nature of the war, just as the antiwar movement had repeatedly pointed out.[79]

President Nixon had begun to withdraw American troops from Vietnam in June 1969, but in December 1972, the United States began large-scale bombing of North Vietnam after the Paris peace talks reached an impasse. Henry Kissinger, Nixon's secretary of state, had been meeting with North Vietnamese Politburo member Le Duc Tho intermittently with no apparent progress toward a settlement. The primary negotiations that ultimately led to the 1973 agreement were carried out during secret negotiations between Kissinger and Le Duc Tho, which began on August 4, 1969. The so-called Christmas bombings led congressional Democrats, at last, to call for an end to US involvement in Southeast Asia.

In late January 1973, the United States, South Vietnam, the Viet Cong, and North Vietnam signed a cease-fire agreement, under which the United States agreed to withdraw from South Vietnam. Under the terms of the settlement, the United States agreed to withdraw its remaining troops within sixty days in exchange for an immediate cease-fire, the return of American prisoners of war, and North Vietnam's promise to recognize the legitimacy of South Vietnam's government and submit future disputes to an international commission. Henry Kissinger and Le Duc Tho were awarded the Nobel Peace Prize in 1973, but the North Vietnamese refused to accept it and completed withdrawal of its forces that year. The military draft in the United States ended January 27, 1973.

In July 1973, White House aide Alexander Butterfield testified under oath to Congress that Nixon had a secret taping system that recorded his conversations and phone calls in the Oval Office. On October 20, 1973, came the Saturday Night Massacre, when Nixon cleaned out the top leadership of the Justice Department to get an acting attorney general who would fire special prosecutor Archibald Cox, who was pursuing the release of ten hours of Nixon's secret recordings. That evening, after the news announcement of the firings, my compatriot Joe Wildberger and I stood in front of the White House calling, "Resign, resign!" Our chants were soon joined by countless more—part of the mass of Americans over the next few days who expressed the same feelings to Congress. The House Judiciary Committee started impeachment proceedings against the president on May 9, 1974, which were televised on the major networks. These hearings culminated in votes for impeachment. On July 24, the Supreme Court ruled unanimously that the full tapes, not just selected transcripts, must be released. Nixon left office August 9, 1974. Gerald Ford gave him a complete pardon, foreclosing any criminal indictment for obstruction of justice.

The North Vietnamese took another year to finish rebuilding supply routes and preparing an offensive. The North Vietnamese Army and the Viet Cong began an offensive that gradually moved south. They entered Saigon on April 30, 1975. The war the United States did not win was finally over, and so was Nixon's presidency.

CHAPTER 3

Winning While Losing

Fighting the Reagan Administration

President Reagan pursued environmental policy consistent with his record. While running for governor of California, he had supported logging the state's centuries-old redwood trees saying, "A tree is a tree, how many more do you need to look at?" As president, he said: "Trees cause more pollution than automobiles do."[1]

RARELY DOES ANYONE STOP to recall the resistance movements and struggles by reformers and activists against some of President Reagan's civil rights and environmental policies or consider how some of it succeeded. I was a member of the US Commission on Civil Rights and was fired by President Reagan for opposing his anti–civil rights policies. He said I served at his pleasure but was not giving him very much pleasure. I gave him even less pleasure then, as I decided to sue, winning reinstatement. I was later appointed by President Clinton as chair of the commission. The commission during the Reagan years, however, was gutted. Reagan used chicanery to tarnish the commission and change it from an independent body into an administration mouthpiece. Notably, this defeat was the only civil rights campaign that anti-Reagan protesters failed to win.[2]

Opposition to Reagan ran the gamut: from his expenditures to fund an American military capable of submerging the Soviet Union in an arms race and to stop El Salvador from being controlled by a communist government, as had happened in Nicaragua; his budget cuts in the domestic arena and tax policy; and his determination to reduce the role of the federal government in domestic affairs, including social programs and civil rights.

Before he was a politician, Reagan, as president of the Screen Actors Guild during the successful 1960 strike, experienced opposition from management when he was on the more progressive side. When he was governor of California, he expressed his ire toward administrators at the University of California, Berkeley, for not quickly ending student demonstrations. During the 1969 People's Park protests on the campus, which grew out of attempts to debate the Arab-Israeli issue, Reagan used the highway patrol to suppress the protests. On "Bloody Thursday," one student was killed and a carpenter blinded, and 111 police officers were injured. Reagan instructed the National Guard to occupy the city of Berkeley, camping in People's Park for seventeen days to end the protests. A year later, asked about campus protest in general, Reagan stated, "If it takes a bloodbath, let's get it over with. No more appeasement." He responded to the United Farm Workers grape boycott of 1969 by repeatedly eating grapes on television and vetoing legislation designed to improve their wages.[3]

Given his responses as governor, the nonviolent protests against his policies during his presidency seemed unlikely to affect Reagan's decisions, but protesters hoped they would influence public opinion and members of Congress concerned about their electoral prospects. The Republicans controlled the Senate by a small margin until the Democrats regained control in the 1986 elections, but the Democrats had a majority in the House throughout Reagan's presidency.

By this time, marches on Washington were the first, most obvious major resistance to federal policies. On May 3, 1981, while Reagan's tax cuts and budget proposals were being debated, the All People's Congress, a coalition of several hundred community-based organizations opposed to Reagan's economic, social, and military policies, sponsored a march on Washington. They drew almost one hundred thousand people to the Pentagon to protest Defense Department budget increases and United States involvement in El Salvador's civil war while social programs were slated for cuts.

Founded in May 1981 in New York and Washington, the All Peoples Congress also sought equal rights for people of color, women, and gays; nuclear disarmament; abortion rights; remedies for unemployment; and an end to cuts in federal social programs and unfair treatment of refugees and undocumented persons. Their use of "Congress" as the name of the organization signified the belief that the US Congress was just "a rubber stamp for Reagan."[4]

In August 1981, Reagan fired striking air-traffic controllers, though they had supported his election, and signed his drastic tax cuts into law. He also got the defense increases he wanted. The deficit grew, interest rates rose even more, from around 12 percent in the Carter years to over 20 percent, which kept the economy in recession. Unemployment increased and the stock market plummeted.

The Air Traffic Controllers Union firing and Reagan's tax, budget, and civil rights policies led to a Solidarity Day march and rally in Washington on September 19, 1981. Lane Kirkland, president of the AFL-CIO, said the marchers were there to show that the president had no "mandate" to destroy social programs. Benjamin Hooks, president of the NAACP insisted, "We will not sit idly by while the bare necessities of life are taken from the needy and given to the greedy." Jesse Jackson, president of Operation PUSH, noted, "Many of the white workers here today voted for Reagan," but they were marching "because they feel betrayed." But Jerry Wurf, president of the American Federation of State, County and Municipal Employees, with the largest number of demonstrators, warned that the turnout didn't guarantee successful opposition and predicted, "This is a beginning of a long, difficult, frustrating process to turn the country around."[5]

By the midterm congressional elections in 1982, unemployment reached nearly 11 percent, and the Reagan tax cut, along with a higher interest rate, induced recession, causing a change in administration policy.[6] Reagan supported a tax increase and a measure to preserve funding for Social Security. However, he and Congress eliminated general revenue sharing to cities, cut funding for public service jobs and job training, almost dismantled federally funded legal services for the poor, cut the antipoverty Community Development Block Grant program, and reduced funds for public transit. Cities with high levels of poverty that depended on federal aid had a hard time keeping services operational. Cuts in low-income housing subsidies, combined with an increase in the number of Vietnam veterans, the mentally ill, and the unemployed and their children on the street led to increased homelessness. Mitch Snyder in Washington, DC, became the best-known national advocate for the homeless during the Reagan years. During the 1984 Reagan campaign for reelection, Snyder went on a fifty-one-day hunger strike, demanding that the president give an abandoned federal building in Washington to his group for a shelter.

Two days before the election, on the fifty-first day of Snyder's fast, the government gave homeless people the building he demanded. Then he fasted twice more to gain the promised money for renovations.

Snyder started his activism while serving time in federal prison, where he met Daniel and Philip Berrigan, the two antiwar priests who had been imprisoned for destroying draft records. He became a follower of radical Catholicism. While there, he fasted for thirty-three days, protesting the treatment of prisoners in Vietnam. In 1973, after he served his sentence, he moved to DC and joined the group Community for Creative Non-Violence. In the homeless movement of lawyers, social workers, priests, and politicians, Snyder was the guerrilla engaged in street theater.

In 1986, CBS aired a television movie about his life and work called *Samaritan: The Mitch Snyder Story*, starring Martin Sheen. In 1987, several celebrities joined Snyder in protesting inattention to homelessness by conducting street sleep-ins, but by the late 1980s, homelessness in the United States had increased to about six hundred thousand people, and Snyder faced increasing public disinterest in the issue.[7] In 1990, he committed suicide.[8]

Before Reagan took office, urban budgets received about 22 percent of their revenue from the federal government. By the end of Reagan's second term, it was only 6 percent.[9] Many cities began to recover from the financial crisis that started during Reagan's presidency only when they gentrified, which increased local tax bases but forced the poor into more homelessness or out of the cities.

In response to the Reagan budget and tax cuts, the All People's Congress designated the week of April 24 through May 2 as "Days of Resistance to Roll Back Reaganism," with local demonstrations. On May 1, 1982, on the first anniversary of the Congress, about eight thousand demonstrators showed up in Washington's Franklin Square and marched to the Capitol.[10]

Farmers, like air traffic controllers, had supported Reagan, but became disaffected. He withdrew the grain embargo President Carter had placed on the Soviet Union because of their invasion of Afghanistan, causing a drastic decline in farm income. Also, the continued high interest rates and credit crunch created by Reagan's policies led to foreclosures, the decline of family farms, and no funds to plant new crops. Farmers protested locally and in Washington by wearing work clothes and baseball caps, though they didn't bring tractors and block roads as they had against Carter. They prayed and planted crosses in memory of farmers forced out of business or who had committed suicide. Led by three tractors, they marched to the Ellipse, behind the White House, testified in Congress, and eventually got

Congress to pass an act providing debt relief. However, Reagan vetoed the bill, announcing that the government couldn't bail out farmers and that the bill would add to the deficit.[11]

Reagan's response to the AIDS crisis also ignited resistance and protests. Since the Centers for Disease Control (CDC) identified the disease, in 1981, it announced, on December 19, 1983, that there were 3,000 reported AIDS cases in the United States, of which 1,283, or 43 percent, were fatal.[12] The CDC warned that the numbers were untrustworthy because they did not have information on all of the cases nationwide and because some health officials were still having difficulty identifying the disease. It was met with silence from the president and no policy response. When the 1984 Democratic National Convention met in San Francisco, the city health department reported at least five hundred cases. This was at a time when it was thought to be a disease that only affected gay men. To gain support for AIDS research, education, and treatment, more than one hundred thousand protesters marched from the Castro district to the Moscone Center convention complex.

The numbers of people with AIDS and the deaths continued to grow. But Reagan did not take a public position until his friend Rock Hudson died of AIDS in August 1985. In September of that year, Reagan called fighting AIDS one of the administration's "top priorities," but demonstrations against the slowness of federal attention continued. AIDS Coalition to Unleash Power (ACT UP), founded in March 1987, carried out protests to speed up the approval process for the drug AZT, which promised treatment. In response, the Food and Drug Administration reduced the time required for approval.

The National March on Washington for Lesbian and Gay Rights, designed to nationalize the work already being done by local movements, had taken place in October 1979. The AIDS crisis and the Reagan administration's negligence on the issue and a 1986 US Supreme Court decision in *Bowers v. Hardwick*, which upheld the enforcement of sodomy laws between people of the same sex in the privacy of a home, led gay and lesbian activists to propose a new march. A conference to discuss the prospects was labeled "For love and for life, we're not going back!" The groups decided to include bisexual and transgender individuals. They also embraced the antiapartheid movement, which had been mounting protests and seeking congressional sanctions against Reagan's opposition.

On October 11, 1987, police reports showed that an estimated 325,000 people marched. The NAMES Project AIDS Memorial Quilt, founded by Cleve Jones to honor those who died from the disease, was first shown at the march. After the march, ACT UP continued protests over the price of AZT until 1989 when the price was reduced. In 1990, two years after leaving office, Reagan apologized for his neglect of the AIDS issue.

On the environment, Reagan pursued policy consistent with his record. While running for governor of California, he had supported logging the state's centuries-old redwood trees, saying, "A tree is a tree, how many more do you need to look at?"[13] In 1986, when the White House needed roof repairs under the solar thermal panels Jimmy Carter had installed years before, Reagan had quietly removed them, explaining that they weren't cost-effective.

Not surprisingly, the administration weakened enforcement and protection of natural resources and antipollution measures. The officeholders seemed not to care that natural resources policy had been Republican initiatives and the Environmental Protection Agency was proposed by President Richard Nixon. Democrats in Congress and moderate Republicans responded to media and grassroots groups that interrupted some of their plans. In addition to national protests and marches, local protests were already under way on some issues and helped fuel opposition to Reagan.

Working-class whites and black community protesters organized against toxic waste dumps and to call attention to lead paint's effect on their children. The Love Canal disaster in an area of Niagara Falls, New York, where a chemical company had dumped waste decades before, heightened public awareness in the 1970s. The area had initially been covered up in 1972, and homes and schools were built there. But after heavy rains, the waste resurfaced and the disease and ill effects became a national news story. Investigative newspaper coverage and grassroots door-to-door health surveys reported otherwise unexplainable asthma, migraines, kidney disease, birth defects, and miscarriages in the Love Canal neighborhood. In local communities in North Carolina, and in other places, toxic waste dumps were found, and in Louisiana, petrochemical refining sites in "Cancer Alley" became a major issue, causing local protests and the development of an environmental justice movement.[14]

Responding to public anguish, Congress overrode Reagan's veto of the reauthorization of the Clean Water Act in 1987. Congressional Democrats fought industry attempts to rewrite the Clean Air Act. They also protected wilderness areas from efforts to permit fossil fuel drilling and blocked Reagan's plan to lease the entirety of the 1.4 million acre outer continental shelf, which constitutes the nation's coastline, for oil drilling.[15]

Reagan's Interior secretary, James Watt, and Environmental Protection Agency administrator Anne Gorsuch (Supreme Court associate justice Neil Gorsuch's mother) made outrageous statements and were intransigent when dealing with Congress. In 1983, Watt told listeners about his Coal Advisory Commission: "I have a black, I have a woman, two Jews, and a cripple."[16] As criticism swelled, he resigned. Gorsuch became the first cabinet-level appointee to be cited for contempt of Congress. On Reagan's orders, she refused to give subpoenaed documents to a House committee investigating the Superfund operations. Fifty-five Republicans voted with 204 Democrats to issue the contempt citation. These episodes increased the number of grassroots environmental group protests, membership in the organizations, and even *Doonesbury* comic strips on the subject.

The long-standing nuclear freeze movement curtailed Reagan's embrace of nuclear proliferation, through political action committees and lobbying groups, which donated increasingly large sums to congressional campaigns. They also organized a march in New York City, not Washington, on June 12, 1982, that drew a million protesters. Their grassroots organizing for arms control and against increased defense spending so motivated voters that Democrats added twenty-six seats to their House majority in the 1982 midterm elections. A freeze resolution was then passed in the House in 1983. Reagan, of course, won reelection in a landslide in 1984, but the millions of dollars donated by freeze-based groups moved the House toward arms control and helped Democrats regain the Senate in 1986. Reagan subsequently abandoned talk of nuclear war and talked peace.

Opposition to Reagan's policies energized other national movements, including the twenty-fifth anniversary of the March on Washington movement and Jesse Jackson's political work, which led to his runs for the presidency in 1984 and 1988. Experience in these movements prepared the grassroots for the resistance needed to oppose Reagan's civil rights policies.

President Reagan attempted to turn back the clock on civil rights gains that had increased opportunity and alleviated discrimination against women and people of color. His appointees in the Justice Department stopped enforcing the laws they didn't like and were emboldened when Republican appointees to the Supreme Court struck down civil rights legislation. Reagan also attempted to add to the conservatives on the Supreme Court by nominating Robert Bork. Using inside and outside strategies—working both within and outside federal agencies—a bipartisan coalition of moderate congressional Republicans and Democrats, professional organizations, and civil rights groups, in coordination with a grassroots movement across the country, enacted legislation four successive times that overturned negative court decisions and Reagan's actions. That informal coalition also killed Robert Bork's Supreme Court nomination. Bork had been promised an appointment since he carried out Nixon's Saturday Night Massacre as acting attorney general, but the coalition regarded him as a racist "ideological extremist" who would tilt the balance on the court.

The victories included enacting the Voting Rights Act Extension of 1982, the Civil Rights Restoration Act of 1988, the Fair Housing Amendments Act of 1988, and the Civil Rights Commission reauthorization in 1984. They succeeded, even though until 1986, Republican senators Orrin Hatch (Utah) and Strom Thurmond (South Carolina) controlled the Senate Judiciary Committee, from which most civil rights legislation emerges. The reactionary policies caused pain but fueled effective organizing and support for resistance and positive change.[17]

Although the coalition of civil rights organizations and activists won legislatively, they soon lost much of the law and policy struggle in the courts and had to renew the battles to restore gains. Struggle seemed endless. After the coalition defeated Robert Bork's Supreme Court nomination, Reagan appointed three associate justices—Sandra Day O'Connor, Antonin Scalia, and Anthony Kennedy—and William H. Rehnquist to chief justice. Reagan also succeeded in gaining confirmation of more than 350 youthful judges to lower federal courts. In the thirty years since Reagan's election, the interpretation of the law by federal court judges has weakened the civil rights laws the coalition achieved.

Reagan succeeded in disabling the United States Commission on Civil Rights, though he failed to expel me as his most vocal critic, whom his supporters urged him not to endure. The commission had been a symbol since 1957 of the nation's commitment to equal opportunity and an end to discrimination for invidious reasons. It had not hesitated to criticize government at all levels, including presidents, based on its investigations.

Reagan and his advisers objected to the commission's watchdog role, because it interfered with their goal of seeming to support civil rights while undercutting enforcement.[18]

Reagan's victory in the 1980 presidential election was decades in the making. Opposition to elements of the black freedom struggle, denying the existence of discrimination, and limiting the availability of remedies were part of the conservative tide that Reagan rode to office.

As advocates pressed for public school desegregation and for remedying economic inequality, job and residential segregation in the North, and an end to police brutality, Richard Nixon expanded the Republican base in the South and in the North. His Southern strategy and construct of the "silent majority," a susceptible demographic left behind by the social and cultural changes of the 1960s, consolidated a conservative political identity to empower the Republican Party.

Nixon was a complex figure. On domestic policy, he hired the first female assistant to the president in history; he appealed to moderates by proposing the Environmental Protection Agency and expanded aid to education, among other social improvement positions. He appeared to remedy the effects of sex and race discrimination in government contracting, but then backtracked. Politically, he had to fend off Alabama governor George Wallace, who in two presidential campaigns appealed to Southern and Northern whites opposed to desegregation in schools and neighborhoods, and experiencing class anxieties, and yearning for the good old days. After the attempted assassination of Wallace in 1972, Nixon won reelection over George McGovern, a real antiwar candidate, in a landslide.

After the Watergate crisis, Nixon's resignation, and Gerald Ford's presidency, President Carter tried to revitalize civil rights enforcement. But massive inflation, the Iranian hostage crisis, the gas crisis, and other issues made it relatively easy for Reagan to defeat him in 1980. Embracing Nixon's Southern strategy, Reagan began his general election campaign in August pledging to defend states' rights in a speech he gave at the Neshoba County fairgrounds in Philadelphia, Mississippi, the town where the young civil rights workers James Chaney, Andrew Goodman, and Michael Schwerner were murdered in 1968. Three months after the Philadelphia speech, Reagan won the election. He sought to extend the race-polarizing strategies that Republicans had used since Nixon, while reminding correspondents that he lacked personal bigotry. Such strategies drove the wedge deeper between the Democratic Party and Northern white working men who felt threatened by efforts to end long-standing employment discrimination by hiring blacks and women. Adding this constituency to others—anti–civil rights Southern whites, the Christian right, economic conservatives, and a few blacks to provide political cover—Reagan worked to consolidate a sustainable conservative majority. On taxes and spending issues, Reagan achieved early success, but when he turned to civil rights issues, he could not seduce Republican moderates. Their votes did not mean they agreed that civil rights should be deemphasized.[19]

The first legislative battle was fought over voting rights, and the victories won are still under attack with the Supreme Court decision in *Shelby v. Holder* in 2013 and the continuing refusal to reenact major features of the Voting Rights Act of 1965. The 1965 act transformed the electorate in the South. Registration, for example, rose from 29 percent of eligible black voters in 1965 to 57 percent in 1980. Critical to the act's success were the provisions of Section 5 requiring Justice Department or federal court pre-clearance of any proposed change to voting practices in jurisdictions where blacks had long been systematically prevented from voting—by violence and intimidation and by means such as poll taxes, literacy requirements, and sham tests of constitutional knowledge. The covered jurisdictions included the states of the former Confederacy in their entirety and several smaller jurisdictions elsewhere. Initially scheduled to expire in 1970, the "temporary" provisions had been renewed that year and again in 1975, and they were scheduled to expire again in 1982. Their renewal was the first front in the battle over voting rights.[20]

A second front opened in April 1980, when the Supreme Court decided *Mobile v. Bolden.*[21] Five years earlier, the veteran civil rights activist Wiley L. Bolden and other African American residents of Mobile, Alabama, filed a lawsuit challenging the at-large electoral system for the city's three commissioners, who exercised all executive and legislative power in the city. Although African Americans constituted 35 percent of the city's population, none had ever been elected commissioner. The plaintiffs contended that the system violated the First, Thirteenth, Fourteenth, and Fifteenth Amendments to the Constitution; Section 2 of the Voting Rights Act of 1965; and the Civil Rights Act of 1871 by diluting African American votes. District court judge Virgil Pittman ruled only on the Fourteenth and Fifteenth Amendment claims, finding that the city had violated both by intentionally discriminating against African American voters, and he ordered that a new mayor-council system be installed. The Court of Appeals for the Fifth Circuit affirmed and the Supreme Court granted the city's petition for review.

As it stood at the time, Section 2 of the Voting Rights Act provided that

> no voting qualification or prerequisite to voting, or standard, practice, or procedure shall be imposed or applied by any State or political subdivision to deny or abridge the right of any citizen of the United States to vote on account of race or color.[22]

Before *Mobile v. Bolden*, there was little case law interpreting Section 2, but it was generally agreed that, based on the legislative history of the act and its 1970 extension, the statute required only a showing of discriminatory effect: that a challenged electoral system infringed the voting rights of racial minorities, regardless of the motivations of those who created and ran the system.[23]

The Supreme Court disposed of the case in conflicting opinions. Four justices, in an opinion by Justice Stewart joined by Chief Justice Burger and Justices Powell and Rehnquist, addressed the Section 2 claim even though the lower courts had not ruled on it. Stewart declared that a claim under Section 2 required evidence that the challenged electoral system was established with the *purpose* or *intent* to discriminate against minorities. He ignored relevant parts of the legislative history in holding that Congress intended to require the same showing under the Voting Rights Act as required for Fifteenth Amendment claims. Then Stewart said that Mobile's system did not violate either the Fifteenth Amendment or the Voting Rights Act, because some African Americans registered and voted without interference. He simply ignored evidence in the record that even when blacks voted, the at-large system intentionally diluted their vote by keeping them from winning a seat that was possible with a single member system. Essentially, the at-large system kept blacks from exercising political power.[24] Justice Stevens concurred in the decision, because he didn't want to increase lawsuits drawing the courts into the "political thicket" of reviewing election district drawing.

When the case was sent back to the lower court for trial on the question of intent, the black plaintiffs' lawyers found a turn-of-the-century document in which one of the system's designers acknowledged that the electoral system was manipulated intentionally to deny African Americans meaningful electoral participation. This finding was important, because the Supreme Court had required proof of intent as the standard the lower court must use. In April 1982, trial judge Virgil Pittman found that "one of the principal motivating factors for the at-large election system for the Mobile City Commission was the purpose (intent) to discriminate against blacks, and to deny them access to the political process and political office . . . [and] that the effects of this discriminatory intent continues [sic] to the present." Mobile's at-large system therefore violated Section 2 of the Voting Rights Act, and also the Civil Rights Act of 1871 and the Fourteenth and Fifteenth Amendments.[25]

Elsewhere, the Supreme Court's decision on Section 2 left cases of vote dilution unaddressed. Requiring intent was the bane of civil rights litigation, for plaintiffs could not often find a "smoking gun" like that used by Judge Pitman. They were a rarity; officials were not usually careless or not brazen enough to leave evidence of their intentions. Lower courts repeatedly rejected challenges to at-large voting systems because of insufficient evidence of intent. With one exception, challenges were sustained only when plaintiffs, like those in Mobile v. Bolden, managed to produce a smoking gun.[26]

The case also showed the continued necessity of the Section 5 preclearance provisions, which are mandates that nine states and parts of seven others seek approval from the Justice Department or from a federal court before changing voting laws or maps.[27] In Mobile, because of compliance with the trial judge's order, eventually, in July 1985, the first three African Americans since Reconstruction were elected to the city council. This was after ten years of litigation and $2.2 million in legal fees, which the city taxpayers had to pay as part of the settlement to give African Americans their right to representatives of their choice.[28] Unless the preclearance provisions were renewed, election officials could do what Mobile's leaders had done in 1911, leaving blacks without political power for years.

Civil rights advocates decided to ask Congress to void the court's ruling in Mobile v. Bolden, because proving intent was usually impossible and left problems with voting rights unresolved. They wanted to reinstate the long-standing interpretation that Section 2 did not require proof of intent, along with renewing Section 5. The lobby group to which the civil rights organizations belonged, the Leadership Conference on Civil Rights (LCCR), took the lead in executing the strategy, introducing the 1982 Voting Rights Act extension bill in April 1981.

The LCCR was founded in 1950 by A. Philip Randolph, head of the Brotherhood of Sleeping Car Porters, whose threatened March on Washington gained Executive Order 8802; Roy Wilkins of the NAACP; and Arnold Aronson, a leader of the National Jewish Community Relations Advisory Council. The LCCR staff would lobby administration officials and Congress while the civil rights member organizations rallied the grassroots. Other movements, including the anti-Vietnam War protests and the civil rights movement of the 1960s, had sometimes acted in coalition, but not in the formal, long-lasting, structured pattern of LCCR. Using the model established in 1950, LCCR played a major role in securing the passage of every federal civil rights statute in the twentieth century. By 1980, when Reagan won the presidential election, civil rights maintained bipartisan support in Congress and most of the country.[29]

The LCCR had a proven track record of using grassroots activism, using the media, formulating and implementing legislative strategy, providing expertise in the substance of the law and legislative drafting, building and sustaining relationships with congressional leaders, and identifying and preparing witnesses for congressional hearings. The conference included at least one organization with expertise in every field of civil rights. LCCR had grown by 1981 to include nonprofits representing women, disabled persons, Indigenous peoples, Asian Americans, Latinos, older Americans, and gay and lesbian Americans—165 national organizations representing 65 million individuals.

The LCCR's efforts were directed by Ralph Neas, its newly hired executive director. Neas, a white Republican Catholic, was the former chief legislative assistant to two Republican senators, Edward Brooke, the first black senator from Massachusetts, and David Durenberger of Minnesota. Neas was experienced at working across party lines at a time when each party in Congress included moderates and liberals along with conservatives. Though some members of the LCCR were wary because of his Republican credentials, Neas's appointment turned out to be a great decision for the times. As he arrived at LCCR, its leading congressional lobbyist, Clarence Mitchell, and other key founders retired. Neas needed all his political experience, ties to staffers and members on the Hill, and ability to manage his diverse coalition to shepherd the Voting Rights Act extension through Congress.[30]

The Reagan administration unsurprisingly wanted to eliminate or weaken the preclearance provisions of the Voting Rights Act of 1965 and to keep the intent standard the Supreme Court had announced in Mobile. The president warned that an effects standard would mean a quota system. Reagan also supported a proposal from Jesse Helms, Orrin Hatch, and Strom Thurmond to apply the preclearance requirements nationally. They knew the problem was not national, but an overwhelmed Justice Department wouldn't be staffed adequately to enforce the law where the problems existed.[31]

In the House of Representatives, the Judiciary Committee and its subcommittee on Civil and Constitutional Rights were chaired by strong civil rights advocates Peter Rodino (Democrat-New Jersey) and Don Edwards (Democrat-California) respectively. LCCR proceeded with a weekly steering committee meeting with groups divided into policy, media, advocacy, and grassroots. In LCCR, accommodations had to be made between the litigators, who wanted to make sure they were well positioned to win cases, and the legislative pragmatists, who were concerned with what would work well enough and could pass. Neas practically took up residence in congressional committee offices as committee members and staff worked with the LCCR to decide on witnesses for hearings in Washington and in the South and Southwest. Meanwhile the grassroots organizations had to attend the hearings and help their members successfully challenge key members of Congress and hold events to show their deep concern about the issue. Everyone had to stay on the same page even as the legislation evolved.

The six weeks of hearings with 117 witnesses showed that systematic, disguised historic discrimination persisted. The evidence was so overwhelming that something rare happened. Henry Hyde (Republican-Illinois), ranking Republican on the Judiciary Committee who had been the leading House opponent to renewing the preclearance provisions, changed his mind and switched sides, and then he switched again. A great deal of back and forth negotiations and friction occurred between the litigators and others on the LCCR steering committee as most wanted something that Hyde could support without harm to voting rights. When the resulting compromise was put forward by Hamilton Fish (Republican-New York), James Sensenbrenner (Republican-Wisconsin), with Rodino and

Edwards, and the LCCR accepted it, Hyde climbed aboard. The House Judiciary Committee reported a bill on July 31 with a results test and with the preclearance requirements intact. Only Congressman Caldwell Butler (Republican-Virginia) voted no. Grassroots mobilization could be directed at rolling up a big vote in the House to influence the Senate vote.[32]

On August 4, 1981, Hyde published an opinion piece in the *Washington Post* supporting extension of the Voting Rights Act. On August 3, Alpha Phi Alpha, one of the major black fraternities, gave $600,000 to heads of the Urban League, NAACP, and United Negro College Fund. Alpha president Ozell Sutton announced that they wanted to support a major effort to gain extension of the Voting Rights Act.[33]

The NAACP mounted Operation Network in each congressional district. Members called their legislators and reported what they said. To report, they used worksheets that included a detailed analysis of the bill and the legislator's answers to their questions, and then reported back on whether the legislator had made a commitment. Other organizations followed a similar procedure, devoting time, energy, and all available resources to the effort. On August 10, at least three thousand blacks waving signs and chanting "We shall overcome" marched in Birmingham, Alabama, to promote extension of the Voting Rights Act. On October 5, 1981, the House passed the Judiciary Committee's bill by an overwhelming majority, 389–24.[34]

LCCR wanted to move quickly in the Senate, drawing on the grassroots pressure that had been applied and the momentum of the vote in the House. Within two months, sixty-one senators, including twenty-one Republicans, had cosponsored the Kennedy-Mathias bill in the Senate, identical to the House bill. The Republicans included Dan Quayle of Indiana, Paula Hawkins of Florida, and William Roth of Delaware. By spring 1982, the number of Senate cosponsors had risen to sixty-five, nearly enough to override a veto. However, the Senate Judiciary's Committee's Subcommittee on the Constitution, chaired by Orrin Hatch, rejected the results test. In its report, the subcommittee majority recommended "the retention of the intent standard in place of the new results standard adopted in the House-approved measure," and it defended the *Mobile v. Bolden* standard. The proposed bill then went before the full Senate Judiciary Committee, chaired by Strom Thurmond. He had the power to delay consideration of the bill as the deadline for renewing Section 5 approached, which all knew would weaken the LCCR's hand.

The coalition was helped when the unexpected occurred: Reagan's fiasco involving Bob Jones University and the lesser known Goldsboro Christian School. Both were private Christian institutions that excluded African Americans. Bob Jones University, located in Greenville, South Carolina, was founded in 1927. The Goldsboro Christian School was founded in 1963 at the height of Southern resistance to *Brown v. Board of Education* and just before school desegregation began in the North Carolina county where it was located. Until the 1970s, both schools enjoyed exemption from federal taxation under section 501(c)(3) of the Internal Revenue Code, which exempted corporations organized exclusively for educational purposes, among others. Donations to 501(c)(3) organizations were deductible from the donor's income. In 1970, the Internal Revenue Service concluded that it could no longer maintain the tax exemption for any school engaging in racial discrimination, and after nearly five years of legal wrangling, the IRS formally revoked Bob Jones University's tax-exempt status in 1975. The school sued the agency in federal court in South Carolina to block the revocation, arguing that the policy was inconsistent with section 501(c)(3) and violated the school's First Amendment right to the free exercise of religion. The school won at trial, but the appeals court reversed the decision, agreeing with the IRS.[35]

While the *Bob Jones University* case proceeded, the Goldsboro Christian School made similar arguments for tax-exempt status in federal court in North Carolina. The district court found for the IRS, and another panel of the appeals court summarily affirmed the ruling based on their decision in the *Bob Jones University* case. In October 1981, the Supreme Court agreed to review the decisions together. The government supported review and in its brief, filed nine months after Reagan took office, argued that decisions and the IRS policy denying tax exemptions were correct.[36]

Much had changed in the eleven years since the IRS initiated its policy. In 1970, memories of Jim Crow, de jure school segregation, violence hurled at civil rights activists, and resistance to school integration in the South were recent. Thousands of private academies, many of them calling themselves Christian, had been established to preserve white-only elementary and secondary schools. By 1981, however, the racial origins of private religious schools like the Goldsboro Christian School had faded, and a reactionary view of civil rights had gained ground. Nixon, Reagan, and many in the new Republican Senate majority had entered office decrying efforts to achieve school desegregation, supported by Christian fundamentalists, who had become a potent political force.[37]

Segregationists began lobbying the administration, supported by Strom Thurmond, a Bob Jones University trustee, urging that it reverse its position. House Majority Whip Trent Lott (Republican-Mississippi) wrote to Solicitor General Rex Lee urging reversal. As Don Edwards, chair of the House judiciary subcommittee described him at the time, Lott was one of the young House Republicans pushing hard for a rollback of civil rights law: "Tough, eloquent, great speakers, they won't give you nothing. Trent Lott is the toughest of that band; he's a tough son of a bitch, I'll tell you, and he won't give you an inch."[38]

Lott did not persuade Solicitor General Lee, but he found support elsewhere in the administration, including from the president, who wrote next to the entry in the presidential log outlining the letter, "I think we should." Justice's Civil Rights Division head William Bradford Reynolds, who had consulted Attorney General Edwin Meese and Treasury Secretary Donald Regan, changed the Justice Department position to support tax exemptions for the two schools. Treasury announced the reversal of its legal position, and said it would restore the schools' exempt status.[39]

Alarmed civil rights organizations, using their Republican contacts, found that Michael Deaver, Howard Baker, and congressional leaders who would have objected were not even consulted. They then went public, attacking the administration's support of what they called a racist policy. NAACP head Benjamin Hooks, who was also chair of the LCCR, denounced it as "criminal." Democratic leaders in Congress called it "part of a pattern of capitulation to the segregationists." Many Republican leaders were also critical. Career employees of the Justice Department Civil Rights Division, including half the division's attorneys, protested the administration's reversal in a letter to Reynolds.[40]

Deaver and Baker were livid at those who had pushed the IRS policy change and tried to defuse the issue. In January 1982, Reagan released a statement, written by communications director David Green, insisting that the president remained opposed to racial discrimination, as he had repeatedly written to correspondents, and was only attempting to keep agencies from overstepping their bounds. A few days later, the administration retreated, sending a draft bill to Congress that proposed denying tax-exempt status to racially discriminatory schools.[41]

Not mollified, Democrats and many Republicans in Congress rejected the bill, because the IRS had the power to establish its policy and no legislation was necessary. The LCCR rejected the bill as the face-saving ploy that it was and filed an amicus brief urging the Supreme Court to uphold the IRS rule. The court took the extraordinary step of appointing William T. Coleman, a former secretary of transportation, chair of the NAACP Legal Defense Fund board, and a distinguished lawyer, to argue the government's original position before Reagan's intervention in favor of the exemption. The court upheld the IRS rule in an 8–1 decision.

The whole episode put Republicans on the defensive in the Senate proceedings over the Voting Rights Act extension and helped to ensure its passage. All the work that Chief Justice John Roberts, then an assistant to Attorney General William French Smith, put into memos, talking points, speeches, testimony, strategy, and op-eds for Justice political officials went for naught.[42]

In the Senate, Robert Dole of Kansas, a mainstream Republican who had previously been uncommitted within the Judiciary Committee, anxiously suggested a compromise and guided it to acceptance. In the compromise bill, from Dole, Edward Kennedy (Democrat-Massachusetts), and Charles "Mac" Mathias (Republican-Maryland), a revised Section 2 specified the results standard and that it could be met based on the totality of the circumstances. Another provision added to please some Republicans said that proportional representation of minorities was not required. In fact, the LCCR had never suggested such an idea in the first place. The act was renewed for twenty-five years—three and a half times longer than any previous extension—and provisions requiring bilingual assistance for voters were extended.[43]

The bill passed the Senate by a large margin, and Dole persuaded the White House that it could get nothing better. The House approved the Senate bill overwhelmingly, and on June 29, 1982, a smiling Reagan signed the bill into law, looking and sounding like he had been its greatest supporter. At every stage of the process, member organizations with grassroots ran phone banks, held demonstrations, and kept the heat on their senators and representatives. Also, Neas and organization leaders kept the press informed and gave as many interviews as possible while they negotiated the necessary compromises behind the scenes.[44]

They had been lucky that the Bob Jones fight came along, and having moderate Republicans in Congress helped, but the organization of the grassroots and the pressure put on Congress in phone calls and in the media helped them prevail. They would use these tactics and strategies in every legislative fight thereafter, including the considerably more difficult and lengthy fight that began when the Supreme Court decided *Grove City College v. Bell*. A liberal arts college in western Pennsylvania, Grove City College was a bastion of conservatism and the religious right whose students were supported by federal financial aid. The school refused to comply with Department of Education regulations implementing Title IX of the Education Amendments of 1972, which prohibited discrimination based on sex by institutions receiving federal funding. The Carter administration instituted administrative action against the college to enforce compliance, and the college sued the government, seeking an injunction to halt the process, because federal aid to students did not constitute aid to the institution.[45]

After the Court of Appeals for the Third Circuit held that the college received aid within the meaning of Title IX and that the statute applied not only to the specific program receiving aid but also to the entire institution, the college appealed to the Supreme Court. Reversing the Carter administration's position, the Reagan Justice Department sided with the college. On February 28, 1984, in an opinion by Justice White, the court ruled that federal grants to students are aid to the college, but students' receipt and use of federal grants "does not trigger institution-wide coverage under Title IX." The prohibition against discrimination, the court held, applied only to the limited aspect of the institution's operations that specifically received the federal funding, in this case the financial aid office, not to the whole institution.[46]

The court's reading of Title IX meant that institutions receiving federal funding could discriminate based on sex despite the statute's explicit prohibition against sex discrimination. Congressional Democrats and moderate Republicans and the LCCR were shocked. They recognized that the decision logically jeopardized all the civil rights laws with identical language forbidding discrimination by recipients of federal funds. One foundational law was Title VI of the Civil Rights Act of 1964, forbidding discrimination based on race, color, or national origin, upon which all subsequent

legislation was based. The Rehabilitation Act of 1973, outlawing discrimination against handicapped persons, and the Age Discrimination Act of
1975, forbidding discrimination based on age, included the same language.[47]

The same scenarios prevailed as in the voting rights legislative fight.
The Reagan administration, which supported the use of federal funds for
religious institutions, applauded the decision. Attorney General Smith said
he was "very pleased." The Justice Department agreed with the civil rights
groups' view that the ruling also applied to discrimination on the basis of
race, color, religion, national origin, age, or physical handicap and began to
close civil rights investigations based on the pre–Grove City position. The
cases involved not only allegations of sex discrimination but also disability
rights and claims of discrimination by racial minorities.[48]

The LCCR made the smart decision to label its legislative effort to
overcome Grove City the Civil Rights Restoration Act, an effort to restore
existing law, and arguing that taxpayers would not want their taxes to fund
discrimination. Patrisha Wright, head of the Disabilities Rights Education
and Defense Fund (DREDF), had begun to actively involve the organization in legislative campaigns of the LCCR. DREDF was a major player in
the campaign to enact the Civil Rights Restoration Act as Section 504 of
the Rehabilitation Act of 1973 was one of the four statutes weakened by
the Grove City decision. This was the first major piece of legislation where
disability rights advocates were part of the leadership along with minority
and women's groups. Within two weeks of the court's decision, legislation
to remedy the decision passed by an overwhelming bipartisan margin. In
the Senate, Orrin Hatch vowed "to fight it with everything I've got." He fil-
ibustered, and after that was stopped, offered fifteen hundred amendments.
Senator Barry Goldwater (Republican-Arizona) opined at one point that
his colleagues were "beginning to look like a bunch of jackasses," to which
Malcolm Wallop (Republican-Wyoming) added, "Why do you say we're
beginning to look like a bunch of jackasses? We're already there." Unmoved,
Hatch and his conservative bloc succeeded in killing action on the bill for
the rest of the session.[49]

As the wrangling dragged on into 1985, the United States Conference
of Catholic Bishops raised the abortion issue. Realizing there were enough
votes in both houses to add an antiabortion amendment to any legislation,
women's groups and Don Edwards would not allow the bill to go to the
House floor. Neas tried to work out a compromise, which pleased neither

side, and Congress failed to enact the Civil Rights Restoration Act until four years after the Grove College decision.[50]

In the meanwhile, civil rights groups could not prevent the confirmation of Antonin Scalia as associate justice and William Rehnquist as chief justice of the Supreme Court. Grassroots efforts proved again difficult to grow in opposition to judicial appointments. But in a major fight that erupted over Reagan's July 1, 1987, nomination of Robert Bork to the Supreme Court, the civil rights coalition effectively showed Bork's views were not American values. They defeated the nomination because moderate Republicans in the Senate agreed with the Democrats that it was an attempt to move the court rightward, imperiling privacy rights and civil rights generally. Learning from previous fights and the stalling of the Civil Rights Restoration Act, LCCR carefully framed the debate to exclude abortion rights from the discussion. Instead, they focused on the paper trail Bork had left over the course of a twenty-five-year career in government, on the bench, and as a law professor. They also pressed senators to assert their power and right to be an equal partner in the process of seating justices on the high court, not just to rubber-stamp a president's nominees.

The lobbying campaign got off to a bad start when the *New York Times* and *Washington Post* published stories on Ted Kennedy and Senator Joe Biden meeting with LCCR. Their reports that Biden promised he would lead the fight against Bork upset Biden. Cranston said defeating Bork was "doable." They kept track of vote counts, working to freeze senators until after the Judiciary Committee hearings. The grassroots got the message out, skipping August vacations to lobby senators in their district and to find voters to contact them. Labor worked their members hard, and some organizations provided funds for the effort.

This was the most expensive and sophisticated media campaign ever for the Leadership Conference, using polls and focus groups and massive lobbying of print and electronic journalists, including the *New York Times* and *Washington Post* editorial boards. A new twist and highlight of the campaign surfaced when People for the American Way, an LCCR member organization, produced an effective television advertisement featuring the actor Gregory Peck, who had given an Oscar-winning performance as the principled lawyer Atticus Finch in *To Kill a Mockingbird*. In the ad, Peck said of Bork, "He defended poll taxes and literacy tests, which kept many Americans from voting. He opposed the civil rights law that ended Whites

Only signs at lunch counters. He doesn't believe the Constitution protects your right to privacy." Bork's defenders countered that these were merely his views about what was legally permissible under the Constitution, and that he had modified some of them, but People for the American Way noted that if his views had prevailed, the results would be exactly as the ad stated.[51]

The Judiciary Committee hearings took three weeks, with great work coordinated by LCCR, senators, and their staffs. When Bork called the Supreme Court "an intellectual feast," LCCR saw victory near. William Coleman, Andrew Young, and Barbara Jordan gave the opening opposition testimony. LCCR did not testify, although some members wanted to. On October 23, 1987, Bork was defeated 58–42, at that time the greatest number of votes against a Supreme Court nominee.

After initially stating that he would nominate someone his opponents would dislike even more than Bork, and after the unfortunate nomination and withdrawal of Douglas Ginsburg, Reagan settled on the confirmable Anthony Kennedy. Kennedy became a reliable supporter of privacy and gay rights but a major problem on race issues. Ever since, "stealth" nominees for the court—those without extensive paper trails—have been the most easily confirmed, and all have avoided engaging in substantive discussions of the law during their confirmation hearings. Elena Kagan, appointed to the Supreme Court in 2010, as a law professor criticized the confirmation process for lacking substance.[52]

After the Bork defeat it might seem that further civil rights enactments were inconceivable for Republicans. But after Democrats regained control of the Senate in the 1986 election, the majority leader, Robert Byrd (Democrat-West Virginia), scheduled the Civil Rights Restoration Act as the Senate's first order of business. The LCCR renewed its push for the act. However, in early 1987, the civil rights coalition divided once more over abortion. Republican senator John Danforth (Missouri) insisted on a right-to-conscience antiabortion amendment to permit federally funded hospitals and their medical personnel to refuse to perform abortions. It would also allow educational institutions to exclude abortions from health and disability leave plans. The coalition, faced with endlessly being unable to pass the restoration act with the acquiescence of prochoice organizations, except the National Organization for Women, decided not to pull the bill again. With the Danforth Amendment, the Senate passed the

Restoration bill overwhelmingly in January 1988, and in March, the House also passed it by a large margin.[53]

Reagan vetoed the bill, the first veto of a civil rights bill in 120 years. Vice President George H. W. Bush, despite his long-standing prochoice record, supported the president, saying that it was "not the time to become disloyal." Congress easily overrode the veto and the Civil Rights Restoration Act became law on March 22, 1988, making it illegal again to use federal tax payers to fund discrimination.[54]

The LCCR thereafter easily obtained passage of the Fair Housing Amendments Act of 1988, which strengthened the 1968 Fair Housing Act's enforcement provisions and prohibited discrimination against families with children and people with physical or mental disabilities. They worked with the National Association of Realtors, which had come to believe in the LCCR's power as a result of the Bork and Restoration Act victories. Using the same grassroots strategies, the group also lobbied hard for passage of the Martin Luther King Jr. federal holiday and redress for Japanese Americans interned during World War II.[55]

The LCCR prevailed in the legislative arena, but Reagan's greatest victory came in an arena where the LCCR had the least practical opportunity to form coalitions and use grassroots pressure and relationships with political officials to shape law and policy: the control of the federal judiciary.

While the coalition defeated the Bork nomination, Reagan appointed three Supreme Court justices and made William Rehnquist chief justice. At the beginning of Reagan's presidency, the federal bench across the United States was divided by about three to two between Democratic and Republican appointees. When he left office, the proportions were reversed and his appointees accounted for half of the judiciary. Fewer than one in ten of his nominees were women and only four were named to the courts of appeals. He named only six new African American judges and elevated one other from the district court to the court of appeals. One African American woman, Ann Claire Williams, survived the screenings to serve. The large number of lower federal court judges whom Reagan appointed meant that the Senate subjected only a few to extensive questioning and successfully challenged even fewer. One nominee, rejected after testimony about his racist behavior after a long period in the Senate, was President Trump's attorney general Jefferson B. Sessions III.[56]

Reagan made no secret of his ambition to reshape the judiciary, and with few exceptions his nominees were thoroughly vetted for their qualification to advance his conservative political agenda. The 1980 Republican platform signaled the administration's plan. Potential judges would be tested on having "the highest regard for protecting the rights of law abiding citizens," playing the racially loaded law-and-order card that Nixon had perfected. Candidates would have to demonstrate their ideological purity for moving the federal government out of the role of protecting individual rights by showing that their "judicial philosophy" was "consistent with the belief in the decentralization of the federal government and efforts to return decision making power to state and local elected officials." And they would have to take a narrow view of women's rights and oppose abortion rights by showing "respect [for] traditional family values and the sanctity of human life."[57]

Once in office, the administration submitted candidates to an elaborate screening process, handled by political staffers in the Justice Department and the White House, to pick those with the right judicial philosophy. This was the process used for the politicized selection of judges during Reagan's tenure as governor of California, despite his claims at the time and later that it was nonpolitical.[58]

Paul Haarlem, who directed judicial selection for Governor Reagan, told a different story, describing a thoroughly political process. Haarlem set up the committees to which Reagan alluded. The lay members "were usually people who had been active in the Reagan campaign," Haarlem explained, and "the judges I'd usually pick in consultation with a Republican lawyer." Close Reagan associates not on the committees, including William French Smith and Edwin Meese, were also involved in vetting. The names of the Republican candidates were then submitted to the state bar association for rating, and Reagan's nominees were selected from those rated "qualified" or better. Haarlem also described how he rejected recommendations in favor of political cronies. In Monterey County, Reagan appointed his local campaign manager over two qualified candidates recommended by the selection committee. He appointed his aide Bill Clark to successively higher courts, rejecting committee recommendations. Reagan also traded judgeships for legislators' votes on several bills.[59]

President Reagan's judicial selection process for federal courts followed the California playbook. First, the 1980 Republican platform criticized

Jimmy Carter for "his partisan nominations" and pledged "to reverse that trend," echoing Reagan's criticism of Brown and his promises in California. Then Republicans took political judicial selection to a new level. They dispensed with the pretense of desiring independent input and diminished the importance of senators and local party leaders in selecting candidates. They also insisted on marginalizing the ratings of the American Bar Association's Standing Committee on the Federal Judiciary.[60]

The administration subjected candidates for the district courts and courts of appeals to an unprecedented, systematic screening process to support Reagan's plan to use the judiciary to achieve the legal and political change he sought. The process was directed by the White House counsel, and Meese, who as attorney general campaigned publicly for the reversal of decades of constitutional jurisprudence in civil rights, privacy rights, the rights of those accused of crimes, and federalism. In the Justice Department, the screening was centered in the newly created Office of Legal Policy, the name of which connoted its political purpose. It included the attorney general, the assistant attorney general for legal policy, the special counsel for judicial selection, and some of their staff. This group made recommendations to the federal Judicial Selection Committee, another Reagan administration innovation, which was based in the White House. Later called the Working Group on Appointments, because it also recommended US attorney candidates (which George W. Bush's Justice Department shamelessly politicized twenty years later) and US marshal positions, this body formalized White House control. Beyond receiving recommendations from Justice, the White House group also created a roster of candidates.

At Justice and in the White House, candidates' records were scoured and analyzed to gauge their ideological and political bona fides. Finalists were subjected to daylong interviews (another Reagan administration novelty, which many candidates found offensive) in which they were asked about their judicial philosophy and positions on specific issues, especially abortion. In short, the process delivered nominees who passed a litmus test designed to assure their devotion to interpreting the law in accordance with Reagan's political objectives. The selection committee's consensus recommendations were presented to the president, who generally did not play an active role in the process and rarely failed to approve the candidates placed before him.[61]

With Stephen Williams's seating in June 1986, Reagan's appointees made conservative judges a majority on the Court of Appeals for the District of Columbia Circuit, the second most important federal court. Conservatives celebrated it as among the important victories of Reagan's presidency. By the end of his presidency, Reagan appointees were the majority on the Courts of Appeals for the Second, Sixth, and Seventh Circuits, and they were a near majority elsewhere, joining Nixon's and Ford's appointees to create Republican dominance in the courts.[62]

The Reagan administration also tried to ensure the staying power of their agenda in the courts by appointing young judges. The justices Reagan placed on the Supreme Court (average age 49.3) were notably younger than President Clinton's nominees (average age 57.3). Presidents George H. W. Bush and George W. Bush followed Reagan's lead (average age 49.3). In making his first nomination, President Trump followed the pattern, naming Neil Gorsuch, age 49, for the Supreme Court.[63]

During Reagan's first term, 11.4 percent of his judicial appointees were under forty, a higher percentage than any recent predecessor, and the average age of his appeals court judges in his first term was 51.5, the youngest average among his and the previous four administrations. Youth was especially emphasized during Reagan's second term, when his nominees to the district and appellate courts were younger than those of any other president in the twentieth century. Of his second-term judges, 34.2 percent of were under forty-five years of age. The next highest percentage of nominees under forty-five was 22 percent, by Theodore Roosevelt.[64]

The Supreme Court's right turn—which began before Reagan's presidency and continued with his associate justice appointments, his elevation of Rehnquist, and the subsequent Republican appointments of Clarence Thomas, John Roberts, and Samuel Alito (all of whom were Reagan administration veterans)—is undeniable and widely recognized. It is perhaps unsurprising that O'Connor and Kennedy, while contributing to the court's rightward shift, became swing votes in cases involving disputes over divisive issues like abortion and affirmative action, since their nominations were atypical in ways that short-circuited the process of guaranteeing their conservative qualifications. O'Connor was simply not subjected to the same screening applied to other nominees. Doubts were raised about her fidelity to the antiabortion creed, but with a president concerned to keep a campaign pledge to name a woman to the first opening on the court, and

Goldwater and Rehnquist backing her, those charged with vetting her set aside the doubts, and Reagan chose her after a brief Oval Office meeting. Anti-abortion activists and other forces of the GOP right had little opportunity to mount effective opposition. Kennedy was thoroughly screened and was passed over repeatedly for lacking the necessary conservative bona fides. But with an election year looming, he was a safe nominee for Republicans in the wake of the Bork defeat and the embarrassment when Douglas Ginsburg was nominated and then withdrew over his past marijuana use. On the other hand, Rehnquist, as chief, continued performing as he had as an associate justice, and for nearly thirty years, Scalia performed as Reagan and Meese knew he would. On the eve of his retirement in 2010, Justice John Paul Stevens trenchantly observed that, with the exception of Ruth Bader Ginsburg and potentially Sonia Sotomayor, each of the eleven justices who joined the court since 1975, including himself, was more conservative than the justice he or she replaced. As a group, the Republican nominees moved the court sharply in that direction.[65]

Less well recognized is how Reagan's expectations informed the lower federal courts, where cases are so numerous and generally lacking in publicity as to elude widespread appreciation.[66] Shortly before Reagan left office, Gary L. Bauer, one of his domestic policy advisers and later head of the Christian Coalition, asserted that although Reagan might not have succeeded in pushing through most of his conservative social agenda, he had pleased conservatives by appointing federal judges who would promote the Right's policy views. "You've got to look at where the courts are going," added Dan Lofgren (Republican-California), who sat on the House Judiciary Committee. "They're far more conservative."[67]

The satisfaction of conservatives like Bauer and Lofgren's confidence in the courts' direction were well placed. That and the success of the Federalist Society, founded in 1982, in identifying and nurturing judges for the process early led to a decades-long effort by the Right to reshape the national discourse and redirect federal law and policy on civil rights. Reagan lost every legislative battle he fought with the civil rights coalition, but in capturing the federal courts and using the Civil Rights Commission to help shape public opinion, the Reaganites won.

What the successes and failures of the resistance against Reagan's domestic agenda show is that protesters were successful in mounting grassroots opposition on legislation and developing new strategies, such as the

Gregory Peck ad. What was desperately needed, however, was some way to mobilize sufficiently to routinely thwart bad judicial appointments. This would include deterring White House nominations, consolidating senatorial opposition to confirmation, and more and better ways of explaining the stakes to the grassroots to win. The founding of the American Constitution Society in 2001, which for progressives identifies and promotes those who might become judicial appointees, did not come until almost twenty years after the Federalist Society was formed.

In confronting Reagan, the LCCR won some important battles, but his judicial appointees would make clear that the war was never over. Victories had to be re-won.

CHAPTER 4

The Free South Africa Movement

After singing the lines of the reggae song we have sung so many years, we at last saw him "walking hand in hand along the streets with Winnie Mandela."

And now here I was, privileged to be among those in the Cape Town mayor's office to greet him after his release from prison. It had been a long day for him, us and the thousands of people massed outside, pursuing their own celebratory waiting.

Rumors flew; he is on his way; he is not coming. The hours passed in debate over whether the crowd was too unruly and wondering what was taking so long. Then suddenly he was there in the room. After he greeted each of us warmly and personally, he went out to speak to the masses of South Africans.

Finally, the man they called "Baba"—father—was here. They had danced the toi-toi a million times at demonstrations, legal and illegal, and prayed for his release. They had suffered miseducation or none at all, bad or inadequate food and housing in the townships and squatter villages. But today they were here to celebrate—pressed up against each other hour after hour in the hot sun with no water, no lavatories and a loudspeaker system that did not work. When it did, they heard speakers in a language many of them did not understand.

But when Baba began to speak, the restless crowd became still. Those who spoke only Xhosa watched those who understood the English, cheering when they did. When he spoke Xhosa directly to them at the end, the cheering became louder. He told them to go home and they did. They had seen and heard Nelson Mandela.

When he came in again to sit with us, mainly everyone laughed and made small talk as one does among family and friends. Tomorrow we would begin again worrying what comes next and what we must all do. But for the moment I was content. My wait for Nelson Mandela had come to an end.

—Mary Frances Berry, *Philadelphia Inquirer*, February 22, 1990[1]

ON THE NIGHT BEFORE Thanksgiving in November 1984, Randall Robinson, executive director of TransAfrica; Eleanor Holmes Norton, a Georgetown law professor; Congressman Walter Fauntroy, a Democrat representing the District of Columbia; and I kept an appointment at the South African Embassy with Bernard Fourie, South Africa's ambassador to the United States, to discuss growing brutality and repression in South Africa, which had instituted apartheid in 1948. Throughout 1984, the international media had covered a large number of labor strikes and youth protests violently suppressed by corporations and government military forces. In addition, reports revealed the horrendous effects of the apartheid regime on the daily lives of black South Africans in rural areas and the townships, who protested against rent increases, poor education, housing and apartheid policies.[2]

The South African government, also, installed a new constitution that continued to exclude blacks from participation in Parliament while giving Indians and "coloreds," people of mixed black and white race, limited representation. South Africans protested this newly constituted Parliament designed to signal that the apartheid system was undergoing reformation. But any pretense of reform was misleading. Not only had nothing changed for the better, but the system was becoming worse.

We talked with the ambassador for forty minutes about the treatment of demonstrators and the need to imagine a future beyond apartheid, and then Eleanor Holmes Norton, as previously planned, made excuses and left the meeting. After another ten minutes, Randall said to the ambassador, "Please convey for us to your government our basic demand, which is twofold. All of your government's political prisoners must be released immediately. These would include, among others, Nelson Mandela, Walter Sisulu, Govan Mbeki, the thirteen labor leaders arrested recently without charge, and the three black leaders who have taken refuge in the British Consulate in Durban. We are further demanding that your government commit itself immediately and publicly to the speedy dismantlement of the apartheid system with a timetable for this task."

TransAfrica staffer Hazel Ross and intern David Scott back at the office made calls to ensure the media knew we had begun a protest. Television, radio, and print media journalists arrived outside the embassy on this slow news night before Thanksgiving. Acting as spokesperson, Norton explained that if our government was prepared to pressure South Africa to end its repression, we wouldn't be protesting. Cecelie Counts, a Harvard law graduate and founding member of the Southern Africa Support Project, and a TransAfrica staffer, had about fifty demonstrators gathered to march and chant "Freedom yes! Apartheid no!"; "The people united will never be defeated!"; "Free Nelson Mandela!"; and other slogans.

Ambassador Fourie looked out the window and seemed astounded. He couldn't believe what was happening. He looked at Walter Fauntroy to ask whether, as a member of Congress, he would help to quell the protest. Walter told him he was present because he had devoted his life to racial justice, and that cause had brought our group there. Fourie left his office to call for advice. We sat there as time passed. After about twenty minutes, Herbert Beukes, deputy chief of mission, who had been silent throughout the previous forty minutes, asked if there was anything they could do to work things out.

I responded, "You can comply with the demands." His reply indicated anything but compliance. I answered, "No."

Fourie came back into the room after his phone consultations. We remained seated as he called in uniformed US Secret Service officers, who arrested us. We were elated; if he had locked us in the office and left for the holiday or had us dumped on the lawn, our protests would have failed like others who had protested at the doors of the embassy. But instead, handcuffed images of Walter Fauntroy, Randall Robinson, and me being taken away in a police wagon in handcuffs were broadcast widely and repeatedly—over cable news and international television.

While we were being charged with trespassing by unlawful entry of an embassy, punishable by a hundred-dollar fine and six months in jail, at the northwest Washington, DC, police station near the embassy, the press coverage brought a swarm of supporters and politicians to wish us well. Fauntroy and Robinson spent the night in the central cellblock downtown. I was taken to spend the night in the DC women's prison. The lights were kept on all night, so I passed the hours following nonviolent protest protocol, talking through the bars with the other inmates about what brought them there and explaining apartheid, hoping the guards also listened while they kept trying to shut us up.

On Thanksgiving, the next day, we refused to post bond but were released on our own recognizance. At 11 a.m., we went to the House of Representatives Rayburn office building, where we held a press conference in a full committee room. A crowd of journalists watched as we announced the Free South Africa movement (FSAM) as a TransAfrica project and the goal of ending US complicity with apartheid by the passage of comprehensive sanctions legislation. To accomplish the goal, it took our steering committee chaining itself to the embassy entryway and others bringing caskets to the embassy symbolizing those killed in South Africa, sitting in at Shell Oil Company, and then all of us working with labor, religious, and civil rights groups in an international campaign against the Royal Dutch Shell Corporation and the corporations tied to the South African regime. Also, those of us on the steering committee shut down Deak-Perera, a major money-exchange dealer, to educate people not to buy South African gold Krugerrands. When Deak-Perera had the office heat turned off, we slept on the cold slate floor at night, kept our signs in the windows, used a portable toilet we had sneaked in while posing as customers, and ate the snacks we'd brought with us. The demonstrations and arrests were to continue for two more years, and each of us was arrested several times.

We experienced moments of sheer elation and optimism. We held marches in Washington, DC, and other places, with celebrities increasingly joining in. Desmond Tutu came to the embassy protests one day to receive a petition that had been signed by a million Americans demanding an end to apartheid. Cecelie Counts was there every day coordinating the protests rain or shine, and we continued even on the day Reagan's second inaugural parade was canceled because it was too cold.

The press could count on a demonstration and arrests every weekday at 5 p.m., with either large numbers of arrestees or celebrities or both. Car traffic in front of the embassy proceeded as drivers responded to the signs saying: "Honk Your Support," car horns filling the air until the arrested were taken away. Some critics thought we shouldn't have engaged in civil disobedience. A distinguished lawyer in Southern Africa Support Project (SASP) advised us that we would look silly, and we should litigate instead. Harry Belafonte, a TransAfrica board member, was shocked that there had been no discussion of this secret initiative we started. Nevertheless, he came, spoke, and was arrested and gave every support to the effort.

Thousands of people were arrested at the embassy. Groups scheduled days to march and protest, bringing large numbers usually in the range of hundreds. Gay McDougall, a Southern Africa Support group member and the head of a lawyers' international human rights group, brought other lawyers; William Lucy, AFSCME secretary-treasurer and president of the

Coalition of Black Trade Unionists, brought unions; and black Baptists and AMEs came by the busloads. Politicians, mayors, and others came to get arrested. Lowell Weicker became the only US senator ever arrested in a direct-action, nonviolent protest. Tennis star Arthur Ashe and musician Stevie Wonder, Coretta and her children Yolanda and Marty King, and most of the Congressional Black Caucus members came. Rosa Parks not only got arrested but also spoke.

There were mishaps. A publicity stunt went awry when we couldn't find the glo-lites we'd planned to have protesters aim at the sky. We had persuaded a TV station to send a helicopter to fly over the Capitol and broadcast the protest. On another occasion, we couldn't find the keys to Fauntroy's church bus when we were ready to carry two hundred demonstrators to the embassy to protest. I don't recall what happened to the keys or how the demonstrators got to the embassy.

In the meantime, there were shantytowns erected and more divestment pressure applied on college and university campuses and across the country. Massachusetts, where divestment campaigns had a long history, enacted the first statewide divestment law in 1983 and served as a model for other state and local jurisdictions. Mel King, a lifelong community activist in Boston and former Urban League affiliate head, who was elected Massachusetts state representative in 1972, and Jack Backman, a liberal, white state senator, introduced the bill and shepherded its passage, an effort fueled by continuing divestment campaigns. The first school in the country to divest was Hampshire College in western Massachusetts in 1977. The Southern Africa Solidarity Committee at Harvard brought members of African liberation groups to campus, held material aid drives for Zimbabwe, and sponsored fund-raising concerts. The Boston Coalition for the Liberation of Southern Africa (BCLSA) included different groups of interested people and individuals in the Boston area. Themba Vilakazi, the Boston representative of the African National Congress (ANC), in 1985 worked to coordinate local antiapartheid work.

Willard Johnson, a professor of political science at the Massachusetts Institute of Technology, founder and head of the Boston chapter of TransAfrica, and also a member of its national board, guided much of the African solidarity work in the city from the late 1960s onward. He deliberately set up an interracial steering committee, even though nationally TransAfrica made clear from the beginning that the Free South Africa movement and the congressional sanctions drive was a black-led campaign. It focused on racism and understood apartheid as being analogous to segregation in the South, which the civil rights movement attacked. The FSAM was essentially a new phase of the civil rights movement.

The Boston chapter was enormously successful. They announced a demonstration outside the South African consul's office when Desmond Tutu visited Boston. When chapter representatives arrived, the consul met with them, agreed with their position, and gave them a copy of his letter of resignation. The local chapter also mounted protests against the sale of Krugerrands in late 1984, which coincided with TransAfrica's national campaign. The campaign spread, and Deak-Perera discontinued its sale of Krugerrands in August 1985.

In New York City, the Reverend Herbert Daughtry and others organized successive protests at the South African consulate. In August 1985, the American Committee on Africa and a coalition of religious, community, and labor groups led by Cleveland Robinson, the secretary-treasurer of the United Auto Workers (UAW), had a major march in the city. Maxine Waters, then a member of the California legislature, led a group of protesters who sat in at the South African consulate in Beverly Hills.

In the San Francisco Bay area, labor activist Leo Robinson, of Local 10 of the International Longshore and Warehouse Union, recalled that the April 1977 two-day shutdown at the docks to prevent the unloading of South African cargo was effective because Local 10 members who were sympathetic took those jobs, knowing that were not going to work. They tied up the ship for two days. They continued demonstrations at the docks over the years, but they received the most attention on November 23, 1984, after FSAM, a project of TransAfrica, launched its campaign. On that day, when they refused to offload cargo from South Africa, some 250 people came out in the rain to support their protest. But the effort was becoming better organized and apartheid atrocities and protests were attracting increasingly intense media attention. The movement continued demanding the release of Nelson Mandela and added an entertainer boycott of South Africa, and in 1985, specifically of the Sun City resort for white South Africans. The slogan was "Don't go, and if you do, demand to speak to Mandela."[3]

After more than two years of what became a nationwide movement of direct-action protest, local constituents were telling their representatives to change US policy. On October 2, 1986, Congress handed President

Reagan his first major foreign policy defeat by overriding his veto of the Comprehensive Anti-Apartheid Act of 1986. Apartheid began to crumble.

To understand why FSAM and the antiapartheid movement succeeded in the Reagan administration when other antiapartheid organizations and protests were not able to stop US support of apartheid requires one to consider the history of US policy and protest and antiapartheid activities. A confluence of factors made it possible for FSAM to influence American policy that then helped destroy the apartheid regime. The people in South Africa took risks, struggled, died, went to prison, and lived "banned" and isolated lives in their own cause to make their country ungovernable as long as their lives were suppressed. Antiapartheid activism and support for the ANC by some Western European countries helped to sustain the ANC and those exiled. Organizations, leaders, and ordinary people in the United States tried repeatedly to upset US policy that sustained apartheid. This all laid the groundwork for the successful FSAM campaign.

The South African government formalized apartheid in 1948. In the United States the NAACP in 1951 tried unsuccessfully to end World Bank loans to South Africa. In 1960, after the Sharpeville massacre, in which police fired on protesters leaving sixty-nine people dead, the ANC, which was the principal antiapartheid party, was banned.[4] In November 1962, the UN General Assembly passed a resolution setting up a Special Committee on Apartheid and called for sanctions against South Africa, which only led Western nations to boycott the committee. The antiapartheid movement in Britain began to pressure politicians, holding a conference in London in 1964. The Labor Party endorsed sanctions during the election campaign that year, but it retreated after winning and gave the standard "Sanctions might hurt the very people we are trying to help" rationale for inaction.

In the United States, Students for a Democratic Society (SDS), founded at the University of Michigan in 1960 and at the time a multi-issue organization seeking university reform, civil rights, and community organizing, responded to the Sharpeville massacre by protesting against Chase Manhattan Bank. In the spring of 1965, SDS protested the bank's involvement in a revolving credit arrangement that bailed out the South African government by attempting sit-ins and distributing Chase Partner in Apartheid buttons. The bank went to court and enjoined their activities. The SDS bulletins and materials publicized the protests, but the national media gave it scant mention.[5]

In 1964, Nelson Mandela, then serving a five-year sentence for leaving the country without a passport and for incitement, and ten other leading apartheid opponents were convicted in the Rivonia trials. At Mandela's trial, he gave his often-quoted last speech before emerging from prison twenty-seven years later, saying he "cherished the ideal of a democratic and free society in which all persons live together in harmony and with equal opportunities."[6] He hoped to live for this ideal. But if necessary, he said, "it is an ideal for which I am prepared to die." Britain and the United States, hoping to suppress international negative opinion, and with some degree of success, issued a statement opposing death sentences for those charged in the Rivonia trials. By 1965, the antiapartheid struggle had receded from public attention and consciousness.

The civil rights movement and anti–Vietnam War protests expanded the space for civil disobedience in the United States. After the assassination of Martin Luther King Jr. in 1968, higher-education affirmative action measures brought more black students to predominantly white campuses. Civil rights activists and black students at white institutions and historically black colleges and universities became especially interested in colonialism in the Caribbean and Africa and ties between blacks in the United States and on the continent. Continued restiveness and resistance among southern African blacks gave rise to some intermittent protest actions. Though the Nixon administration was dominated by expansion of the Vietnam War "in order to make peace," and then by the president's Watergate troubles and resignation, it pursued some activity that reinforced the apartheid regime. Nixon's national security adviser at the time, Henry Kissinger, in a memorandum, rejected the decolonization emphasis of the previous administrations and recommended a relaxation policy advocating closer ties with the white governments of Mozambique, Angola, Rhodesia, and South Africa.[7] American companies were urged to increase business with South Africa, and South Africa once again could buy aircraft and other military materials in the United States.

In Congress, change toward more support for ending apartheid developed. In the House, Charles Diggs became chair of the Subcommittee on Africa, in 1969, the first black chair of that committee. The committee invited testimony from scholars, experts, and black activists, and not just the usual corporate leaders and government officials. Hearings on events and policy in southern Africa became routine. As the number of black members of Congress grew, the Congressional Black Caucus (CBC), founded in 1971, included more members interested in Africa.

Throughout the 1970s, antiapartheid activism remained for the most part decentralized. Any number of organizations, including state and local governments, churches, civic organizations, foundations, peace groups, labor, colleges and universities, played roles in keeping the fight alive. The American Committee on Africa (ACOA) was the oldest antiapartheid organization. George Houser, Bayard Rustin, and Bill Sutherland of the Congress on Racial Equality founded it in 1953 to support the 1952 Campaign to Defy Unjust Laws (Defiance campaign) called by the ANC. In 1954, Houser traveled to Africa to meet with leaders of liberation struggles throughout the continent, including Chief Albert Luthuli and Walter Sisulu in South Africa. When Houser returned, he went to work for ACOA full time, serving as executive director until 1981, when Jennifer Davis, who served during FSAM's campaigns, took over. ACOA hosted African leaders in the United States, lobbied the United Nations and the US government, arranged meetings for Africans leaders who came to the United States, produced reports, and raised funds for African university students and refugees. In 1972, ACOA joined with Methodist, Episcopalian, Presbyterian, and United Church of Christ denominations to form the Washington Office on Africa as a lobbying arm for African issues. In the labor movement, the international units of the AFL-CIO and the United Steelworkers educated local members and provided congressional testimony.

Several short-duration grassroots organizations also emerged during this period. Black employees at Polaroid headquarters in Cambridge, Massachusetts, started a revolutionary movement to spread information and education in opposition to the use of Polaroid photographs in the South African passbook system. The National African Liberation Support Committee of elected officials and community-based organization coordinated African Liberation Day marches in 1972 and '73. Scholars whose research trips to Africa had been funded by the government and foundations became vocal critics of apartheid. In 1975, banned activist and poet Dennis Brutus moved from Britain to the United States, settling at Northwestern University, in Evanston, Illinois, and traveling the country talking about apartheid. Between 1981 and 1983, US government efforts to deport him led to a successful fight waged by ACOA, TransAfrica, and other groups to gain asylum for him.[8]

The overthrow of the forty-year dictatorship in Portugal in 1974 left the way open for the liberation of Portuguese southern Africa, including the present countries of Angola, Mozambique, and Guinea-Bissau. Kissinger, in the environment of Watergate and Nixon's resignation, and ignoring America's colonialism and apartheid hypocrisies, tried to define the southern Africa issue as helping South Africa contain communism. This focus involved encouraging civil war in Angola, keeping Marxism that was already ensconced in Mozambique from spreading to Rhodesia, and demonizing protesters in South Africa as communists. But the conflict in Angola acquired global dimensions, with antiapartheid activists in Europe and the United States finding openings for shattering Kissinger's anticommunist mantra. Activists countered with charges that South Africa was pursuing an anti-liberation goal and only interested in shoring up apartheid from all geographical sides.

In June 1976, the Soweto uprising was the catalyst for new energy and sustained mobilization and protest by antiapartheid activists. Beginning on June 16, about twenty thousand children protested in streets against teaching Afrikaans in the schools. The number of children killed by police ran into the hundreds, enough to gain international press attention. In the United States, campus protests, local candlelight vigils, picket lines, and groups aligned against apartheid grew exponentially.

The Interfaith Committee on Corporate Responsibility, founded in 1973, gained momentum and pushed the antiapartheid principles promoted by Leon Sullivan, a black minister from Philadelphia and member of the General Motors board. GM was the largest employer of blacks in South Africa. The principles, known as the Sullivan Principles, embodied social responsibility for corporations doing business in South Africa. Corporations would have a policy of equal treatment of employees and an integrated environment without race discrimination. The idea was that companies would be forced to stop doing business in South Africa, since the principles directly conflicted with apartheid. At the same time the antiapartheid movement lobbied individual businesses to adopt and comply with the Sullivan Principles, the movement opened an attack on institutional investors.

Activists advocated for withdrawal from investments in South African–based companies and divestment from any US-based companies with business in South Africa that had not adopted the Sullivan Principles.

Pension funds became a major target. Some companies ceased doing business in South Africa while others endorsed the principles but remained. The principles did shelter companies that stayed in South Africa from criticism during the disinvestment campaigns before the FSAM protests started. In 1987, after the movement had gained momentum, Sullivan would renounce his own principles as not going far enough.[9]

Students at the University of California, Michigan State, Stanford, and other schools protested until their universities divested completely. Some state and local governments passed limited disinvestment laws. In 1978, the City of San Francisco opted not to invest in corporations and banks doing business in or with South Africa.[10]

Starting in 1977, the antiapartheid movement briefly became a strong contender for more public attention and for interest not just locally but also in the administration and Congress because of regional developments in Africa. In 1976, Portugal left Africa, stripping and taking off with whatever they could. South African officials continued to use armed insurgencies against the new, rising internal independence movement and independent neighboring countries that had joined forces to overthrow the apartheid regime.

President Carter appointed people who had experience and interest in Africa. Goler Butcher, who had served as Diggs's counsel on the Subcommittee on Africa, became Africa bureau chief in the US Agency for International Development (USAID). Andrew Young, a Georgian, who was rewarded for his early support of Carter with the UN ambassador post, said the civil rights movement had put them in good position to attack apartheid, since it was essentially a civil rights issue. They had to fight off National Security Council chief Zbigniew Brzezinski, who linked Ethiopia and Angola to Cuba and the Soviet Union, still advancing the Kissinger East versus West priority, an anticommunist framing of the African situation.

None of this activity seemed to make a dent in changing US policy or the apartheid regime. Further, the bright prospects for change quickly evaporated. Charlie Diggs left because of corruption charges in early 1979, and Carter fired Andrew Young for violating the no talk-with-the-Palestinians policy. Stephen Solarz (Democrat-New York) became chair of the House Subcommittee on Africa, and Howard Wolpe (Democrat-Michigan) took the post in 1981. Despite Reagan's election and Republicans gaining control of the Senate, the House Subcommittee on Africa tried to move forward. The new chair and staff kept up study missions to countries in southern Africa and Namibia and held serious hearings. As members of Congress from the Black Caucus and others interested in Africa grew in numbers and seniority, additional committees began to investigate matters such as US financial dealings with South Africa.

After TransAfrica was founded in 1977, it joined with ACOA, the Washington Committee on Africa (WCOA), the American Friends Service Committee (AFSC), and other groups to educate the public and to advocate for socially responsible investment. Harry Belafonte and Arthur Ashe formed Artists and Athletes Against Apartheid to ask entertainers to stop working in South Africa and the Sun City resort for white South Africans. Randall Robinson of TransAfrica testified before congressional committees, wrote letters to politicians, and was increasingly frustrated because there was too little public interest in changing American policy toward Africa. He concluded that the media showed political interest when something happened that threatened places with a significant number of whites. The obvious answer was that the precarious future of whites in South Africa, Namibia, and Rhodesia made those places the best possible sites to redirect policy.

In May 1981, an anonymous government employee informant, whom Randall did not know, gave him classified papers about Secretary of State Alexander Haig's meeting with South African foreign minister Roelof Botha on furthering the United States' "constructive engagement policy," a label coined by Chester Crocker, assistant secretary of state for African affairs, to relieve South Africa's "polecat" status in the world. Randall gave the papers to the press, which led to stories in the *Washington Post* and other media outlets, and he also went to an Organization of African Unity meeting and distributed copies of the secret papers to representatives of the African countries.

Zimbabwe gained its independence in 1980, joining with an independent Angola, even though its South African–fueled military conflict continued. Namibia, however, was still under the control of South Africa, and black Namibians and black South Africans still suffered under apartheid. Blacks in South Africa grew increasingly restive and repressed. In 1982, AFSC published a citizen's guide for local people on how to withdraw funds from banks and corporations involved with South Africa. Antiapartheid protesters joined in a June 1983 national antinuclear march and the August 1983 March on Washington. The Dennis Brutus asylum campaign was another avenue for protests. In the fall of 1983, Randall suggested civil disobedience, but congressional staffers thought it was too soon. In October 1983, three hundred attendees at a national students' conference in New York planned demonstrations against apartheid for March and April 1984.

In September 1984 came the parliamentary change in South Africa that gave the franchise to coloreds and Indians but not blacks. Protests and repression grew and US constructive engagement continued. Then, in October 1984, the United States, guided by Ronald Reagan, abstained from a United Nations General Assembly resolution condemning protests against the continued suffrage policy restriction. The assembly had repeatedly denounced apartheid as racism since 1962. Apartheid also had been an issue in Jesse Jackson's 1984 presidential campaign.

Richard Hatcher, chair of TransAfrica's board, felt that the organization needed to protest the White House since Reagan's reelection in 1984 ensured continued American complicity with apartheid. Hatcher was the first black elected mayor of a large city (Gary, Indiana), in 1968, and chair of Jackson's presidential campaign. Sylvia Hill and the other SASP members and TransAfrica decided to engage in a nonviolent protest at the embassy, the official symbol of South Africa in the United States.

There had been other protests against South Africa in the United States before FSAM. None had dented apartheid. But this history provided the context for the FSAM campaign. When TransAfrica announced the Free South Africa movement, we initially thought the protests might go on for a week. TransAfrica lined up prominent people who, if the first day was successful, had agreed to be arrested: Congressman Charles Hayes (Democrat-Illinois) and the Reverend Joseph Lowery, chair of the Southern Christian Leadership Conference on the 26th of November; Congressman John Conyers (Democrat-Michigan) and William Simons, president of the Washington Teachers Union, on the 27th; Congressman Ronald Dellums (Democrat-California), Marc Stepp, UAW vice president, and Hilda Mason, DC Council, on the 28th; Yolanda King, daughter of Martin Luther King Jr., Gerald McEntee, president of AFSCME, and Richard Hatcher, mayor of Gary, Indiana, on the 29th; Congressman George Crockett (Democrat-Michigan), Congressman Don Edwards (Democrat-California), and Leonard Ball, Coalition of Black Trade Unions, on the 30th.[11]

Pulitzer Prize–winning journalist Roger Wilkins, former assistant attorney at the Justice Department and nephew of the NAACP's Roy Wilkins, and Bill Lucy, AFSCME secretary-treasurer and president of the Coalition of Black Trade Unionists, joined the FSAM steering committee in the first week. Randall, Walter, Bill, Roger, and Sylvia Hill, founding members of the Southern Africa Support Project, and Cecelie Counts, as both a founding member and coordinator for FSAM, met early every morning at my house to plan our activities. At first, Randall and his staff may have seen Congressman Walter Fauntroy and me mainly as celebrities who could attract the media spotlight, but with our first meetings, it became clear that our committee collectively had the experience to sustain a movement and make mostly good decisions.

Unlike those students who started the anti–Vietnam War protests twenty years earlier, the original FSAM steering committee members had a great deal of activist experience and knowledge of civil disobedience and of Africa, which informed decisions during the movement. Also, we had experience in government and dealing with government to help us understand how to move legislation. Randall Robinson had spent time in Tanzania in the fall of 1970, which, after Nkrumah fell in Ghana, was the most welcoming African country for black Americans. He and fellow Harvard law students Henry and Rosemary Sanders had trouble getting funded for research fellowships in Africa after law school. They went to the black assistant dean Walter Leonard, who got the Ford Foundation to create a Middle East and Africa Field Research Program for Afro-Americans. The Sanderses went to Nigeria; Robinson went to Tanzania.

Randall, back in Boston in the winter of 1971, worked in a legal assistance office for three years, then at the Roxbury Multi-Service Center as a community organizer. He was an organizer of a protest asking for a Gulf Oil boycott and demanding Harvard's divestment of Gulf Oil stock because of the company's key support of colonialist regimes in Africa. Harvard held the largest block of Gulf stock of any American university. In Angola, the oil the company pumped provided 48 percent of Angola's budget. The protests included a graveyard of one thousand black crosses, which were built on the Harvard campus, and the takeover on April 21, 1972, of the administration building. Harvard didn't relent, but the educational value was enormous.

Then Robinson went to work for Congressman Charles Diggs, chair of the House of Representatives' Africa Subcommittee. Before Diggs was felled by a corruption scandal dating to before Randall's time, every black American who wanted to do policy work on Africa came into his orbit. By the late fall of 1976, Portugal had retreated from Africa and Rhodesia's government was on the run. Randall went to Cape Town in December 1976 as part of a congressional delegation chaired by Diggs, who offended South Africans by asking when blacks would get the right to vote.

During the Congressional Black Caucus weekend in 1976, the NAACP, black church labor unions, Greek letter organizations, the National Council of Negro Women, and business leaders met with Herschelle Challenor, counsel to the House Africa Subcommittee. These organizations and leaders decided to form TransAfrica, which was incorporated July 1, 1977, as an organization of black Americans to influence US foreign policy on Africa and the Caribbean. Randall became executive director. Because funding was always shaky, the organization started with a fund-raiser, led by his brother Max Robinson, a leading TV newscaster.

Walter Fauntroy was a student at Virginia Union University when he met Martin Luther King Jr. Fellow Baptist ministers, they became friends. Fauntroy joined the Southern Christian Leadership Conference (SCLC), and upon his return to his hometown, Washington, DC, he became a congressional lobbyist for civil rights. Fauntroy also helped to coordinate the 1963 March on Washington and became pastor of New Bethel Baptist Church and director of the Washington bureau of the SCLC. He served as DC coordinator of the 1963 march, the Selma-to-Montgomery march, and James Meredith's 1966 Mississippi "March Against Fear." President Lyndon Johnson appointed Fauntroy vice chair of the White House Conference on Civil Rights in 1966 and vice chair of the DC Council in 1967. He founded and headed the Model Cities organization in DC and tried to stop the violence when riots overcame parts of DC after King was assassinated in 1968. Fauntroy served on the city council and then became the district's first nonvoting delegate to Congress in 1971. Based on his local prominence, experience as a civil rights activist, and service in Congress, Walter was a good choice to become one of the first FSAM protesters.[12]

I was a member of the US Civil Rights Commission and had a great deal of very recent and extensive national press coverage because of fighting Reagan's attempt to turn back the clock on civil rights. Reagan had fired me for opposing him, but I sued him and won reinstatement in a federal court suit. I also had a great deal of nonviolent protest experience. Between graduate school and law school at the University of Michigan, I had gone to Vietnam to report on the war. I had been involved in anti–Vietnam War protests on campus. And I had been one of the students who took over the university president's office on April 9, 1968, the day of Martin Luther King Jr.'s burial in Atlanta, to demand more funding for African American students and African American faculty hires.

In 1970, I was a new faculty member at the University of Maryland, College Park, when an antiwar protest that was bigger and possibly more raucous than the one at Kent State erupted. Thousands of demonstrators occupied and vandalized the university's main administration building and ROTC offices, set fires all over the campus, and blocked Route 1, the main artery into College Park. Armed with bricks, rocks, and bottles, the protesters continuously skirmished with police, who were armed with riot batons, tear gas, and dogs. As the campus raged, Maryland governor Marvin Mandel finally sent in National Guard troops in an effort to quash the uprising. Fortunately, unlike Kent State, no lives were lost at College Park. The chancellor asked me and a few other faculty members to sit with him and advise him. I had also gone back to Central Michigan University to help talk the students into ending an armory protest after Kent State, when the university president did not want to let the governor send in the National Guard to arrest protesters because his daughter was one of the protesters.

Also, when I was chancellor at the University of Colorado, Boulder, I went outside to meet with students who thought they had to take over a building to get my attention on an issue of academic policy. So, I had lots of nonviolent civil disobedience experience and from both sides.

I also had experience with the African liberation struggle. I had participated in the sixth Pan-African Conference in Tanzania in the summer of 1974, where African heads of state and other speakers argued over Marxist-Leninist reforms as opposed to capitalistic measures against black oppression. Some black nationalists agreed that a socialist revolution might be necessary, but they didn't think the racism of white workers could be overcome and felt blacks could be liberated only by their own efforts. During the Carter administration, I had also visited South Africa. At that time, I met in the country secretly with some of the freedom fighters. While at the University of Maryland, I had also become acquainted with Zimbabweans and had visited some of the guerrillas in Zambia before independence. When independence came, as a Carter administration political official, I took the opportunity to talk with Zimbabwean president Robert Mugabe at the White House on his first visit to the United States. I went again to Zimbabwe and observed whites screaming loudly, objecting when traffic stopped for the motorcade of the new president, calling him a "monkey."

Eleanor Holmes Norton was an experienced civil rights activist. While in college and graduate school, she was active in the civil rights movement and an organizer for SNCC. By the time she graduated from Antioch College, she had already been arrested for organizing and participating in sit-ins in Maryland, Ohio, and Washington, DC. While in law school, she traveled to Mississippi for the Mississippi Freedom Summer and worked with civil rights stalwarts like Medgar Evers. Her first encounter with a recently released but physically beaten Fannie Lou Hamer forced her to bear witness to the intensity of violence and Jim Crow repression in the South. Upon graduation from law school, she clerked for Judge A. Leon Higginbotham. She was a litigator at the ACLU, head of the Human Rights Commission of New York City, and head of the Equal Employment Opportunity Commission, named by Carter. She then was a professor at Georgetown and a member of FSAM.

A key activist who was not in the room at the meeting with the ambassador when we started the protest, because she was not as obviously newsworthy at the moment, was an academic, Professor Sylvia Hill of the University of the District of Columbia. She had been a leader working for the liberation of southern Africa since the 1970s. She had been the North America regional secretary general for the Sixth Pan-African Congress, held in Tanzania, which I attended. At that time, she was a professor at Macalester in St. Paul, Minnesota, and some of her students helped with the conference and the movement. She and her husband, James, had been in SNCC in Mississippi and moved to Minnesota, which was his home. After SixPac, they moved to Washington, DC, bent on organizing to help the liberation of southern Africa. She and Joseph Jordan, Sandra Hill, Cecelie Counts, Adwoa Dunn-Mouton, and others founded the Southern Africa Support Project (SASP), which did a study of local churches and other organizations to find out which ones were most likely targets for organizing. They gave presentations and formed a network of local volunteers interested in the liberation cause. In 1980, Sylvia persuaded ANC head Oliver Tambo, who visited with SASP while in Washington, that Americans could be as responsive to the antiapartheid movement as Europeans, who were its major supporters. Tambo began to allocate resources in the United States. Thereafter, Lindiwe Mabuza, who was assigned to Washington, DC, and Johnny Makatini, serving at the United Nations, gave our movement knowledge and a sense of the ANC's visions and goals. They traveled, met, and talked with people and collaborated with antiapartheid, traditional civil rights, and women's groups and appeared in the media wherever they traveled. Adwoa Dunn-Mouton, a SASP member, was the group's most important black staffer on the Hill serving on the Subcommittee on Africa. SASP organized and delivered the core daily demonstrators, drummers, and picketers when the movement started and as it continued in Washington.[13]

In massive resistance to apartheid, black South Africans mobilized to make the townships ungovernable, black local officials resigned in droves, and the government declared a state of emergency in 1985 and used thousands of troops to quell "unrest." That, and the success of FSAM and antiapartheid protests around the United States, brought routine media coverage to the South African issue, and congressional action on sanctions became possible. Randall and his staff met weekly with members of Congress, usually in Senator Edward Kennedy's office.[14]

The antiapartheid public mood became so strong a month after the FSAM embassy protests started that in December 1984, twenty-five conservative Republican House members wrote an open letter to Prime Minister Botha threatening sanctions if apartheid continued. The explanations of inaction by corporations, which were saying, "We're against apartheid but oppose sanctions," sounded increasingly hollow. Ever more frustrated as the FSAM push toward legislation gained force, Sullivan said his principles wouldn't end apartheid and companies should withdraw from South Africa after the FSAM protests continued.[15]

Ending apartheid had become a dominant civil rights issue, and the legislation that had been introduced by Congressman Ronald Dellums, supported by the members of the Congressional Black Caucus in the House, and piloted through the House by Congressman Howard Wolpe, chair of the House Africa Subcommittee, passed. President Reagan's September 29, 1986, veto was overridden by the House on October 2, while Coretta King, Jesse Jackson, Randall Robinson, and others sat in the gallery and CBC members prowled the Senate floor as the veto was overridden 78–21. The Comprehensive Anti-Apartheid Act of 1986 became law. Soon Britain and the European Union would also pass sanctions.

The Comprehensive Anti-Apartheid Act of 1986 banned new US investment in South Africa, sales to the police and military, and new bank loans except for the purpose of trade. Specific measures against trade included the prohibition of the import of agricultural goods, textiles, shellfish, steel, iron, uranium, and the products of state-owned corporations. The legislative work was not over. Representative Charlie Rangel (Democrat-New York) in 1987 successfully added an amendment to the Budget Reconciliation Act prohibiting US corporations from receiving tax reimbursements for taxes paid in South Africa. This meant that these corporations essentially had to pay double taxation until they extricated themselves from South African apartheid.

The apartheid system remained in place, but not for long. Resistance continued. In February 1987, the United States and Britain vetoed a UN Security Council resolution that would have made the sanctions imposed by the 1986 act international. In 1988, South Africa detained thirty thousand people without charges, arrested thousands of children, and banned every civic and political organization. Consistent with its constructive engagement policy, the Reagan administration used every loophole in the 1986 law to work in favor of the South African economy.

By September 1988 the House passed HR 1580, the Anti-Apartheid Amendments of 1988. Even though Shell Oil Company funded a vigorous lobbying campaign against the sanctions bill that was also supported by Prime Minister Margaret Thatcher's British government, the bill passed, but with a strategic loss. The bill mandated disinvestment. However, the Senate voted to permit US aid to South African–backed forces in Angola, which meant indirectly giving to South Africa through funding the continued conflict and supporting South African–backed forces there.

The South African government tried to fake out the antiapartheid forces by appearing to reform again. In February 1989, P. W. Botha resigned as head of the ruling National Party and was replaced by F. W. de Klerk. Government representatives began to meet openly with representatives of the ANC. Like the ANC, FSAM feared that the political leadership in Congress would accept de Klerk's leadership as fundamental change in the apartheid regime. We felt that we had to do everything we could in solidarity to expose this effort by the apartheid regime to only appear to make changes.

Unsurprisingly, none of the FSAM leadership had been allowed in South Africa since the protests and the passage of sanctions. Even when Desmond Tutu invited us to his installation as archbishop of Cape Town, none of us could attend. In February 1990, I was permitted to join Jesse Jackson; his wife, Jacqueline Jackson; the novelist John Edgar Wideman; and H. Beecher Hicks, pastor of Metropolitan Baptist Church in Washington, DC, in wangling permission to visit by persuading the ambassador, Piet Koornhof, that if we found progress, we might have something positive to say. When we got there, we went all around the country, accompanied by a large press contingent, speaking, meeting with activists, demanding to see Mandela, and calling for the release of political prisoners.

The government informed us on the evening of February 10 that we could essentially stop agitating because Mandela would be freed the next day. On February 11, at about 7 p.m. South Africa time, the waiting for Nelson Mandela, which had been a constant companion most of my adult life, came to an end. On February 11, 1990, after spending twenty-seven years in prison, he was released. There our group was in the Cape Town City Hall to greet him, with the mayor and his official welcoming coterie. Leading antiapartheid activists Allan Boesak and Frank Chikane were also there, as were Mandela's prison compatriots, Raymond Mhlaba and Walter Sisulu, accompanied by his wife, Albertina Sisulu. Also there waiting quietly were Mandela's daughter, Zindzi, and his youngest grandchild, Bambata, still a babe in arms, and Mandela's mother and sister.

The speech he gave at the Cape Town City Hall reemphasized the need for struggle and for sanctions until the end of apartheid and the institution of democracy. His manner and demeanor, the favorable press, along with continued resistance, seemed to foreshadow eventual political victory for the foes of apartheid.[16]

The Free South Africa movement organized an eleven-day, seven-city trip to the United States for Mandela and the ANC delegation in June 1990, for which Roger Wilkins had the major responsibility. Thousands of people greeted Mandela and the delegation throughout the seven-city tour. The ANC viewed this visit as an opportunity to demonstrate to the politicians that Mandela and the African National Congress had large popular support and to help raise funds for ANC to establish a new South

Africa. Mandela was the fourth private citizen in the history of the United States to address both houses of Congress. This represented a major political achievement, since he and the African National Congress had long been viewed by the State Department as terrorists. After Mandela's visit, the Free South African movement came to a close, although supporting organizations and individuals continued to work on African and other international issues.

FSAM was a catalyst for making the antiapartheid struggle visible both inside South Africa and around the world. The visual, radio, and print media crossed borders to tell and show this struggle. Witnesses against apartheid, numbering some five thousand in the United States, made their opposition visible with their arrests. The bravery and momentum of the struggle inside South Africa became the visible example of all that was wrong with apartheid. I still affirm what I said when first asked whether I'd willingly get arrested at the South African embassy: "It is the right time and the right thing to do!"

The Free South Africa movement had to make a place on the US government's foreign policy agenda for a continent usually ignored. In retrospect, it is clear that the 1984 antiapartheid campaign had an inside and outside strategy. We had some access to political leaders and the process, because some of us had been or were political officials. The people we mobilized did not have routine access to a range of policymakers, and the people on whose behalf we protested had none. As Sylvia Hill best explains, we were not acting because of direct harm we suffered but because of the suffering of others and the use of our taxpayers' funds, which made us complicit in the suffering. Defeating apartheid would help them, and race consciousness and political solidarity on race issues might occur elsewhere and in the United States, but FSAM had no personal benefit in mind beyond the goals of the campaign.[17]

We showed how to mobilize a movement, but not, Cecelie Counts suggests, how to organize coalitions. Some other leaders and organizations who had labored long in the human rights field resented Randall, TransAfrica, and our movement because it was unlike what had existed. But our secrecy, holding information within a small group, and keeping the demands simple had worked. Some established organizations, seeing ending apartheid as a human rights issue much like, say, the Palestinian question, were uneasy with the race-based arguments we used, analogizing apartheid to Jim Crow and framing apartheid as a civil rights issue. But we thought correctly that defining apartheid as a civil rights issue would embarrass opponents, mobilize constituencies, and likely achieve the passage of legislation.

We forgot when apartheid was overthrown that the only thing South African leadership owed us was thanks for getting sanctions. This reality hit Randall hard. I recall the way Barbara Masekela, who later became South Africa's ambassador to the United States, put it after Mandela came to the United States, "We did what we needed to do, and that was then and this is now." South Africa's postapartheid government would have a government-to-government relationship with the United States and essentially didn't need a protest movement anymore. We had done our work.

CHAPTER 5

A "Kinder and Gentler" Presidency

George Herbert Walker Bush

On March 12, 1990, American Disabled for Attendants Today (ADAPT), the Center for Independent Living, and other groups brought hundreds of people with disabilities to rally in Washington. At the bottom steps of the Capitol they denounced the slow movement of the Americans with Disabilities bill. Then some abandoned their wheelchairs, got down on their hands and knees, and began crawling slowly up the eighty-three steps toward the building's west entrance. Eight-year-old Jennifer Keelan, from Denver, with cerebral palsy yelled: "I'll take all night if I have to!" Others yelled, "Pass the bill, pass it now!"

PROTEST MOVEMENTS BEGAN TO shift tactics in the late 1980s. Unlike earlier movements, which had identifiable leaders who demanded specific policy changes, political protests increasingly relied on creative expression to influence the public and public policy. Using storytelling, graffiti, alternative music, street theater, puppetry, and new media technologies, protests sought to change popular culture and mobilize support for progressive change. The medium became the message, as Marshall McLuhan had recommended decades earlier. Now there was rap music, zap actions by the Guerrilla Girls, and Critical Mass, which brings hundreds of people together for bicycle riding in the streets, and which San Francisco Mayor Willie Brown was finally forced to accept. Disruption remained the aim of these gatherings; however, it would be misleading to draw sharp distinctions between protest styles of the 1960s and 1990s. The "Don't Buy Krugerrands" campaign and the movement against sweatshop apparel all disrupted business as usual and helped persuade politicians to respond favorably.

Protesters against George H. W. Bush's policies used some cultural forms, but they mainly used the "inside/outside" strategy typical of other movements. These included lobbying and marches, statements from public figures, and ads. At the start, Bush experienced what happens to every president-elect: at least one objection to a cabinet appointment. Bush's choice of Louis Sullivan, president of Morehouse Medical School in Atlanta, who would be the only black cabinet member as secretary of Health and Human Services drew the ire of antiabortion advocates. They cited remarks he made in a news interview indicating his support for a woman's right to choose abortion. Bush, avoiding questions about the protests, canceled a news conference at which he had been expected to name additional cabinet choices. Sullivan said he supported the right to choose but without the use of federal funds to no avail. Bush deflected the protests by having Sullivan say he agreed with Bush's policies and would accept only people "knowledgeable" on abortion issues and recommended by antiabortion groups as his key subordinates. When Bush followed through on appointments, the issue mostly died and Sullivan was confirmed.[1]

AIDS activists used street theater and other tactics in their protests. ACT UP had held its first action on Wall Street during the Reagan administration, in March 1987, to protest the profiteering of pharmaceutical companies such as Burroughs Wellcome, manufacturer of AZT, the first drug approved to fight AIDS. In April 1989, ACT UP members went to Burroughs Wellcome's headquarters and chained themselves to office furniture to protest the high cost of AZT. On September 14, 1989, ACT UP members chained themselves to the VIP balcony at the New York Stock Exchange, closing trading. Four days later, Burroughs Wellcome reduced the price of AZT by 20 percent, effective immediately, reducing the price to wholesale distributors from $1.50 to $1.20 per capsule. Secretary Sullivan said he was pleased and that the price cut, combined with recent findings that lower dosages could be effective, would reduce the cost of AZT treatment. Peter Staley, an ACT UP activist, said the 20 percent reduction was too little, only a "step in the right direction, but a very small step."[2]

Protests on the AIDS crisis continued throughout Bush's four years and during his reelection campaign as so many people died from the disease. Thousands of AIDS activists, organized by ACT UP, stretched a red ribbon around the White House after a debate between presidential candidates Bush, Bill Clinton, and independent Ross Perot in October 1992. The ribbon was in support of AIDS sufferers. Protesters liked Clinton's proposal for an AIDS czar and even Perot's call for speedier drug approval, but dismissed Bush's talk as only being about his supporting more research.[3]

From April 15 to June 4, 1989, there were also successful protests, mainly on the West Coast and in Washington and New York, as part of the international backlash against China in response to its suppression of the popular national democracy movement. The Chinese government used the military to kill many demonstrators and clear out Tiananmen Square, where they had been protesting. Bay area congressional representatives quickly sought recourse for Chinese students. Bush issued an executive order to give permanent residence to protesters and those at risk of repression. The Chinese Student Protection Act of 1992 established permanent residence for Chinese nationals, targeted toward students. Chinese students who were in the United States during the time of the protests participated in TV interviews, demonstrations, and rallies, and were featured in newspaper articles. Chinese nationals were eligible to apply for permanent residency, even with expired passports. Over the years, the act granted green cards to an estimated fifty-four thousand Chinese nationals.

Unlike the Chinese student protests, Bush's perpetuation of a no-entry policy toward Haitian refugees did not result in policy improvements. I first met Bush after I went to Rome during the last years of the Reagan administration, along with a small group organized by Jesse Jackson. It was part of our protest against Haitian refugee detention and deportation. We met with Pope John Paul II to discuss what the church might do to help the refugees incarcerated in Florida until they could be returned to Haiti, since they were mostly Catholic. The Catholic bishops responded by trying to alleviate the material deficiencies of their detention. When we returned, we met with then vice president Bush to give the briefing Americans are expected to do when they meet with foreign leaders on matters of US policy and to ask the government to relent. We found him affable, sounding very agreeable but stuck on the policy of returning the Haitians immediately or incarcerating them until they could be returned.

Bush's engagement in the almost seven-months-long (August 1990 to February 1991) Persian Gulf War stimulated some protests. In October 1990, antiwar protesters across the country demanded an end to the deployment of US military in the war, proposing instead a diplomatic solution. Protesters, in these first coordinated protests, objected to sending two hundred thousand troops to the Persian Gulf as protection for Saudi Arabia's oil after Iraq's invasion of Kuwait. In New York City, a large crowd, variously estimated at four to fifteen thousand people, gathered at Columbus Circle and marched to Times Square, chanting, "Hell no, we won't go; we won't fight for Texaco!" In Washington, DC, picketing of the White House and a sit-down on Pennsylvania Avenue closed the streets for two hours. Protests also took place in San Francisco, Los Angeles, Atlanta, Boston, Chicago, and other cities.[4]

Activism against Bush's return of Haitian refugees continued throughout his administration and accelerated after a coup in Haiti on September 30, 1991. The military ousted Jean-Bertrand Aristide, the island nation's first democratically elected president. Aristide came to the United States, and an increased flow of refugees left on creaky boats for the United States. US policy became a demand for negotiations to bring him back to power, despite qualms among some US officials concerning his militant leftist politics. "It's an election year, and people don't want poor black folks coming here," said Democratic congressman Charles Rangel in a televised interview. "If these people came from a country that had oil or if they had some wealth, there would be adjustments made."

The House and its committees took several actions during 1992 to protest the Bush administration's policy of returning Haitian refugees. But none of those measures became law. In September 1992, TransAfrica, the NAACP, and other groups organized a protest at the White House. Coretta King, tennis champion Arthur Ashe, and others joined us in marching and getting arrested along with ninety or so others. Arthur was physically very weak from illness, and this was the last time he could come with us to demonstrate on human rights issues. He was hospitalized soon thereafter and died of complications from AIDS, which he contracted from a blood transfusion, on February 6, 1993. The policy of no entry to Haitian refugees was inherited and retained continuously by presidential administrations, except for a brief period after one of the hurricanes.

For civil rights advocates, domestic civil rights challenges in addition to AIDS sparked resistance. An insider strategic lobbying strategy was crucial, but targeted grassroots activism made a difference at key points in successful legislative campaigns. Bush vetoed the family and medical leave bills twice, even though women's groups took the lead on mobilizing bipartisan support in Congress. The terrain remained particularly difficult on race issues. Just as blacks who undermined civil rights were appointed in the Reagan years, they continued to spring up all over the Bush administration, in Congress, and at the Supreme Court with the confirmation of Clarence Thomas as an associate justice. The Reaganite color-blind society theatrics had taught that black or female appointees were just as likely as the white men they served to spout anti–civil rights rhetoric and take retrograde actions accordingly.

But at first an "era of good feelings" prevailed, based on Bush's history and the hope that he would be "kinder and gentler" than Reagan. He and his appointees were generally more low key than the Reagan group. Attorney General Richard Thornburgh, a former Pennsylvania governor, and low-profile John Dunne, assistant attorney general for civil rights, went along as the White House denounced "racial quotas" repeatedly and deliberately invoked this catchphrase to imply unfairness to whites in favor of unqualified blacks in employment. The administration's goal was to undermine the passage of a new job discrimination bill, which was urgently needed. In the states, the Steel Belt rusted as a recession and unemployment grew, with black unemployment twice as high as that of whites. Reagan's deficit and tax cuts exacerbated class and racial tensions. Klansman David Duke ran a nearly successful race for governor of Louisiana against Edwin Edwards, who would later uphold the state's tradition of governors being jailed for corruption. Duke's popularity with voters in and out of the Pelican State underscored the visibility of white supremacy in American politics.

Bush's soothing calls for a "kinder and gentler America," with a "thousand points of light," perversely brought more victims of injustice seeking justice. Individuals filed more complaints of discrimination against employers, police officers, rental agents, schools, and real estate brokers than they had since the beginning of the Reagan administration. In 1990, the Department of Justice received 9,800 civil rights complaints, well over the 7,500 received in 1986.[5]

Though African Americans filed most race discrimination complaints, a spike in complaints from Hispanics and Asian Americans also occurred. Interracial conflicts between minority groups constituted an even more disturbing development. A series of violent and deadly racial clashes between blacks and Hispanics in the Miami metropolitan area during the 1980s dramatically displayed this trend. Repeated episodes of racial discord and violence between Korean merchants and black customers in South

Central Los Angeles and other cities around the country increasingly fueled tensions.

The first legislative foray by human rights advocates did not focus on race, and it succeeded. On May 9, 1989, the Americans with Disabilities Act (ADA) was introduced in Congress with bipartisan support. There had been some slight improvement in attention to disability rights before. In 1977, when I went to Washington to head federal education activities, the 1976 Education of All Handicapped Children law was funded for the first time in the first budget we submitted to Congress. Before that time, disabled children were most often not permitted to attend public schools. Even those who did attend were not given services to meet their individual needs. Individualized education plans were required under the law, but implementation was a major problem.

State residential treatment institutions for the disabled had long been horrific, and rehabilitation was most often a myth. Public transportation was mostly inaccessible to the disabled. This included both the visually impaired and those who had mobility deficits. The right to vote was denied through inaccessibility to polling places and the means of casting a vote. Section 504 of the Rehabilitation Act of 1973 was designed to solve some problems. It provided that no program receiving federal funds could discriminate against people with disabilities. But enforcement persistently lagged. From the Nixon through the Ford administrations, required regulations were written but not implemented.

Disability advocates' earlier protests to gain federal attention prepared them to launch direct action in support of the ADA. It doesn't take much to protest, but disability service programs received grants from the federal rehabilitation program that helped them organize.

DISABILITY PROTESTS

When Jimmy Carter took office in 1977, the disability rights advocates who voted for him demanded that he sign and implement the regulations immediately. Instead, Health, Education, and Welfare (HEW) secretary Joseph Califano appointed a task force to review the regulations. Fearing dilution of the regulations, the American Coalition of Citizens with Disabilities insisted that he proceed with signing and implementation. Activists also engaged in nonviolent direct action. For twenty-five days in April 1977, about 150 disability rights activists took over the fourth floor of a federal building in San Francisco. Some carried signs reading "Handicapped Human Rights Sign ADA." The protesters announced they would stay until the regulations were issued. They received some outside assistance. By the third day of the protest, McDonald's, Glide Memorial Church, Safeway, and the Black Panther Party gave food. Safeway also gave medicine, and a Hispanic group, the Mission Rebels, provided hot breakfasts. The Salvation Army provided food, coffee, and blankets. On day three HEW officials turned off hot water, reduced phone lines to two pay phones, and limited all other phones to incoming calls. HEW also prohibited occupiers leaving the building from reentering.[6]

The Black Panther Party newspaper covered the protests in its April and May 1977 issues. The coverage included a photo of Dennis Billups, described in one *Black Panther* feature article as "a young blind Black man from San Francisco . . . one of the active and enthusiastic participants in the ongoing occupation of the HEW offices by handicapped and disabled people fighting for their civil and human rights."[7]

A group of protesters also entered the HEW headquarters building in Washington where Califano and senior officials had offices. When Califano met with them on April 4, they demanded issuance of the regulations without delay; when he didn't promise to do so, they walked out. The next morning, three hundred people gathered downstairs in HEW's headquarters and in other offices around the country. They were helped by the International Association of Machinists; McDonald's also gave food, but the local community didn't come out to join the protest. Califano stayed in his office the first night. He had phone service cut off and allowed them a doughnut and cup of coffee in the morning. On April 6, 1977, the sit-in ended and the occupiers left the building. They said that no food or access to medicine and unsympathetic guards made it impossible to stay.

In other cities, protests failed to gain momentum. But in DC, newly arrived protesters from San Francisco rented a windowless Hertz truck with a hydraulic tail lift to travel to Califano's house and hold a candlelight vigil until dawn. Most stayed at the Luther Place Memorial Church, sleeping on foam mattresses on the floor and eating food provided by the local Washington International Machinists Union. They also demonstrated outside Carter's church and held vigils outside HEW. Reporters questioned Califano when he went to a hotel event to speak. On April 28, 1977, Califano signed the existing Section 504 regulation.[8]

In March 1988, in the last months of the Reagan administration, disabilities rights advocates, along with other human rights activists, joined in supporting the students at Gallaudet University, a school for persons who are deaf, in Washington, DC, in their Deaf President Now protests. Established under a charter signed by President Abraham Lincoln as an institution for educating the hearing impaired, Gallaudet is private and nonprofit but receives most of its funds from a dedicated federal appropriation in the federal Education Department budget. By early 1988, students believed it was time for the institution to appoint its first deaf president. Enough deaf scholars had earned PhDs, and numerous deaf professionals had experience serving in educational institutions. On March 6, 1988, the trustees announced they had chosen Elisabeth Zinser, an administrator from North Carolina, as president. Zinser, who could hear, was selected over two other finalists who were deaf. Students barricaded the campus gates using heavy-duty bicycle locks and hot-wired buses, moving them in front of the gates and letting the air out of the tires. The locked gates kept people from coming onto campus grounds while forcing the board of trustees to come to hear the protesters' demands. When the board ignored their demands, the supporters of Deaf President Now marched to the US Capitol. The students continued blockades, marches, class boycotts, and rallies, and were joined by disability activists and other supporters from elsewhere. The board gave in and named I. King Jordan as the first deaf president. He had been dean of the College of Arts and Sciences and one of the three finalists in the search.

Disability rights activists were well prepared to support the ADA through the legislative process. But the inside players and strategy relied on supporters who were political appointees and members of Congress and the Senate. Two Republicans who were disabled were advocates for persons with disabilities. One was Evan Kemp Jr., named by Bush as chair of the Equal Employment Opportunity Commission and also wheelchair-bound. Another was Justin Dart, a successful businessman whose grandfather founded Walgreens drugstores. Dart's father, one of an informal group of advisers known as Reagan's "kitchen cabinet," was a Reagan appointee as vice chair of the National Council on Disability, which recommended the language in the bill. Kemp was a friend and bridge partner of White House counsel Boyden Gray. Kemp and Dart worked with Patrisha Wright and others in the Leadership Conference on Civil Rights to pass the act.

The bipartisan bill included the protections for the rights and opportunities of the disabled that the US Commission on Civil Rights had developed in its report, *Accommodating the Spectrum of Individual Abilities*, written by consultants Robert L. Burgdorf and Chris Bell, and published in 1983. The report gave me the opportunity to take a big-picture look at disability rights law and where it ought to go. A key finding of the report was that discrimination based on disability was "a serious and pervasive social problem." When the National Council on Disability (NCD) was created in 1984, it produced a report on how federal laws and programs could be improved. Burgdorf, who had been appointed their counsel, was responsible for the report *Toward Independence*, which was based on consumer forums around the country. NCD concluded that discrimination was the biggest problem facing those with disabilities. Unlike the commission's report, they recommended enactment of a comprehensive law prohibiting discrimination based on disability. Bergdorf prepared a draft of such an act, even before the NCD published its report.

The first bill was introduced in April 1988 by Representative Tony Coelho, who had epilepsy, and Senator Lowell Weicker, who had a son with Down syndrome. It held to the principled insistence by activists for disability rights that any legislation and regulations for the disabled had to track provisions for women and people of color. They wanted the same category of rights. Without public funds, Justin Dart and his wife, at their own expense, held public hearings throughout the country documenting the injustice of discrimination in the lives of people with disabilities. Thousands of people with disabilities attended, along with their friends and families.[9]

Then came months of Congressional hearings, during which advocates produced witnesses who persuasively explained their personal need for civil rights protection. The legislative process took months because it required back-and-forth exchanges between members, the civil rights leaders Ralph Neas, Patrisha Wright, and others, as well as the relevant staff of four committees and the White House. Grassroots activists worried that something might derail passage. Attorney General Dick Thornburgh informed House leaders that the administration wanted an amendment in the Senate-passed bill that would rule out monetary damages for discrimination against disabled persons. LCCR insisted that the administration had to accept that the principle of parity, which required that disability discrimination be treated just like discrimination based on race, sex, national origin, and religion, ruled out the proposal.

Disability activists became totally impatient with the pace of the legislative effort and engaged in a timely targeted protest. On March 12, 1990, American Disabled for Attendants Today (ADAPT), Center for Independent Living, and other groups brought hundreds of people with disabilities to rally in Washington. At the bottom steps of the Capitol they denounced the slow movement of the Americans with Disabilities bill. Then some abandoned their wheelchairs, got down on their hands and knees, and began crawling slowly up the eighty-three steps toward the building's west entrance. Eight-year-old Jennifer Keelan, from Denver, with cerebral palsy yelled, "I'll take all night if I have to!" Others yelled, "Pass the bill, pass it now!"[10]

"The Capitol Crawl" made national news and headlines and pushed lawmakers toward passage of the bill. Activists kept up the pressure. In late April, protesters occupied the office of Jack Brooks, chair of the House Judiciary Committee, urging passage of the legislation. In May, the House passed the bill by a unanimous voice vote. Patterned after laws against discrimination based on sex, race, or national origin, the ADA signed by President Bush on July 26, 1990, for the first time broadly protected disabled persons from discrimination.

The bipartisanship fueled by grassroots pressure that helped ADA passage was in short supply when six Supreme Court decisions undermined unemployment discrimination law in June 1989. The rulings made it much harder for persons who experienced discrimination to win a case. It took all the energies of activists, the grassroots, and proponents in Congress to pass legislation remedying the damage. The first legislative attempt overlapped somewhat with the ADA campaign.

In 1990, Senator Kennedy and Congressman Augustus F. Hawkins introduced a bill to overturn the Supreme Court decisions and for the first time to provide monetary damages for those who suffered intentional discrimination, which would include the disabled. Bush had an approval rating of 70 percent among blacks, which some pundits attributed to his not being Reagan. His staff wondered if he should oppose the bill to gain conservative support. He asked for an administration bill that would undo two of the negative Supreme Court decisions. One was the *Patterson v. Mc-Lean Credit Union* ruling, which narrowed the ability of minorities to win monetary damages for job discrimination. The bill would also restore the burden of proof to defendants in cases where employers' hiring practices had a discriminatory impact. A second case, *Wards Cove Packing Co. v. Atonio*, overturned a 1971 Supreme Court ruling in *Griggs v. Duke Power Co.* that the employer had the burden of proving that a hiring practice was required by business necessity. The administration proposal did not touch the other four negative 1989 court decisions. In one, *Price Waterhouse v. Hopkins*, the court decided that when an employer had mixed motives for making an employment decision, only one of which was sex discrimination, the employee's complaint was invalid if the same decision would have been made without the sex discrimination. In another case, the court had also restricted the use of a law that prohibited race discrimination in contracts, saying that it outlawed only an original hiring decision and not any actions taken thereafter, even if the actions were discriminatory. In *Martin v. Wilks*, the court let white firefighters in Birmingham, Alabama, sue to overturn a consent decree years after a lower federal court approved it, even though they were notified of the consent decree beforehand and had a chance to object.

Attorneys for the civil rights groups prepared an analysis of both bills to present to Attorney General Thornburgh and President Bush. On May 14, the White House asked African American leaders, including Arthur Fletcher, whom Bush had designated chair of the US Commission on Civil Rights, to meet with the president. In addition to the heads of major civil rights organizations and their lawyers, Bush invited what the White House described as "conservative blacks who did not emphasize civil rights," such as Robert Woodson, the president of the National Center for Neighborhood Enterprise. The meeting, which the White House called "a listening session" for Bush, would be followed by meetings with other groups, including "Hispanics, Jews, Roman Catholics, the disabled, Asians and women."[11]

Although Bush had asked Congress, after the Supreme Court decisions, to pass a bill broadening protection against job discrimination, Thornburgh threatened to urge a presidential veto of the Kennedy-Hawkins legislation, characterizing it as requiring quotas. Fletcher said he did not agree. By this time the label "quotas," signifying some unfair, unjustified advantage to blacks over whites, had been used effectively by Republican conservatives and served to inflame much of the public against any civil rights measure to which the term was applied. The issues in the bills, as in the Supreme Court decisions, though decisive, were so technical on whether a case could be won or lost that public interest was minuscule —until administration officials who wanted to protect employers from winning suits highlighted the specter of racial quotas.

"The major hang up, is whether it would produce so-called quotas," Fletcher said after the ninety-minute meeting. He insisted that the Kennedy-Hawkins bill had goals, not quotas. "You're talking to the person who wrote the Philadelphia Plan, who put goals, targets and timetables in the first plan that was ever issued 20 years ago," Fletcher said. "A quota is a flat number that has to be satisfied irrespective of whether the person can do the job. . . . All businesses pursue goals."[12]

Woodson, downplaying the need to remedy discrimination, commented that the president should forget both the administration proposal and the congressional bill. Using a standard conservative tactic of minimizing discrimination issues by directing attention solely to other major problems in black communities, Woodson said Bush should "go back to the drawing boards and really construct legislation that addresses the critical needs of people whose brains are being blown out in these inner cities, whose families are in crisis."[13]

On May 19, 1990, the former head of the National Urban League said that President Bush risked widespread protests and destruction of his popularity among blacks if he vetoed civil rights legislation pending before Congress. "Black people may have forgiven George Bush for the Willie Horton ads, but there will be no forgiveness for vetoing a bill that saves basic civil rights from the tender mercies of the Reagan Supreme Court," Vernon Jordan, who served as the Urban League's president from 1972 to 1981, told the George Mason University graduating class in suburban Fairfax, Virginia. "A veto would unleash a firestorm of protest that would permanently rupture the administration's credibility and galvanize black people and white people who believe in the power of the law to right the wrongs of racism," he said.[14] Critics said that 1988 presidential campaign ads to boost Bush's image as a tough-on-crime candidate were racist in their use of Horton, a black convicted killer who raped a woman while on furlough from a Massachusetts prison.[15]

The negotiations continued over the summer as Fletcher did everything he could in the media and with other black Republicans to persuade Bush to support the Kennedy-Hawkins bill. To no avail, they argued that a presidential veto could trigger an angry response from minorities and hurt Republican efforts to recruit African Americans as GOP voters. In early October, Bush proposed a compromise that would allow race discrimination for "legitimate community or customer relationship efforts." The president did not give any examples of when discrimination would be appropriate. Arthur Fletcher was apoplectic as he told the media that Bush's proposal would "take us back to the 1940s. I cannot believe anyone sincere about civil rights could have proposed such language."[16]

On October 16, the Senate passed the Kennedy-Hawkins bill 62–34, without Bush's suggested language. The House followed suit, passing the bill on October 17, 273–154, but the White House reiterated the president's intention to veto it.

Former Ford administration transportation secretary William Coleman, a leading lawyer and chair of the NAACP Legal Defense Fund board, met with Bush for one last attempt at persuasion and left feeling "reassured." Civil rights leaders and women's rights advocates marched at the White House on October 19, chanting, "Sign the bill!" They sought a meeting with President Bush, but press secretary Marlin Fitzwater said it "probably would not be that helpful," and unless Congress changed the bill, Bush would veto it.

The efforts of civil rights advocates, including Fletcher, failed. Bush decided to stick with the conservative opponents. The veto came two weeks before the November 6 congressional elections. Civil rights organizations and women's groups called the bill a test of Bush's support for the interests of minorities, and the veto seemed likely to serve as a focal point in the remaining days of campaigning.

On November 21, Bush vetoed the Civil Rights Act of 1990, and the Senate voted 66–34 to override, failing to gain the required two-thirds majority by one vote. Kennedy called the veto "tragic and disgraceful."[17] It meant that "when the chips are down, the White House is against civil rights." Neas noted that Bush had joined "Andrew Johnson and Ronald Reagan as the only presidents to veto a civil rights bill." Arthur Fletcher told the press that the Civil Rights Commission was on record as strongly disagreeing with Bush's stand. *Boston Globe* columnist Derrick Jackson pointed out that "none other than David Duke," the former grand wizard of the Ku Klux Klan, who had just lost a US Senate race in Louisiana but won 44 percent of the vote in a "rabid campaign against affirmative action," came to the Hill to praise the failure to override the veto. Duke proclaimed, "The President and the Congress are getting my message."[18] Outside the White House, the activist and comedian Dick Gregory protested President Bush's veto.

Civil rights advocates and supporters in Congress prepared to reintroduce the legislation in the next Congress. Meanwhile, Bush's ratings among African Americans receded to Reaganesque levels. While Congress and civil rights advocates worked on the Clarence Thomas nomination and other issues, they also concentrated on passing a civil rights bill in 1991 to overcome Bush's veto of the 1990 act. The employment discrimination bill was reintroduced in January 1991, and this time in addition to grassroots pressure, the LCCR negotiated with corporate leaders on the substance of the bill. White House staff promoted media attacks on corporate participants. Thus, key people dropped out. At first, the bill did not pass.

On July 1, 1991, the nomination of Clarence Thomas to the Supreme Court ignited a flurry of protests against the Senate confirmation proceedings and George H. W. Bush. The hearings devolved into a discussion of Anita Hill's sexual harassment charges rather than his reactionary civil rights record. Eleven Democrats voted to confirm him and two republicans voted against him. National civil rights organization carried the fight to Washington and grassroots mobilization never caught fire. The NAACP came late to opposing Thomas because his race complicated their decision. Other groups waited on them, and then the Anita Hill issue overshadowed everything else. But it is important to note that the fallout from this issue led Congress to pass the employment discrimination bill from 1990, and Bush signed it on November 21, 1991.

In achieving passage of the Civil Rights Act of 1991, the key players were Ralph Neas, within the Leadership Conference on Civil Rights; National Women's Law Center president Marcia Greenberger; Women's Legal Defense Fund executive director Judith Lichtman; and Elaine Jones, then legislative advocate in the Washington office of the NAACP Legal Defense Fund. After considerable negotiations in which Senator John Danforth (Republican-Missouri) played a major role, Bush decided to accept the slightly revised bill. He claimed that new language allowing businesses to defend themselves against charges of unintentional discrimination settled the quota issue. Danforth and Bush administration officials settled another major issue concerning a new provision under which women, religious minorities, and the disabled who won discrimination lawsuits could claim damages, in addition to back pay, just as racial and ethnic minorities could. The agreement included a sliding scale of punitive and other damages with a cap ranging from $50,000 to $300,000, depending on the size of the business. In announcing the compromise, Bush stated, "I can simply certify it is not a quota bill; it is a fair bill, and it's going to hit a lick against discrimination in the workplace. And I couldn't be more happy."[19]

However, White House counsel Gray unhappily fielded criticisms from conservatives. He published an opinion-page column in the *Washington Post* saying, "Contrary to a rapidly congealing press myth, President Bush did not 'cave' or 'surrender' on quotas in the new civil rights bill." He asserted that a legislative compromise became possible "only after the Democrats beat a total retreat on quotas, thereby paving the way for the president to make concessions on other, less fundamental, issues."[20]

Civil rights lawyers Vernon Jordan and William Coleman responded on November 18, 1991, that the bill had in fact restored the law to its meaning before the 1989 Supreme Court decisions, with improvements on damages. Most important, with Senator Danforth leading the charge, Congress had passed a bipartisan bill. The president helped to put civil rights back where it belonged: "as part of a national consensus." They were dismayed, because Gray's column "attempts to rip that consensus apart just as it was forming again," which "ill serves the President and the country."[21]

The fallout from the Rodney King beating by police in Los Angeles created other difficulties for Bush and further eroded his standing with civil rights supporters. On March 3, 1991, Lake View Terrace resident George Holliday videotaped the police beating King, an African American man whose automobile they had pursued in a high-speed chase.

After the trial in the King case, the long-standing problems of police-community relations and the Justice Department's ineptness in alleged police cases came glaringly into public view. Between 1982 and 1991 the Justice Department conducted 720 investigations of police and sheriff's departments. Only four cases resulted in indictments, and only three cases, one involving the Border Patrol, resulted in convictions. The US Civil

Rights Commission held hearings in Los Angeles and reported on festering police-community relations, despite obstructions to the hearing process and denials of wrongdoing from the police and sheriff's departments.[22]

After a Simi Valley jury acquitted Sergeant Stacey Koon and officers Laurence M. Powell, Theodore J. Briseno, and Timothy E. Wind in the beating of Rodney King, which triggered the Los Angeles riot, President Bush suggested the impossible: that the assumed acquittals might be reversed on appeal, which showed his ignorance about the judicial process and the unwillingness of his Justice Department to bring a federal prosecution.

On May 1, 1992, the president held a meeting with civil rights leaders to consider responses. Accompanied by Vice President Dan Quayle; Missouri governor John Ashcroft, the chair of the President's Commission for Urban Families; his two highest level African American appointees, Constance Newman, director of the Office of Personnel Management, and Louis Sullivan, secretary of Health and Human Services; and also Fletcher, the president met in the Roosevelt Room with an array of civil rights leaders. They included Benjamin Hooks, executive director of the NAACP; John Jacob, president of the National Urban League; Raul Yzaguirre, executive director of La Raza; Dorothy Height of the National Council of Negro Women; Bush aide Thaddeus Garrett; and the Reverend Edward Hill, pastor of Mt. Zion Missionary Baptist Church in Los Angeles, whom Reagan had proposed for US Civil Rights Commission chair. The leaders suggested a blue-ribbon race relations panel to investigate the issues, but Bush rejected that idea. Perhaps the staff recalled how the Kerner Commission went much beyond what President Johnson had expected.[23]

While Bush tried to downplay the injustice seen in the King case and the trials of the officers, Ben Chavis Jr., executive director of the Commission for Racial Justice of the Cleveland-based United Church of Christ, disagreed, as did other African Americans. He spent three days in Los Angeles among church and community leaders and residents. He "hovered with several Los Angeles citizens around a television set, all of them with smoke in their lungs from the fires from burning buildings, and heard President Bush say the protests were about mob brutality and not civil rights." But Chavis said he's "absolutely wrong" and leaders should "deal with problems of racial inequality." He thought outbreaks of protest would occur again unless political and religious leaders accepted the moral challenge to work to assure justice for all Americans.[24]

➤ ➤ ➤

Bush's shift to an antiabortion position and the Reagan-Bush appointees to the Supreme Court inspired prochoice activists to organize to protect a woman's right to choose. They were successful in influencing the retention of *Roe v. Wade*, despite fears that it would be overturned by the court. Every year since the first 1974 antiabortion march, a March for Life has commemorated the anniversary of *Roe*. Presidents Reagan and George W. Bush both sent telephone messages of support to the protesters. When Missouri's antiabortion restrictions in *Webster v. Reproductive Health Services* came before the Supreme Court in 1989, the Bush administration urged the court to overturn *Roe v. Wade*. In April 1989, before the decision, the National Organization for Women's (NOW) March for Women's Lives brought about 500,000 protesters to the National Mall in Washington. In April 1992, another NOW March for Women's Lives drew about 750,000 people to the mall.[25] Film stars, politicians, and civil rights activists joined demonstrators in the rally. NOW wanted to make abortion rights a major issue in the upcoming presidential and congressional campaigns. Although white women were the overwhelming majority, the marchers also included people of color, the old and the young, men and women.

Patricia Ireland, president of NOW, insisted, "We're going to turn out of office people who don't support us." It took more than two hours for the crowded rows of marchers to pass the White House on the way to the foot of Capitol Hill, where speeches, songs, and slogans filled the afternoon. The crowd gathered at the Ellipse from midmorning and began marching shortly after noon toward the mall.

NOW said the event was the biggest abortion rights rally ever held. A much smaller crowd of antiabortion activists held a counter-rally on the west lawn of the Capitol, not far from the mall. But there were apparently no confrontations.

Students and others who could not get to Washington also marched on the day of the protests. For example, Students for Choice, a prochoice group based on the University of Wisconsin, Madison, campus, held a march down State Street to the capitol in Madison Sunday afternoon to rally for abortion and reproductive rights for women. About two hundred people took part in the peaceful march. No arrests were reported.[26]

The court was about to consider the constitutionality of Pennsylvania's abortion restrictions in *Casey v. Planned Parenthood*. In June 1992, it reaffirmed *Roe v. Wade* in the *Casey* decision by a vote of 5–4. In dissent, Justice Scalia made clear that the court paid no attention to protests, though his remarks had just paid attention to them. The justices, while upholding the *Roe v. Wade* decision, permitted the states to impose some restrictions.

They upheld Pennsylvania restrictions, which imposed a twenty-four-hour waiting period before an abortion, forced most teenagers to get parental consent or judicial permission for abortions, and required doctors to keep detailed records on abortions they perform. Also, they affirmed an informed consent rule that a woman seeking an abortion must be told by a doctor about fetal development and alternatives to ending her pregnancy.

Supporters of abortion rights insisted that the regulations could have a dramatic impact on many women's access to abortions. For example, clinics would need to pay more to doctors to comply with the waiting period and informed consent measures, which required two visits to a doctor rather than one, and perhaps more consultation time. The twenty-four-hour waiting period could result in a week's delay for some women at clinics that perform abortions only once or twice a week. Wanda Franz, president of the National Right to Life Committee, responded that a mandate to provide women more information before an abortion was beneficial and should not be criticized.[27]

The leaders of seven national women's organizations, including the National Gay and Lesbian Task Force, NOW president Patricia Ireland, and Eleanor Smeal of the Feminist Majority, held a protest against the restrictions upheld in *Casey* on July 1, 1992, blocking the sidewalk outside the White House. Their supporters rallied across the street by Lafayette Square with signs and banners. The leaders were released later on their own recognizance. "We are defying the law in the rich tradition of our foremothers, who fought for their rights. We will oppose all unjust laws that restrict women's reproductive rights," said Ireland. "We deplore the terrorist violence" of antiabortion groups that block abortion clinics, intimidating women seeking abortions and doctors who perform them, she said. Smeal told the noontime rally, "Yesterday it was in my home state of Pennsylvania that women lost their rights. Tomorrow it will be another state."[28]

Responding to abortion rights proponents, Congress began action on the Freedom of Choice Act to codify the guarantees provided in *Roe v.*

Wade. They wanted to pass the legislation and force a Bush veto before the fall election. But they were not able to obtain congressional enactment.

An antiabortion group in Palm Bay, Florida, which had been harassing patients and endeavoring to close clinics where abortions were performed, began posting "Wanted" posters that provided detailed personal information about doctors who performed abortions. Their campaign, called "Operation Goliath," mailed posters to neighbors, employees, and business associates of the doctors. Bruce Cadle, the leader of the group, was a thirty-four-year-old former real estate salesman and full-time, paid antiabortion activist. One of the physicians targeted was Frank Snydle of Melbourne, Florida, who said he was more upset about calls to his eighty-two-year-old mother than he was about the poster with his picture and a description of him as a "hired assassin." The poster also included the addresses and phone numbers of his fiancée and mother.[29]

Snydle reported that his mother had been followed by two men in a van and that she finally pulled into a store parking lot and they pulled their van up beside her. "Then she got out and called 911, but the police can't do anything because the stalking law isn't in effect," he said. People who stalked their victims could go to prison under new legislation approved by the Florida House of Representatives that went into effect July 1, 1992, three months later.

Snydle was one of three Central Florida physicians singled out on wanted posters offering up to $1,000 for information leading to their arrest or the revocation of their medical licenses. The other doctors were R. Monthree of Winter Springs and Carlito Arrogante of Lake Worth. The posters say the data is being provided "for informational purposes, not to encourage harassment." But abortion providers saw the posters as one more tactic in an escalating campaign that could lead to violence as abortion rights activists marched in Washington, DC.

Lynn Rosenthal, president of the Florida Abortion Council, a professional association of eighteen clinics, warned, "The people involved in Operation Goliath are terrorists." She regarded the threat as serious, pointing out that in 1989, the last time there was a national abortion rights march, two Florida clinics were destroyed by fire.

Though the posters claimed they were only for informational purposes, Cadle said they wanted to inspire demonstrations at the homes of doctors and their families to embarrass them publicly. They had "some doctors quit once we exposed them."[30]

Protests continued in the run-up to Bush's reelection campaign against Bill Clinton. In Cleveland in August 1992, two groups held rallies. More than one hundred people turned out for a morning prochoice rally on Public Square, which was followed by a march through downtown and an afternoon Womanfest. About forty people showed up at a counter-rally in Willard Park.

At the Public Square rally, Barbara Otto, spokeswoman for 9to5, the National Association of Working Women, one of the sponsors of the rally, noted that "many women don't have a choice to go to college, stay at home or go to work." Most women are born into the working class, Otto observed. Working women need medical care, family leave, protection from sexual harassment, and child-care programs, but President Bush has opposed legislation backing such issues, she said.

About a dozen antiabortion advocates picketed the prochoice rally, prompting Jessie McGuinness, chair of the rally, to tell the crowd, "Do not confront them. It won't do any good." The antiabortion protesters carried signs such as "Peace in the Womb" and "Not NOW, Not Ever."

At the antiabortion protest, Marilyn Kopp, a spokeswoman for the National Women's Coalition for Life, said, "Not all feminists are pro-death." Her group claimed to represent 8.1 million women in local groups. Jean Graham, vice president of the Ohio Chapter of Feminists for Life, said antiabortion feminists wore the mantle of early feminists and that the prochoice groups were not the only feminists.[31]

During the years of the Bush administration, activists' legislative responses to Supreme Court cases were effective, well targeted, and well timed. The AIDS protesters, under the mantle of ACT UP, used guerrilla tactics and gained a reduction in price of AZT and accelerated an FDA drug-safety review. The Civil Rights Act protests did not become a movement, and the technical nature of the decisions inhibited understanding. The Thomas embarrassment, combined with protests over his opposition to the Family and Medical Leave Act, as well as attacks from leaders such as Vernon Jordan and criticism from the media, eroded Bush's popularity and helped lead to the passage of the Civil Rights Act of 1991. The course of events and the Supreme Court opinions imply that the massive prochoice marches influenced the court not to overturn *Roe v. Wade*.

Bush lost the 1992 election to Clinton because he seemed bored at times, and there didn't seem to be a rationale, beyond experience, for his reelection. Additionally, his violation of his promise to not raise taxes turned off some in the Republican base. Bush also seemed not to have a policy to deal with the ongoing economic recession, while Clinton's deployment of the slogan coined by James Carville, "It's the economy, stupid," was successful. Ross Perot's candidacy also contributed to Bush's defeat. Perot took almost 20 percent of the popular vote, making Clinton a minority president.

CHAPTER 6

The Adaptable President

William Jefferson Clinton

Before the cameras, Mrs. King read a wonderfully supportive statement recalling the debate over the role of Bayard Rustin, a gay man and a well-known civil rights organizer, in the 1963 March on Washington. Mrs. King said, "Like Martin, I don't believe you can stand for freedom for one group of people and deny it to others."[1]

AS THE 1993 CONGRESSIONAL BLACK CAUCUS dinner approached, caucus members had refused to meet with the forty-second president, Bill Clinton. The CBC's temporary expression of disaffection with the Democratic Party president they had helped to elect occurred because many of their constituents felt betrayed. On November 3, 1992, civil rights supporters, including a majority of black voters, voted for Clinton despite his special trip back to Arkansas to witness the execution of Ricky Rector, a mentally disabled man with an IQ of seventy, and his attack on Sister Souljah, whom Jesse Jackson, the most popular black leader at the time, had invited to appear at his Rainbow PUSH convention, in Jackson's presence. African Americans were also unnerved by Clinton's actions since his inauguration, including the June 1993 dumping of Lani Guinier after he had announced her appointment, because of conservative attacks on her views about voting rights, though he had the cover of his friend Vernon Jordan's approval. They also felt deeply troubled by his support of budget cuts, which hurt the poor. At the local level, people expressed disapproval of Clinton to their political representatives, who therefore had to show some wariness about him. The day before Clinton's CBC dinner speech, the White House "decided to placate the CBC by showcasing the administration's leading African American officials onstage at a news conference." My appointment as chair of the US Civil Rights Commission was a major announcement. As a result, at the dinner, Clinton was met with loud applause rather than boos and hisses.[2]

I knew from talking to Clinton staffers that some people objected to my appointment because I had criticized the president and because of the controversy when Reagan tried to fire me for criticizing his policies. They didn't want me to have a larger platform for denouncing the administration's positions. White House personnel director and Clinton confidant Bruce Lindsey asked me directly if, as chair, I would criticize Clinton. I assured him that if the president did nothing to undermine civil rights, he had nothing to fear from me. Also, I was questioned by the White House counsel's office about news articles in which I criticized some of Clinton's actions. I was forced to explain, once again, the independence of the commission, that I was exercising my responsibility as a member of a watchdog agency. I kept noting what I felt to be true—that I believed Clinton appreciated an independent commission.

Bill Clinton seemed to be another "friendly" president who liberals and progressives thought would do the right thing, despite some suspicions about his promises and actions. In fact, he was an adaptable president. I first encountered Clinton in the Carter administration, where his quick intellect, charm, and easy embrace and reinterpretation of every idea were on display. He came to Camp David in August 1979 when the president was inviting opinion leaders to advise him on themes to use in his reelection campaign. Those of us who worked for President Carter listened while we noticed that no matter what anyone said at the table that day, Bill Clinton had a suggestion or an easily given, almost persuasive answer. He reminded me of some of my talkative and likeable students. I whispered to Anne Wexler, an assistant to the president, "Who is he?" And she said, "Oh! Vernon Jordan [then head of the National Urban League] brought him. He's the new governor of Arkansas who says he's going to be president someday."

Throughout his two terms, President Clinton used my history as presidential critic to his advantage. He liked to tell audiences that whenever he asked how he was doing, I'd say he deserved about a C or C+, but that was all right by him, because criticizing him was my job. For his entire administration, White House staffers alerted me about anything affecting civil rights, probably in the hope that I would not criticize them unnecessarily in the press. I do not recall any real surprises.

On unusual occasions, for example, when racial profiling became almost endemic, I would fax a letter to the president and receive a reply. Given our experience with Reagan, I was more concerned about protecting the commission's independence than having Clinton's approval. I was also aware of the need to prevent access from subverting my responsibility as a commissioner to remain an honest critic. I was more interested in ensuring that the agencies enforced civil rights and that bad policy was avoided. I also talked to Clinton directly, at small dinners and at informal meetings, about civil rights issues, and took the opportunity to gently harass him about the persistent Haitian refugee problem and the need to end the exile of the elected Haitian president Jean-Bertrand Aristide, a former Catholic priest. He always appeared concerned though noncommittal.

By halfway through his first term, the reelection prospects for Clinton, who was a minority president (winning in a three-person race against George H. W. Bush and Ross Perot and receiving only 43 percent of the popular vote), looked dismal. The base voters who elected him were disaffected, and turnout was depressed in the midterm election. In fact, Republicans, in 1994, gained control of both houses of Congress for the first time in forty years. A great deal had happened to stimulate grassroots protest and disaffection on the Left: health-care reform failed, equivocating over gays in the military continued, the North American Free Trade Agreement (NAFTA) portended Democratic voters losing jobs. And as the Whitewater allegations against Hillary Clinton persisted, rumors spread about President Clinton's extramarital affairs. All this served to erode his popularity.

But the Republicans in control of Congress overreached, and with the government shutdowns, when Clinton vetoed proposed cuts in education and Medicaid, they lost control and Clinton recovered. The US government in 1995 closed its doors twice: first for six days in November and again for twenty-one days in December. Voters, who had once urged the Republicans onward in their attacks on big government, now applauded Clinton for protecting their working-class interests.

Now whetted and looking toward reelection, Clinton moved politically further to the right with policies on crime, welfare reform, the federal budget, and affirmative action. Progressives denounced him. With the shift in policies, Clinton also effectively used public appearances and media strategies in dealing with breaking events to improve his reelection prospects. In 1995, the president responded passionately to the Oklahoma City federal building bombing and the killing of 168 people, including 19 children in the building's day-care center.[3] He responded with vigorous investigations of church burnings in the South and approved a successful cease-fire in Bosnia, all actions that burnished his reputation.

The economic boom, mainly due to expansion of the technology sector, low interest rates, low unemployment, and a reduction in the deficit, helped to undermine opposition to Clinton's presidency. In the end, Clinton won reelection easily as a successful centrist president, but he had again faced two challengers, Senator Robert Dole (Republican-Kansas) and Ross Perot, and did not win the popular vote. In addition, Republicans retained control of the House and Senate.

As a Democratic president, Clinton enjoyed the usual reluctance of dependable Democratic voters and beholden officeholders to criticize him or his policies, and despite his moves to the right, he benefited from party stalwarts' assumption that whatever he did would be "friendly." But in point of fact, despite the president's affable everyman, "I feel your pain manner," Clinton's policies increased economic inequality. Cuts in programs in housing, transportation, job training, environmental protection, and economic development continued to burden the neediest Americans. And welfare reform, a cornerstone of Clinton's move-to-the-right platform, embraced a catch-22 pitfall. It ensured continued poverty by codifying time limits and eligibility requirements that diminished the possibility of recipients achieving the education needed for obtaining jobs to pursue lives independent of public assistance.

When Clinton supported a two-year limit on staying on the welfare rolls, Peter Edelman, acting assistant secretary for planning and evaluation, and Mary Jo Bane, assistant secretary for children and families, executed an inside the administration protest. They submitted their letters of resignation, both citing the welfare measure as the reason. Edelman was a longtime expert on remedying poverty, and Bane was a leading scholar on welfare policy. Both had been members of the government task force working on the issue. One of Hillary Clinton's first jobs in Washington had been working for Edelman's wife, Children's Defense Fund (CDF) president Marian Wright Edelman.

Peter Edelman said he resigned because he believed the reform ended a "sixty-year commitment to aid all needy families with children who met the federal eligibility requirements." This meant that once the economy was no longer improving, those now denied support and their children would suf-fer more. But, loyal party stalwarts—even members of Congress from urban areas—voted for Clinton's policies on welfare that undermined the poor. As political scientist Cathy Cohen has pointed out, the persistence among blacks of a respectability ideology means that middle class people and the politicians don't want to be associated with the unrespectable, including the impoverished, the homeless, addicts, and people with AIDS.[4]

This perspective also applied to the muted protests when Clinton supported keeping mentally disabled drug users and other addicts out of public housing. This policy, coupled with a decline in the overall avail-ability of public housing and housing subsidies, had the effect of increasing homelessness already growing under Reagan. Local housing development agencies and tenant organizations, advocating for those with low incomes, issued complaints, but they were unable to organize a major protest. Other than a Children's Defense Fund rally several weeks before the congressional votes, there was little evidence of grassroots mobilization, which is difficult to achieve when only the poor seem affected. Clinton's tough-on-crime posture in the Ricky Rector execution was just a prologue to the party's policies during his administration that generated little opposition in real time but twenty years later are widely viewed as socially, economically, and culturally devastating. The party's embrace of a war on crime fit a defini-tion that researchers had been verbalizing in the 1990s and led to the Vio-lent Crime Control and Law Enforcement Act of 1994. It mandated harsh penalties for minor drug offenses and adding one hundred thousand new police officers on the streets. It also ended federal student aid to provide education for prisoners to improve their chances for avoiding recidivism. The legislation led to the president's public labeling of black teenagers as superpredators and blamed these children for the rise in violence perpe-trated by youths—particularly in inner cities—which effectively served as a rationale for overly aggressive policing. Overall, the legislation resulted in even higher black incarceration rates.[5]

Senator Joe Biden gets the credit for writing the Violent Crime Con-trol Act with full Democratic Party support at the time, including some members of the Congressional Black Caucus who expressed concern about black on black crime that made some communities unsafe. Women's groups advocated for it and still praise Biden, because the act provided $1.6 billion for enforcement against violent crimes against women, gave automatic and

mandatory restitution, and allowed civil suits when there was no prosecution. It also set up an office on Violence Against Women in the Justice
Department. The office still exists. The major sections of the bill have been
disavowed in recent years, because not only did black incarceration for
minor offenses soar, the effect on black family cohesion has also been horrendous. Also, the enormous financial costs of imprisonment for nonviolent crime, mostly drug offenses, became an issue. During Hillary Clinton's
unsuccessful 2016 presidential campaign, Bill Clinton expressed regret for
signing the bill, and Hillary Clinton, pressured by black critics, apologized
for using the term *superpredators*.[6]

The African American and progressive communities were not the only
losers during this period. Gay people who voted for Clinton and eagerly
joined in celebrating his inauguration also were soon disappointed. Three
national gay-rights groups sponsored the first gay inaugural ball and a spate
of receptions and dinners. Gregory King, of the Human Rights Campaign
Fund exulted, "We now have a president who is committed to ending discrimination and fighting the war against AIDS. He is someone who believes we are a part of America."[7]

During the 1980s, even as social attitudes toward gays became more
positive, the military became more negative toward the continued service
of gays. Perhaps the AIDS crisis and its early association with homosexu-
ality had some influence. In any case, the military increased investigations
and dismissals from the armed forces between 1986 and 1990. Clinton had
promised to end discrimination against gays during the campaign, and the
Pentagon began working on the issue. On January 24, 1993, a news story
broke that Defense Secretary Les Aspin told Clinton in a confidential
memorandum, leaked to the *New York Times* by an Aspin critic, that a
majority of Congress, and top military leaders, would oppose the administration's ending of the ban on gays serving in the armed forces. He advised that if Clinton issued such an order, Congress could reverse it. Aspin
suggested a round of consultations to arrive at a policy that might escape
rejection. The administration's plan for quietly executing the strategy was
upended by the leak.[8]

The controversy over the policy became a major priority for advocacy
groups after the memo leaked. Political repercussions for months helped to
crystallize opposition to Clinton. Urvashi Vaid of the National Gay and
Lesbian Task Force led the organizing for an April 25, 1993, March on

Washington for Lesbian, Gay, and Bi Equal Rights and Liberation. The march was an overwhelming success. About a million protesters gathered to demand passage of a lesbian, gay, bisexual, and transgender civil rights bill and an end to discrimination by state and federal governments, including the military; massive increase in funding for AIDS education, research, and patient care; universal access to health care, including alternative therapies; an end to sexism in medical research and health care; and an end to racial and ethnic discrimination in all forms. The demands included a ban on discrimination and violence based on actual or perceived sexual orientation, identification, race, religion, identity, sex and gender expression, disability, age, class, and AIDS/HIV infection.[9]

Then two developments kept the issue in the forefront of policy news. On May 5, 1993, the Hawaii Supreme Court ruled in *Baehr v. Lewin* that denying marriage to same-sex couples violated the Equal Protection Clause of the state constitution. In the meantime, Clinton set up a six-month review, after which he would announce a decision on the gays in the military policy.

The Service Members Legal Defense Network organized to advocate that Clinton permit gays to serve. They asked me to persuade Coretta Scott King to hold a press conference as part of its effort to influence Clinton to adopt a broad nondiscrimination policy. King had earlier criticized discrimination against gays, but she had not objected to a conditional policy that would discharge anyone whose sexual orientation became known.

Trading on a relationship born of many struggles, I asked King for her help. She told me that "some of the men who had been with Martin" advised her to "stay out of it." However, she firmly believed Dr. King would have stood up for gays because of his unconditional belief in human rights. She finally said if I would come to stand with her, she would hold the press conference. I went to Atlanta, and the Reverend Joseph Lowery broke ranks with the other "men who had been with Martin" to stand with us. Before the cameras, Mrs. King read a wonderfully supportive statement recalling the debate over the role of Bayard Rustin, a gay man and a well-known civil rights organizer, in the 1963 March on Washington. Mrs. King said, "Like Martin, I don't believe you can stand for freedom for one group of people and deny it to others." I chimed in that the president should not issue a keep-quiet-about-it policy, which would essentially make liars out of gays in the military. Clinton announced the unsatisfactory "Don't Ask, Don't Tell" policy decision on July 19, 1993.[10]

Defense Secretary Les Aspin issued enforcement regulations in December 1993 to go into effect in February 1994. The regulations provided that applicants for the services and service members would not be asked about their sexual orientation and that homosexual orientation (absent conduct infractions) would not disqualify anyone from service. The policy was enacted by Congress and signed by Clinton on November 30, 1993. It was not repealed until September 20, 2011, during the presidency of Barack Obama. Openly gay people were finally permitted to serve.

In the meantime, LGBT groups tried to address the problem of job discrimination, though unsuccessfully. On June 23, 1994, Congressman Gerry Studds (Democrat-Massachusetts) introduced the Employment Non-Discrimination Act (ENDA), which would ban discrimination in employment based on sexual orientation in Congress. It failed, was reintroduced in the House again, and failed again.

The issue of same-sex marriage was not much discussed at all until the late 1980s when the AIDS crisis caused increased concern about inheritance and death benefits among gays and lesbians. Then, in response to the 1993 *Baehr v. Lewin* Hawaii decision and developments in the states, Congress considered the Defense of Marriage Act (DOMA), designed to prevent the Constitution's Full Faith and Credit Clause from being applied to a state's refusal to recognize same-sex marriages. The act passed in May 1996, also defining marriage as a union only between a man and a woman and denying federal benefits to same-sex couples. DOMA passed both houses of Congress by large veto-proof majorities and was signed into law by President Clinton on September 21, 1996.

In 1996, after DOMA passed, the advocacy groups pushed for passage of ENDA, which failed only narrowly by a 49–50 vote in the Senate. Some activists regarded the support from some senators as an attempt to even out politically their vote for DOMA. The bill was not subjected to another House vote. As of 2017, ENDA has still not been enacted into law, which means that even today, when same-sex marriage is legal, in the absence of state protection, employment discrimination based on sexual orientation remains legal.

Clinton claimed later that he signed DOMA because of the veto-proof majority passage and to ward off a constitutional amendment outlawing same-sex marriage. He didn't hold a signing ceremony and had no photographs taken, and more than likely he wanted to avoid the political risk of being a same-sex marriage supporter. James Hormel, appointed by Clinton as the first openly gay US ambassador in 1999, recalled that gays were shocked, since Clinton had taken such a favorable position on gay rights during his campaign. By the time the Millennium March for Faith and Family took place in 2000, LGBT activists were divided on issues ranging from how the focus on gay marriage had left ENDA unattended and the mainstreaming of the movement by the Human Rights Campaign. The largely one-sided crowd at the Millennium March rally was addressed, via video, by President Clinton. Politically they had moved on; organizers urged the election of Albert Gore Jr.[11]

One of the major marches during Clinton's first term was not identified as a protest of anything he had done and issued no warnings to him. Though it had a huge turnout, it had no specific demands. It came when the policy conflict over gay rights in the military and same-sex marriage seemed to overshadow everything about rights. On October 16, 1995, a Million Man March, called by minister Louis Farrakhan, brought thousands of people to the National Mall. Controversy over Farrakhan's seeming homophobia and antisemitism did not detract from his status as the only black leader, at the time, whose public call could have brought so many black men to Washington for a rally. The march, according to the leaders, was to put black issues back on the nation's political agenda. They felt that the social and economic issues oppressing blacks were not a policy priority. March organizers noted that blacks' unemployment was still nearly twice that of white Americans, the black poverty rate was about 40 percent, and black median family income was about 58 percent of the median for white households. Though there was much talk of good economic times, about 11 percent of black males were unemployed and sixteen- to nineteen-year-olds had an unemployment rate of more than 50 percent. The speakers also focused on budget cuts in needed programs, severe environmental hazards, and the black incarceration rate and its deleterious effect on families.

The march also sought to dissipate negative racial stereotypes in the American media and in popular culture. March organizers expressed dismay at the sweeping stereotypes they thought white America seemed to draw from the coverage of such figures as Willie Horton, O. J. Simpson, and Mike Tyson. Believing that "black men have been designated by the culture as the sacrificial lambs for male evil," event organizers asked black male attendees to make a public display of their commitment to responsible and constructive behavior that would give the mass media positive imagery to broadcast.

The marchers came to town, and left the same day. The coming together was inspiring. One most important result of the march was that some who had not been at a march on Washington before were astonished that so many people came together in one place and without hostility, violence, or misbehavior. Also, an important take-away was the commitment of many attendees and observers to involve themselves in local voluntary education and mentoring programs to help youth and to overcome social problems.

A Latino immigrant rights march on October 12, 1996, had mixed results. Unlike the Million Man March, it had a distinct policy focus. The protesters cited specifically the budget cuts by the Clinton administration and Congress, the bipartisan anti-immigrant legislation call for doubling the number of INS border police over the next five years, and the addition of six hundred new agents to crack down against "criminal" aliens and visitors who overstay their US visas. The bill also authorized $12 million for a border fence; raised the maximum penalty for document fraud from five years to fifteen years; required sponsors of immigrant relatives to earn at least 125 percent of the federal poverty level; and streamlined procedures for deporting those who arrived with inadequate documents, including asylum seekers. The organizers made clear that, unlike the 1995 Million Man March, they had concrete demands, including free education for all children from kindergarten through college, a seven dollars an hour minimum wage, and legal amnesty for undocumented and illegal immigrants.[12]

MALDEF (Mexican American Legal Defense and Educational Fund) and La Raza, the two largest Latino organizations in the United States, did not formally endorse the march, which may not have benefited their advocacy with the administration and Congress, but Raul Yzaguirre, executive director of La Raza, spoke at the rally. On October 12, 1996, an estimated twenty-five thousand people demonstrated in Washington, DC, against anti-immigrant sentiment. Logistical support came from the American Friends Service Committee and the AFL-CIO, which provided office space in Washington. Many of the march's top organizers came from the labor movement. The turnout was disappointing. A march in 1994 in Los Angeles drew seventy thousand participants, and the Million Man March organized by African Americans in 1995 drew an estimated eight hundred thousand to a million people. Transporting people from outside Washington, arranging for buses, and making sure people knew where to catch a ride proved difficult for the Latino immigrant rights march.[13]

The Million Man March and the Latino Immigrant March were important educational protests. Though the Latino Immigrant March did not turn out large numbers, it gave the groups organizing experience that would stand them in good stead as they developed protest strategies. They did not, however, challenge President Clinton to do anything in particular or otherwise forgo their votes for his reelection.

There were other protests that addressed economic inequality. The National Sweatshop Campaign challenged the private sector and acted outside of insider politics; built resources at the grassroots, tying it together in a national campaign; had campus or local groups as partners in a national campaign; synchronized outreach and used social media and e-mail; and linked local problems to national solutions. The National Sweatshop Campaign effectively evolved into the living wage movement. On the environment, the Sierra Club and state-based Public Interest Research Group (PIRG) working together got new tough standards for the Clean Air Act in 1997, despite a $20 million industry advertising campaign.[14]

The 1999 World Trade Organization (WTO) Ministerial Conference was designed to start a new millennial round of international trade negotiations. It convened at the Washington State Convention and Trade Center in Seattle on November 30 that year. The negotiations ignited one street protest outside the hotels and convention center, bringing to prominence the antiglobalization movement in the United States. Opponents of globalization charged the WTO and other international organizations of facilitating corporations' increasing profits while risking worker's safety, implementing exploitative employment and compensation rules, and undermining environmental conservation and national authority and boundaries. They would accept free trade only if it could benefit poor countries or the poor in wealthy countries. In short, they saw globalization without mandatory regulation as the promotion of inequality.

Antiglobalization protests were among the first major international mobilizations coordinated over the Internet. Online streaming of audio and video clips by the Seattle Independent Media Center let an international audience participate. Throughout the week, nongovernmental organizations (NGOs) also sponsored debates, lectures, and teach-ins. The

Electrohippies Collective let four hundred thousand people conduct a virtual sit-in on the WTO website.

Antiglobalization protests had been building elsewhere before Seattle. Between 1989 and 1992, protesters appeared at Asia-Pacific Economic Cooperation (APEC) meetings. In 1993, President Clinton established the practice of an annual APEC Economic Leaders' Meeting to better coordinate strategic vision and direction for the countries in the region. Mass protests resulted at APEC summits in Vancouver and Manila, over globalization policies, free trade, and the situation in developing countries. On November 24, 1997, the APEC Canada meeting was held at the University of British Columbia campus in Vancouver. Protesters on the campus and in downtown Vancouver clashed with the Royal Canadian Mounted Police and disagreed internally about whether to use civil disobedience. The large number of protesters included leaders of protests held at a Manila APEC summit in 1996, when tens of thousands of labor and social justice groups marched to oppose free trade.

The focus of a protest in Eugene, Oregon, on June 18, 1999, called the Carnival Against Capital, was the twenty-fifth G8, or Group of Eight, summit of the major international powers, in Cologne, Germany. In Eugene, local anarchists, the "black bloc," drove police from a small park, and one anarchist was convicted of throwing a rock at a police officer.

The November 30, 1999, Seattle street protests, called N30, turned out about forty- to sixty-thousand protesters, making it the largest demonstration against the WTO, International Monetary Fund, or World Bank. On November 16, two weeks before the conference, as information developed about the criticism of globalization and the likelihood of protests, President Clinton issued Executive Order 13141, Environmental Review of Trade Agreements, committing the United States to a policy of "assessment and consideration of the environmental impacts of trade agreements." The order stated, "Trade agreements should contribute to the broader goal of sustainable development."[15] This position was supposed to help deflect protests.

Several days before the WTO conference, activists issued a fake-news insert into copies of the *Seattle Post-Intelligencer* that were awaiting distribution. The front-page stories included "Boeing to Move Overseas" (to Indonesia) and "Clinton Pledges Help for Poorest Nations." The byline on the Boeing story attributed it to Joe Hill, a union organizer who had been executed by firing squad in Utah in 1915.

The same day, November 24, the International Center for Trade and Sustainable Development reported concerted planning taking place for demonstrations. Organizers included NGOs devoted to labor issues, the environment, and consumer protection; labor unions, including the AFL-CIO; student groups; faith-based groups; and anarchists. The groups formed a coalition that had credentials to participate in official WTO meetings.

In the run-up to the WTO meeting, developing countries demanded that developed countries honor commitments made at previous WTO meetings before making new rules. They noted the need to implement compliance with agreements on market access for textiles, the use of antidumping measures against developing countries' exports, and over-implementation of the WTO Agreement on Trade-Related Aspects of Intellectual Property Rights. This north-south breach helped to ensure the collapse of the WTO talks and added to the street protests.

By the morning of November 30, and through a variety of tactics, such as street theater, sit-ins, chaining themselves together, and locking themselves to fences, an estimated ten thousand protesters stopped the official opening of the meeting. The police used pepper spray, tear gas, and rubber bullets against the protesters. Some protesters then threw water bottles at the attacking police. At the same time, the AFL-CIO People's Rally and March of more than twenty-five thousand activists concerned about the impact of globalization on jobs and wages, which had an official permit, began at Memorial Stadium and then marched downtown. As the march gradually approached the Convention Center, a few hundred anarchists vandalized Starbucks, Nike, Nordstrom, and other stores. A few protesters burned trash cans and broke store windows. By midday, protesters filled Seattle's central business district and WTO events for the day were canceled. The police ran out of riot-control chemicals. Mayor Paul Schell, seeking to suppress the protests before President Clinton's scheduled arrival the next day, announced a 7 p.m. to 7 a.m. curfew in the area.

On the next day, December 1, police outlawed the use of gas masks by the protesters and identified a fifty-block "no protest zone" in the central business district. At the mayor's request, Governor Gary Locke sent in the Washington National Guard and army troops arrived. As the nonviolent protest continued, the black bloc continued to engage in vandalism and curfew violations. The police arrested more than five hundred people on that day. For the next two days demonstrators held a sit-in outside the

Seattle Police Department to protest police abuse of the peaceful protesters. Late on December 3, US trade representative Charlene Barshefsky, who chaired the conference, and WTO director-general Michael Moore suspended the conference because of both the north-south conflicts between the delegates and the protests. Moore, in his opening address, had said the conference "is doomed to succeed." It would see the wealthier countries make concessions to help the poorer countries succeed, including greater access for their exports. But their poverty was not the fault of "the trading system," he insisted. Some of these poor governments had to pay "up to nine times more on debt repayment than on health. The heavy hand of history has its thumb on the windpipe of many member governments." The Clinton administration hadn't been able to manage the protests, and Moore was wrong about the likelihood of successful negotiations; the conference, under the circumstances, was doomed to fail.[16]

In addition to the increased police and cleanup costs for subduing the protests, Seattle had expensive litigation costs. After protracted judicial conflict, in 2004, the city paid a total of $250,000 to 157 individuals arrested outside the zone the police made off-limits to protests. Three years later, a federal jury found the city had violated the Fourth Amendment by arresting protesters without probable cause. The protests made excellent use of the Internet and social media for grassroots mobilization. They also stimulated public discussion of how globalization affects economic opportunity and made President Clinton and his administration focus on the issue.[17]

The type of protest tactics and police response in Seattle erupted at subsequent meetings of the WTO, other international organizations, and the Democratic and Republican National Conventions. In the last year of the Clinton presidency, April 15–17, 2000, around ten thousand to fifteen thousand protesters demonstrated at the IMF and World Bank meeting in Washington, DC. The International Forum on Globalization, a small research and educational group focusing on globalization, held training sessions on civil disobedience and globalization at Foundry United Methodist Church on Sixteenth Street, downtown. On April 15, as protesters began to gather at Convergence Center, a warehouse on Florida Avenue, police raided the building and made arrests. Police then arrested a small group of protesters demonstrating against the prison industrial complex. Among the 678 people arrested that day was three-time Pulitzer Prize–winning,

Washington Post photographer Carol Guzy. Two Associated Press reporters said they were hit by police batons. On April 16 and 17, during protests and street theater at the IMF, more people were arrested. In the end, the police reported about 1,300 arrests. In June 2010, a class action suit filed against the District of Columbia for the April 15 false arrests and due process violations was settled for a total $13.7 million damage award. The antiglobalization movement continued to develop momentum as the Clinton presidency ended.[18]

The other protests during the last year of Clinton's presidency, labeled "Million" after Farrakhan's Million Man March, were mostly educational and did not demand much of Bill Clinton. A Million Mom rally held in DC on Mother's Day, May 14, 2000, focused on gun violence. Donna Dees-Thomases, a New Jersey mother, organized it after a white supremacist invaded a day camp in Granada Hills, California, on August 10, 1999, and fired seventy shots, wounding five people, including three children. She got a permit for the Mother's Day march, and with friends created a foundation to identify mothers in each congressional district who would support gun control legislation. The rally drew an estimated 750,000 people, with 150,000 to 200,000 people holding events in more than seventy cities across the country, constituting the promised one million. After the march, Million Mom March organized local chapters, and in 2001 united with Handgun Control Inc. and the Brady Campaign to Prevent Gun Violence. The local groups continue to push for gun control.[19]

Clinton's foreign policy beyond the globalization protests involving international organizations and NAFTA did not elicit major protests. He claimed credit for persuading Russia to withdraw troops from the Baltic republics of Estonia and Latvia in 1994 and for special envoy and former Senate majority leader George Mitchell's successful conclusion of peace negotiations in Northern Ireland. On the Middle East, the administration pursued negotiations between Israeli and Palestinian leaders, but they, unsurprisingly, failed. His overall foreign policy projected an activist role but was weak on human rights. He would emphasize human and civil rights only when it was within the power of the United States to achieve without undermining national security or depleting national resources. This sounded reasonable but had jeopardized the Bosnia Muslims, only gave temporary attention to the Haitians, and left unprotected those who would ultimately be killed in the Rwanda genocide.

Somalia and Rwanda were Clinton foreign policy failures. Somalia elicited a strong public reaction that influenced his decisions, but there was little protest about Rwanda at the time. In Somalia, President George H. W. Bush sent troops into that country to help implement a United Nations decision to address the famine devastating the population. The country was in chaos after President Siad Barre was overthrown in a coup in 1991. Clinton had to face the repercussions of Bush's decision. In October 1993, a warlord opposed to the troops protecting aid deliveries shot down two Blackhawk helicopters, resulting in the death of hundreds of Somalis and eighteen American soldiers, whose bodies were dragged through the streets of Mogadishu. It was a widely broadcast, ghastly spectacle. The resulting public outrage in the United States influenced Clinton to withdraw all American troops by March 1994. Criticism that American troops were not properly equipped helped to speed the resignation of Secretary of Defense Les Aspin and raised questions about Clinton's foreign policy heft.

In April 1994, a vast killing spree broke out in Rwanda, in central Africa. An estimated eight hundred thousand Tutsis and their defenders were murdered in a government-sponsored genocide. With the failure in Somalia still very much in the minds of American policymakers, neither the United States nor the United Nations moved aggressively to stop the slaughter. Both Clinton and the world community were criticized for not acting to stop the massacre of Rwandans. In December 1993, Randall Robinson, head of TransAfrica, who had known some administration officials from his law student days at Harvard and others from his political work, had lunch with an official he knew at the White House. His acquaintance told him Rwanda was "going to blow sky-high" and he couldn't get anything done about it, and could Randall mobilize some public pressure. Randall demurred, thinking to do so in a short time was impossible, since most Americans didn't even know where Rwanda was.[20]

According to classified documents made available later, the administration knew Rwanda was being engulfed by genocide in April 1994 but buried the information to justify its inaction. Political officials spoke of the events as genocide but didn't say anything publicly. Finding no American foreign policy concerns at stake, the difficulty of determining what action to take, and having engaged no allies in any action, Clinton didn't want to intervene. Political officials and the president knew of a planned "final solution to eliminate all Tutsis" as the slaughter proceeded. In the three months from April 6, the Hutus had killed about eight hundred thousand Tutsis and moderate Hutus. In 1998, the Clintons embarked on an extensive six-nation tour of Africa, during which the president stopped briefly in Rwanda and explained away his inaction.

Also in April and May 1994, Randall Robinson and I entered Clinton's foreign policy orbit directly on the question of American policy toward Haiti. An accelerated number of refugees were arriving in Florida after the overthrow of their democratically elected president Jean-Bertrand Aristide in September 1991, who was exiled to the United States.

McKinney and McDowell, a black woman–owned public relations firm that represented TransAfrica, was frustrated at their inability to have Randall quoted on the Haitian refugee issue. He had become defined in the media as the antiapartheid activist, and an expanded awareness of human rights was necessary. They agreed with Randall on the idea of a hunger strike, initially to include others. Although I had been working on Haitian refugee issues since the meeting with Pope John Paul II during the Reagan administration, I declined Randall's invitation to participate. I thought he had enough media presence by himself and his individual stance would burnish TransAfrica's image.[21]

The campaign started with a *New York Times* advertisement in which Randall and others who had voted for and supported Clinton criticized his policy. Then on April 12, to get Clinton to change the policy, he began a hunger strike that lasted twenty-seven days. McKinney and McDowell stoked media attention, creating a bandwagon effect. The visits of sympathetic, high-visibility celebrities and politicians got extensive media coverage. Administration officials kept themselves apprised. Mort Halperin, special assistant to the president, and Sandy Berger, Randall's law school classmate and Clinton's deputy national security adviser, had come to visit him on May 1 and promised news in two weeks perhaps. But the days went by, and Randall's physical condition worsened.[22]

I kept telling White House officials that Randall would not give in and they should expect his death soon. He looked terrible, and I became increasingly concerned about how long it would be before he died. On the twenty-first day of his fast, a Monday, as I visited with him, I was so worried that we agreed I should act as an unofficial intermediary to try to move the administration toward a quicker positive decision. He was hospitalized and treated overnight on Thursday and then released as he continued the fast.

A news photograph showed his deteriorated condition. I went to Randall to tell him they promised to call with a decision the next day, a Saturday. On that day, National Security Adviser Anthony Lake called Randall to say that the policy would be changed and that the president would announce the decision and his appointment of former congressman William Gray to implement the new policy. The United States also insisted that the coup perpetrators in Haiti step down, sending troops to usher them out. On October 15, 1994, Aristide was restored as president of Haiti.[23]

One can know about historic icons who went on hunger strikes, such as Mahatma Gandhi, who fasted at least seventeen times, but seeing someone who is your friend and comrade come alarmingly close to death for a cause is not easy. The hunger strike worked, because the White House officials were persuaded of Randall's commitment to die, and they knew him and his record. The widespread media attention as days went by and demands from supporters that the administration do something were major influences on the White House. I was known to Clinton officials. After all, the president had designated me chair of the Civil Rights Commission, I had a reputation for brutal honesty and criticism, and was not just Randall's friend.

Clinton faced other foreign policy challenges that led to criticism and protests. The Bosnian crisis erupted in 1991, stoked by the collapse of the Soviet Union and the disintegration of Yugoslavia, which led to an upsurge of nationalism. The West recognized Slovenia and Croatia but the Serbs were intent on establishing a greater Serbia, and the Bosnians, mostly Muslim, had their own view of the future. Several US State Department officials who had handled Yugoslav affairs resigned their posts in the Clinton administration, because they believed Serbian attacks on Bosnians amounted to war crimes and should have been punished. After two years of mostly staying out of the Balkans conflict, Clinton changed course. A Srebrenica attack in which hundreds of Bosnians were killed and reports of systematic rape of Bosnian women by the Serbs as a kind of ethnic cleansing elicited strong reaction from the West. There were United Nations and European Union reports, and protests were launched in 1993 by the Bosnia Task Force USA (BTF), an alliance of ten national Islamic organizations, and the National Organization for Women in one hundred cities across the United States to protest the rape of women in Bosnia. BTF also organized the largest rally by Muslims for Bosnia in Washington, DC, in May 1993. It was attended by fifty thousand Muslims.[24]

In 1995, Clinton supported the NATO bombing of Bosnian Serb positions and the use of Croatian ground troops. The military and negotiations
handled by Richard Holbrooke, assistant secretary of state for European
affairs, led to the Dayton Peace Accords between the Croats, Serbs, and
Bosnian Muslims. In September 1996, Clinton sent a peacekeeping force of
twenty thousand American troops as part of a larger NATO deployment to
enforce the cease-fire and elections. The lines were drawn sharply, and the
Bosnian Serbs who were close to Russia and had expansive nationalistic
views were the bad guys. Clinton's apparent success in the Balkans added
to his credibility as a leader.[25]

The results of the crises were much on my mind when I attended a
Millennium Evenings lecture on April 12, 1999, in the East Room of the
White House, where Elie Wiesel spoke about "The Perils of Indifference:
Lessons Learned from a Violent Century." The president, commenting
after the lecture, said, "None of this answers any of the difficult questions that a Kosovo, a Bosnia, and a Rwanda present. But Kosovo is at
the doorstep or the underbelly of NATO and its wide number of allies.
We have military assets and allies willing to do their part. President Mi-
losevic clearly has established a pattern of perfidy, earlier in Bosnia and
elsewhere. And so, we act." When he mentioned Rwanda, someone in
the audience gasped.

In the questions after the lecture, the moderator recognized Odette
Nyiramilimo from Rwanda, a physician practicing in Kigali and a survivor
of the Rwandan massacres. Nyiramilimo asked Wiesel what "governments
and individuals around the world who, by their indifference in 1994, allowed the genocide to happen in my country, now could do to show that
they are not still indifferent to our fate?"

Wiesel responded, "Madam, I wish I had an answer. I don't. Why are we
so involved, so nobly, in Kosovo? Why were we not in Rwanda? I am—as
you know, Mr. President, I am not in high councils of your government, so
I don't know the real reason. Maybe Mr. Berger knows more, surely more
than I. But one thing I can't understand. I know one thing—we could have
prevented that massacre. Why didn't we? I don't know."

The president explained his policy and said, "I can only tell you that I
will do my best to make sure that nothing like this happens again in Africa.
I do not think the United States can take the position that we only care
about these sorts of things if they happen in Europe. I don't feel that way.

And I think that we will, next time, be far more likely to have the means to act in Africa than we had last time in a quicker way."[26]

On a 1998 state visit to Kigali, the Rwandan capital, Clinton told the Rwandans and assembled diplomats, "The international community, together with nations in Africa, must bear its share of responsibility for this tragedy, as well. We did not act quickly enough after the killing began. We should not have allowed the refugee camps to become safe havens for the killers. We did not immediately call these crimes by their rightful name: genocide. We cannot change the past. But we can and must do everything in our power to help you build a future without fear, and full of hope."[27]

Clinton was spared open opposition on domestic civil rights issues because the Leadership Conference on Civil Rights groups, whose members were mostly Democratic Party supporters, were relieved to have a Democratic president after the Reagan-Bush years. In 1993, Clinton signed the Brady bill, which imposed a five-day waiting period on handgun purchases and added federal background checks, and he signed the Family and Medical Leave Act of 1993, which Bush had twice vetoed.

Advocates who organized to end toxic-waste dumping and other hazards in poor and racial minority neighborhoods got a 1994 Environmental Justice Executive Order and program. On NAFTA, the labor unions in the coalition were mostly opposed to the agreement, because they perceived it would have an impact on jobs. On the day of passage in the House, four Greenpeace and anti-NAFTA protesters disrupted the proceedings by chanting and dropping fake fifty-dollar bills down on the House floor from the visitors' gallery. Capitol Police arrested them and cleared the area.[28]

Civil rights groups disagreed with Clinton on withdrawing Lani Guinier's nomination for the post of assistant attorney general for civil rights and on the issue of gays in the military, but they were able to preserve some gains. Following a 1995 Supreme Court decision undermining affirmative action, grassroots resistance helped to keep Clinton from endorsing the court's restrictions. The court's *Adarand Constructors, Inc. v. Peña* decision, involving a Latino contractor, held that race-based set-asides in government contracts would be unconstitutional in most circumstances. Given the continued minuscule number of taxpayer-supported contracts awarded to minority contractors, despite a policy to remedy the disparity dating from 1978, the entire civil rights coalition was upset at the news and determined to insist that Clinton find a way to protect the program despite the court ruling.

George Stephanopoulos, displaced by Dick Morris's ascendancy as an adviser, as Clinton moved politically to the right, volunteered to work on a new, positive affirmative-action policy for the president that would withstand legal scrutiny. He hired Christopher Edley to write the report. Edley and Stephanopoulos consulted widely with experts and civil rights leaders as they developed ideas. Clinton received a steady flow of briefing papers and held informal discussions, some of which the vice chair of the Civil Rights Commission, Cruz Reynoso, and I attended. The Democratic Leadership Council conservatives pressured Clinton to abandon the set-asides instead of finding ways to continue them. At one small working dinner near the end of the process, Elaine Jones, director-counsel of the NAACP Legal Defense Fund, and I told the president that, beyond the policy issues, given his rhetorical emphasis on his race relations history, the public would find a statement in opposition to be ridiculous. In the end, he endorsed a solution that held off both sides. At the National Archives on July 19, 1995, Clinton made his "Mend It, Don't End It" speech, preserving most of the policy. The contracting agencies would first use race-neutral approaches in selecting awardees, including, instead of race, such factors as social disadvantage. They would need to justify the use of race as a plus factor. After the agencies made sure their procedures were in compliance, they continued to award a small number of contracts to minority contractors, just as they had done before.

Despite his equivocations and false steps, blacks remained the staunchest supporters of Clinton throughout his presidency. When he was impeached by the House on December 20, 1998, for lying about his relations with intern Monica Lewinsky, Democratic members stood by him hugging and wishing him well as he left the chamber. They joined him on the White House lawn afterward as he made clear he would not resign. MoveOn.org, an e-mail group created by software entrepreneurs Joan Blades and Wes Boyd, got its start in 1998 with a petition asking Congress to "censure President Clinton and move on," as opposed to impeaching him. There were several small in-person demonstrations for Clinton's impeachment, and House members, especially the Black Caucus, demonstrated against the impeachment by walking out of the House chamber.[29]

On August 26, 2000, the Reverend Al Sharpton and Martin Luther King III convened a March on Washington "Redeem the Dream" celebration on the anniversary of Martin Luther King Jr.'s speech at the 1963 March on Washington. The rally highlighted police shootings and racial profiling of blacks. Martin Luther King III told the crowd that the dream had not been fulfilled, "not when an unarmed black man named Amadou Diallo could be shot at forty-seven times by a group of five New York policemen who emptied the clips of their automatic pistols into him for holding up his wallet in the foyer of a Bronx apartment building." On the day before the rally, Marty and Al Sharpton met with Attorney General Janet Reno to insist that the Justice Department withhold federal funds from any police department that engaged in racial profiling.[30]

Amadou Diallo was killed by police in New York City on February 4, 1999, eight days before the Senate vote on Clinton's impeachment. Diallo's body absorbed nineteen of a barrage of shots fired by white police officers in the vestibule of his apartment building for no apparent reason. A few days later, the commission, which I headed, asked Attorney General Reno to investigate the shooting, focusing on our consistent concern with episodes that exacerbated bad police-community relations. We thought that "only by demonstrating a wholehearted commitment to finding the truth" would "public concern about police community relations be alleviated." Reno replied that she had begun an investigation with the involvement of the FBI and would keep us apprised of the results. I also faxed the president, explaining that we were "fed up" with the persistence of unaddressed "alleged police misconduct." He quickly replied, "Janet is on it."[31]

We puzzled over whether we should respond to the demands of civil rights groups that we go to New York to investigate police-community relations. We had been monitoring police-community relations in New York City since the Abner Louima incident in August 1997 and our recommendation that they carry out their duties in a nonabusive way.

At the police-community hearings, audience members hissed and booed Mayor Giuliani; protesters against him and police were gathered outside. Weeks later, when we made our recommendations, Giuliani expressed fury at our conclusion that city police engaged in racial profiling when determining whether to make an arrest.

Although the 250-page report, published in August 2000, praised the police department for trying to improve its relationship with minorities, we characterized the department's overall approach to race relations as flawed in everything from training to promotions. The *New York Times* noted our scrupulous evenhandedness:

> Even though its findings are largely critical, the draft report is re-strained in its language, and there are several discussions of disputed issues in which the commission acknowledges that statistics support the Police Department's version of events. For instance, although crit-ics have suggested that psychological screenings were being used to block minority candidates from the Police Department, the commis-sion found that the statistics did not support that contention.

The Giuliani administration issued a detailed rebuttal of the findings, which we published in the report. The racial profiling section of the report, based on New York Police Department data from 1998, observed that while African Americans constituted only 9 percent of Staten Island's popula-tion, 51 percent of the people stopped and searched by the police in Staten Island were black and most of them were never charged with anything. Throughout New York City, African Americans were stopped well above their population proportion in every community. Instead of issuing an or-der banning racial profiling, President Clinton again found a way to appear to act but fall short of exerting his power. He directed the Justice, Treasury, and Agriculture Departments to collect data on the race, ethnicity, and gender of individuals subject to certain stops by federal law enforcement. He also said he supported legislation to ask police departments to collect the data and wanted increased funding for training and diversity.[32]

Clinton succeeded as an adaptable president. The antiglobalization protesters challenged him. LGBT groups succeeded in mounting major protests that educated the public and helped move forward the social rev-olution that came to fruition after he left office. Civil and human rights groups that would have been the most likely protesters did not make de-mands that required sustained demonstrations. Clinton had the advantages of personality and his party identification, and after the Reagan and Bush years, progressives and liberals were tolerant and glad to have a "friendly" president in office.

CHAPTER 7

Unnatural Disasters

The Presidency of George W. Bush

Brownie, you're doing a heckuva job.

—President Bush to Michael D. Brown, administrator of the Federal
Emergency Management Agency (FEMA), the principal federal official
in charge of the federal government's response to Hurricane Katrina,
September 2, 2005 (Brown resigned on September 12, 2005)

George Bush doesn't care about black people.

—Kanye West[1]

PRESIDENT GEORGE W. BUSH was both one of the most popular and one of
the least popular presidents in American history. His term was marked by
an extraordinary natural disaster, Hurricane Katrina, and several unnatural
disasters—most of Bush's own making. His popularity arose from his com-
forting, seemingly firm manner but also from his denouncement of bigoted
reactions to the terrorist attacks on September 11, 2001. Bush's unpopular-
ity stemmed from the wars in Iraq and Afghanistan; from the federal government's disastrous, failed response to the loss of lives and property when
flooding waters overtopped New Orleans levees following Hurricane Katrina; and from his calamitous financial policies and management, which
led to the economic crash of 2008.

The Iraq war, the death and destruction in New Orleans, and the president's antiabortion positions brought the most numerous protests, though
his economic and civil rights policies elicited complaints and grumblings.
On the domestic side, he had the last, most important word when he named

Chief Justice John Roberts and another justice, Samuel Alito, in his second term, thus solidifying conservative control of interpretation of the Constitution and the nation's laws for years to come.

Before he could even begin implementing his campaign promises, Bush's presidency was under stress because of how he was elected. In addition to being elected by a minority of the people, like Clinton in 1992, many people believed George W. Bush's election was flat out illegal. So, while Clinton's first inaugural events were celebratory, Bush's 2001 inauguration ceremonies brought thousands of demonstrators to Washington. They came to protest the voter suppression in Florida and the Supreme Court decision that gave Bush the election and presidency, even though Gore won the majority of popular votes.

I was still chair of the US Commission on Civil Rights, which was responsible for investigating complaints that anyone's right to vote was denied on the grounds of race, color, religion, or national origin. The commission received numerous complaints on Election Day and the days after from people who said their right to vote had been denied. We sent monitors to Florida over the next few days, who reported as the votes were being counted that while the media discussed only hanging chads and recount possibilities, numerous registered voters complained of being simply prevented from voting at all. The commission voted unanimously to go to Florida to hold hearings with sworn witnesses, including complainants and government officials, to ascertain the facts and to determine what recommendations could prevent such denials in the future.

Based on hearings held January 11–12, 2001, in Tallahassee and in Miami on February 16, 2001, we found unmistakable evidence of voter suppression targeting black, disabled, and older voters. A company hired by the state had purged eligibility rolls using faulty methods, which resulted in many erroneous expulsions of qualified voters. Voters mistakenly categorized as felons were turned away when they had never even been arrested. At the polls, potential voters confronted inexperienced poll workers, antiquated machinery, inaccessible polling locations, and other barriers. Some voters in wheelchairs were reduced to finding someone to carry them in to inaccessible polling places.

Some voters with visual impairments found that the precincts did not have proper equipment to assist them in reading their ballots and, therefore, they had to rely on others—often strangers—to cast their ballots, denying them their right to a secret ballot. Other precincts were not equipped, or otherwise failed altogether, to accommodate potential voters with disabilities. As a result, individuals with disabilities were simply turned away and thus disenfranchised. The commission's findings, published in June 2001, made it clear that widespread voter disenfranchisement—not the dead-heat contest—was the most truly damning aspect in the Florida election.

In its June 2001 report, the commission concluded that Section 2 of the Voting Rights Act (VRA) appeared to have been violated in Florida. The VRA does not require intent to discriminate. Violations of the VRA can be established by evidence that the effect of procedures and practices has interfered with the right to vote.[2]

In counting the votes that were cast, Bush had the advantage. His brother, Jeb Bush, was governor of Florida, and the secretary of state in Florida, Katherine Harris, a Republican, and a member of his campaign committee, had the power to certify who had more votes and had won the election. Facing claims of tainted ballots, Harris rushed through a partial recounting that left Bush ahead.

An appeal to the Democratic majority Florida Supreme Court resulted in an order that Harris not certify a winner and for the recount to resume. Harris set a deadline so that while there were still thousands of ballots still being disputed, she could certify Bush's victory by 537 votes. The Republican Party appealed to the US Supreme Court to foreclose Gore's challenge to Harris's certification.

The Supreme Court decided 5–4 to overrule the Florida State Supreme Court and end any further ballot counting. Rehnquist, Scalia, Thomas, Kennedy, and O'Connor, ignoring their usual ideological objections to interference with state action, overruled the Florida Supreme Court and prohibited continued counting of ballots. They said the recounting violated the constitutional requirement for "equal protection of the laws," because different counties of Florida had different standards for counting ballots. Interestingly, and unusual enough, they indicated this rationale only applied to the case before them, to foreclose other parties from making similar denial of equal protection arguments in other cases.[3]

Justices Stevens, Ginsburg, Breyer, and Souter dissented, arguing that the court should not interfere with the Florida Supreme Court's interpretation of state law. Breyer and Souter concluded that even if there had been no uniform standard in counting that the court majority felt needed remedying, then the proper response was to order a new election in Florida with a uniform standard. Justice Scalia explained years later that the majority just wanted to affirm Bush's election as quickly as possible and end the controversy.

After the Supreme Court gave Bush the election, it seemed possible that protesters might turn out in force at the inaugural parade. After the Seattle antiglobalization protests in 1990, law enforcement agencies, having been surprised by the size of the demonstration, developed a variety of tactics to prevent the disruption of future events, including the deployment of police in massive numbers, infiltrating the groups to determine their plans, and using force to remove protesters. They decided to use tear gas, pepper spray, even concussion grenades, rubber and wooden bullets, night sticks, water cannons, dogs, and horses to repel protesters if necessary. Such methods *were* utilized at the November 2000 G8 antiglobalization protest in Montreal, at which many protesters were beaten, trampled, and arrested. In what was intended to be a festive protest, police started herding protesters into zones and pens to facilitate control.[4]

Most of these control measures were not needed for the large crowd that turned out for Bush's inaugural parade. The police stationed on foot all along the way, backed up by squads on motorcycles and horses, managed to concentrate protesters and the public in small groups along Pennsylvania Avenue, which was designed to eliminate a large group engaging in disruption or violence. This strategy meant Bush heard continuous protests as he traveled the route toward the White House. The city had removed all trash cans and other receptacles that might hide explosives, and for the first time, onlookers had to go through security checkpoints. The only violence reported involved minor altercations between protesters and police.

Perhaps four protesters were arrested altogether, and someone in the crowd struck Bush's limousine with a tennis ball and an egg. Along the route, supporters wielded Bush-Cheney signs and Texas flags. Also, outside Planned Parenthood's Washington office a group gathered to pray that Bush abide by his antiabortion promises. However, thousands of protest placards read "Bush Cheated," "Hail to the Thief," "Selected Not Elected," "Bushwhacked by the Supremes," and "Golly Jeb, We Pulled It Off!" There were also signs saying "Dick and Bush" and "George Wanker Bush." Judging from the signage and chants, the protesters included feminists, prochoicers, death penalty opponents, gay rights activists, and environmentalists. The

Reverend Al Sharpton held a rally in a nearby park protesting the disenfranchisement that permitted Bush's election.

Once in office, Bush's proposals reflected his campaign promises. Not unlike his father, he pledged to be a "compassionate conservative," using traditional conservative ideas such as small government and free-market principles to help the needy. In practice, he proposed tax cuts that appeared to benefit the rich, crafted a weak environmental policy, and planned to "privatize" Social Security by having the retirement funds of citizens tied to the stock market. He also wanted to increase the military budget and implement the antiballistic missile "Star Wars" program, though experts thought it wouldn't work, and even if it did, it would only cause a more aggressive arms race.

At first, a hangover from the disputed 2000 presidential election undermined the administration's political legitimacy. Then the terrorist attacks of September 11, 2001, changed Bush's priorities and polished his first term image. But in 2003, the deceptive rationale for the Iraq war tarnished his image. In his second term, the inadequate response of the federal government to the havoc wreaked by Hurricane Katrina in the South in 2005 and then the 2008 financial crisis savaged his reputation.

Bush's civil rights policies tried to turn back the clock in ways reminiscent of the Reagan era. His administration opposed affirmative action, LGBT rights, reproductive rights, and other human rights remedies and protections in the courts. Unlike the Reagan years, the Republicans had all three branches of the government under their control for most of Bush's time in office. Also, under the protective coloration of a wartime president, resistance to his election in 2000 dissipated. Until the protests against the Iraq war in 2003, opposition to his domestic programs and policies was largely ineffective in changing his policies.

Like Reagan, Bush appointed African Americans, Latinos, and Asian Americans to high government positions, some that had never been held by a person of color. These appointees vigorously defended his policies and certainly did not move civil rights in a positive direction. I left the Civil Rights Commission in December 2004 after Bush's reelection, deciding not to accept a continued appointment by House Democrats.

The last report the commission released under my tenure, in December 2004, evaluated Bush's first term civil-rights performance. The report gave the president credit for being clearer before 9/11 on racial profiling than Clinton had been and for assembling a diverse cabinet. However, Bush's funding requests for civil rights enforcement fell far short; his Justice Department retreated from enforcing voting rights and from increased inclusion and diversity in higher education and employment. He also failed to promote the passage of election reform after the 2000 debacle in time for the 2004 election. In addition, Bush successfully urged Congress to cut billions of dollars from programs to help low-income and disabled persons pay for housing through rent vouchers, and he proposed nothing to replace these initiatives.

The report faulted Bush for doing practically nothing to ensure the reduction of environmental hazards in minority and low-income communities, making a mockery of the environmental justice movement's hard-won 1994 executive order requiring action. Shortly after the commission held public hearings in 2003 to listen to advocates and Environmental Protection Agency officials who had no rationale for their neglect, EPA administrator Christine Todd Whitman resigned.

The commission report detailed how Bush had expanded the discrimination that had long denied asylum to Haitian refugees in Florida, despite a generous policy for Cubans. He had in fact authorized federal agents to hold Haitians in detention indefinitely without bond until their cases were heard by an asylum court, with no firm date set for hearings.

Bush also closed the White House Office for Women's Initiatives and Outreach and attempted to close the Women's Bureau at the Department of Labor. In addition, he embarked on an initiative to undermine the enforcement of Title IX's prohibition against sex discrimination in higher education, and then retreated, but only after an overwhelmingly negative public reaction. The commission report found that one of the most significant wrongs Bush inflicted was his attempt to redefine civil rights to include the bogus claim that denying taxpayer money to religious programs is a denial of civil rights based on religion. This improbable and intellectually dishonest redefinition was used to provide a rationale for supplying religious institutions with taxpayer funds.

In keeping with this rationale and his campaign focus, Bush issued his first executive order, creating the Office of Faith-Based and Community Initiatives on January 29, 2001. He argued that religiously based organizations, charities, and community groups could respond to people's needs more effectively than government. Opponents complained that this use of taxpayers' funds violated separation of church and state, but they were not able to mount effective protests, given the support of some in the Democratic Party constituency for the approach of funding programs operated by religious groups. The office stayed, and the organizations received federal funding, with the White House failing to report on whether this use of funds had indeed been more effective than funding traditional non-faith-based groups. The office remains in the White House and continues to distribute funds, and is likely to stay, since the history of government programs is that they rarely get shut down.

Still implementing his antiabortion views in the period before 9/11, Bush faced down criticism from Democrats and researchers over government funding for stem-cell research. He balanced his moral convictions against practical science in developing treatment of disease when in August 2001 he announced in a prime-time address that federal funds could only be used for research on already destroyed stem cells.

Also in 2001, shortly after taking office, Bush reimposed the gag rule issued by President Reagan, and then rescinded by President Clinton, ordering no funding of international organizations that use money from non-federal sources to offer or provide information about abortions. On April 1 he signed a bill making it a federal crime to harm or kill a fetus during the commission of another federal crime. It defined an "unborn child" as "a member of the species homo sapiens, at any stage of development, who is carried in the womb," alarming prochoice supporters, who challenged the bill in three federal courts even before Bush signed it. It was upheld against repeated court challenges.[5]

On January 23, 2001, Bush, with the support of Senator Edward Kennedy, asked Congress to enact the No Child Left Behind Act. The bipartisan legislation expanded federal funding for education, setting federal standards and testing to measure school achievement, and encouraged more freedom of choice between private and public schools. The act required that 100 percent of US children must have basic reading and math skills by the 2013–2014 school year. Schools that did not meet the standards could be taken over or closed. The bill passed both houses of Congress by June 14, 2001. The bipartisan acceptance of the bill's emphasis showed that Democrats had not found a way to improve and protect public education from inappropriate testing and teachers from being held accountable for social and economic factors over which they have no control.

When Bush left office, No Child Left Behind was just another in a long history of attempts at education reform that failed to remedy the poverty and race achievement gaps. Fourth-grade reading and math scores and eighth-grade math scores improved slightly in some schools, but the racial achievement gap had not improved and dropout rates were abysmal. Parents and teachers complained about "teaching to the test," evaluating teachers based solely on standardized test score improvement, costs, and the loss of state and local control over education.

Instead of distributing funds to hard-pressed city and rural public schools for rehiring laid-off teachers, equipment, and supplies, President Obama created Race to the Top from part of the American Recovery and Reinvestment Act of 2009, the economic stimulus. To compete for part of the $4 billion allocation, states had to agree to policies the administration selected, including teacher evaluations based largely on student standardized testing. A state could also receive additional points for accepting the controversial Common Core standards for curriculum. Race to the Top was discontinued in 2015 and Congress replaced No Child Left Behind with Every Student Succeeds Act, restoring more state autonomy in the same year. Providing more state autonomy was as likely to perpetuate achievement disparities as past efforts at reform if the social and economic environment in which children live and the material conditions and resources in schools were not improved for children in need. A successful movement to implement policy on these realities has not yet been developed.

In February 2001, Bush suggested tax cuts to create jobs and stimulate the economy, proposing a $1.6 trillion reduction in taxes. Republicans in Congress moved quickly to support the bill. Senate Democrats, however, forced a compromise that reduced the final tax cut to $1.35 trillion and set up the tax cuts to expire in 2011. But 2001 was the last time the government had a surplus. Government spending continued to increase; tax revenue declined but entitlements increased, and discretionary spending grew along with military expenses after 9/11. After Republican victories in the 2002 off-year elections, Bush pushed for more tax cuts, which narrowly passed with Vice President Cheney breaking a Senate tie. Bush's 2001 and 2003 tax cuts reduced federal revenue, made wealth inequality greater in the United States, and created an expanding federal deficit. The budget remained unbalanced, and a major economic dislocation was imminent. But it would not come until Bush's second term.

Bush's first term was dominated by the event that occurred nine months into his presidency, on September 11, 2001, and pushed all other issues into the background. Hijackers, nineteen men from the Middle East, most of them from Saudi Arabia, on three different planes, flew the huge commercial jets, loaded with fuel, into the twin towers of the World Trade Center in downtown New York and into one side of the Pentagon in Washington, DC. The towers collapsed, burying thousands of workers and hundreds of first responders, fire fighters, and police who were attempting rescue. A fourth plane headed for the Capitol building in Washington. Passengers and flight crew heard from phone calls that the nation was under attack, and they struggled to regain control of the plane from the terrorist hijackers, but the plane crashed sixty-five miles southeast of Pittsburgh. All forty-four persons aboard, including the four hijackers, were killed.

President Bush immediately declared a "war on terrorism," and Congress quickly passed resolutions for military action without a declaration of war required under the Constitution. Only Democratic congresswoman Barbara Lee, an African American from the Bay Area in California, voted against the resolution.

Bush identified Osama bin Laden as responsible for the September 11 attacks and ordered the bombing of Afghanistan, where he thought bin Laden was located. In the aftermath of 9/11, the American public rallied to support the president in the "war on terrorism."

In October 2001, Walter Isaacson, then head of CNN, directed staff that images of civilian casualties in Afghanistan should be accompanied with an explanation that it happened as retaliation for harboring terrorists. Whether there was specific evidence or not, "it seems perverse to focus too much on the casualties of hardships in Afghanistan," he said. The television anchorman Dan Rather, publicly strained in his relations with both Bush presidents in the past, ironically declared, "George Bush is the president. . . . Wherever he wants me to line up, just tell me where."[6]

In the atmosphere of wartime patriotism, criticism was indeed risky. It was made legally dicey when Congress passed the Uniting and Strengthening America by Providing Appropriate Tools Required to Intercept and Obstruct Terrorism Act (USA Patriot Act), in October 2001, which eliminated or weakened limits on government surveillance, wiretapping, detention, and prosecution. The Department of Justice could detain noncitizens based on suspicion—without charges, without due process—and the secretary of state could designate any group as "terrorist." Anyone who belonged to a designated group or raised funds for it was suspect. The act had a chilling effect on media and potential protesters for fear of being identified as helping terrorists.

In January 2002 Bush secretly authorized the National Security Agency to monitor the international telephone calls and e-mail of American citizens and others in the United States without the approval of a Foreign Intelligence Surveillance Court, as required by law since 1978. He later explained that these steps were necessary to keep Americans safe after 9/11.[7]

President Bush, along with other political leaders and government agencies, including the Commission on Civil Rights, published ads and made statements asking the public to avoid hostility toward Arab Americans. However, the government began to round up people for questioning, almost all of them Muslims, holding a thousand or more in detention without charges. Some were held, despite judicial orders, on secret evidence.

A few protests to Bush's military response took place immediately. On September 29, 2001, the Act Now to Stop War and Racism (ANSWER) coalition of peace and civil rights groups held a rally and marched to downtown DC from Malcolm X Park. An estimated eight thousand people participated. There were also protests in San Francisco, Los Angeles, and other cities. However, before entry into the Iraq war was imminent, the protests were not as large and widespread as they became later. The ANSWER protesters bore signs reading, "Justice, Not War" and "Our Grief Is Not a Cry for Revenge." Some family members of those who died in the World Trade Center or the Pentagon wrote to President Bush, urging him not to match violence with violence, asking him not to bomb the people of Afghanistan. Amber Amundson, whose husband, an army pilot, was killed in the attack on the Pentagon, told the press, "If you choose to respond to this incomprehensible brutality by perpetuating violence against other innocent human beings, you may not do so in the name of justice for my husband." Despite the new laws and the social climate's chilling effect, protests arose and continued until they grew in intensity with the Iraq war.

Some families of victims traveled to Afghanistan in January 2002 to meet with Afghan families who had lost loved ones in the American bombing. Critics of the bombing campaign argued that terrorism was rooted in deep grievances against the United States, and that to stop terrorism, these grievances needed to be addressed. Complaints cited included US troops stationed in Saudi Arabia, site of the most holy of Islamic shrines; the sanctions against Iraq, which, by the United Nations account, had resulted in the deaths of hundreds of thousands of children; the continued billions of dollars in US military aid to Israel and support of Israel's occupation of Palestinian land.

Despite 9/11 and the Patriot Act, in September 2002, an estimated 1,500 to 2,000 people demonstrated in Washington, DC, against the annual meetings of the International Monetary Fund (IMF) and World Bank. Protesting groups included the Anti-Capitalist Convergence and the Mobilization for Global Justice. Police arrested 649 people, including at least seventeen reporters. Five were charged with destruction of property, while the others were charged with parading without a permit or failing to obey police orders to disperse. As in Seattle, protesters sued in federal court, objecting to the arrests. After protracted litigation, in 2009, the District of Columbia agreed to pay $8.25 million to almost four hundred protesters and bystanders to end a class-action lawsuit over mass arrests during the 2002 protests.[8]

When, on February 5, 2003, Secretary of State Colin Powell told the UN Security Council that Iraq had weapons of mass destruction, he triggered major protests, as war seemed probable. On February 15, 2003, a coordinated day of protests took place across the world in which people in more than six hundred cities declared opposition to war in Iraq, yet the conflict began with the US invasion on March 20. Social movement researchers have described the February 15 protest as the largest such event in human history. United for Peace and Justice helped to coordinate the worldwide demonstrations. UPJ began as a national campaign to coordinate work against a US war on Iraq. At an initial meeting in Washington, DC, on October 25, 2002, more than seventy peace and justice organizations agreed to form the organization.

According to the BBC, between six and eleven million people took part in protests in up to sixty countries over the weekend of February 15–16; other estimates range from eight million to thirty million. Some of the largest protests took place in Europe. Mainland China was the only major region not to see any protests on that day, but small demonstrations, attended mainly by foreign students, were seen in the United States. CBS News reported protests in 150 cities, with the largest in Chicago, Los Angeles, and New York.

Organizers of the New York City protest had hoped to march past UN headquarters. However, a week before the march, the city persuaded district court judge Barbara Jones that police could not keep order along the suggested route. They were restricted to a rally. Donna Lieberman, executive director of the New York Civil Liberties Union, complained that marching and parading through streets to protest should have been permitted as a core First Amendment value. However, post 9/11, security concerns constrained civil liberties.

On that day, organizers brought more than three hundred buses and four special trains of protesters to New York from across the country. The BBC estimated that one hundred thousand protesters took part in a rally near the UN headquarters. Among those taking part was a group of relatives of victims of the World Trade Center attacks. Speakers included politicians, church leaders, actress Susan Sarandon and other entertainers, and South African Anglican archbishop Desmond Tutu. A march, though unplanned, occurred anyway, as three hundred thousand to a million people clogged the streets of Manhattan, making their way twenty blocks down First Avenue and overflowing onto Second and Third Avenue. The protests were largely peaceful, though police arrested forty protesters who caused some property damage in Union Square and threw rocks at police officers.[9]

The local Independent Media Center produced a short video claiming to show inappropriate and violent police behavior, including backing horses into demonstrators, shoving people into the metal barricades, spraying a toxic substance at penned-in demonstrators, using abusive language, and raising nightsticks against some who couldn't move. However, the NYPD denied the charges, claiming the tape was "filled with special effects" and did not prove the police had no basis for their actions. Individual protesters complained that the police blocked streets and confirmed that they were penned. At the end of the day, police reported that there had been roughly 275 arrests; organizers claimed there were more: 348 arrests. CNN journalist Maria Hinojosa reported that the crowd included "older men and women in fur coats, parents with young children, military veterans, and veterans of the antiwar movement."[10]

At the Los Angeles demonstration, fifty thousand to sixty thousand protesters, including actor Martin Sheen, then regularly appearing on television as the US president in *The West Wing*, said, "None of us can stop this war. . . . There is only one guy that can do that and he lives in the

White House." In San Francisco on Sunday of that weekend, in order not to conflict with the city's Chinese New Year's parade, a crowd of two hundred thousand people, according to organizers and the police, rallied and marched.

In Austin, Texas, ten thousand protesters marched down Congress Avenue from the state capitol building. In Colorado Springs, four thousand protesters were dispersed with pepper spray, tear gas, stun guns, and batons. In Seattle, organizers hoped for twenty thousand to thirty thousand people to join a march from Seattle Center, following a giant blue planet, the emblem adopted by the march organizers. But about fifty thousand people turned out to protest the war on Iraq and the war on immigrants, more than those who protested the WTO Ministerial Conference of 1999 in Seattle. Demonstrations also took place in Philadelphia, where thousands marched to the Liberty Bell, and in Chicago, where ten thousand people demonstrated.

After these large protests, US demonstrations against the war continued, but were not comparable to those during the Vietnam War or to the initial February protests. Not having a national draft may have been a factor in lessening the urgency for grassroots protesters, but more likely 9/11, the Patriot Act, and new FBI guidelines successfully stifled dissent and stoked notions that attacks on Bush and the administration could seem unpatriotic.

After 9/11, the country still acknowledged the legality of freedom of expression, but utilizing it became risky. This became the new normal, and free speech, including at protests, had become subject to suspension. The police increasingly used tactics they had used during the IMF-World Bank protests, creating areas where no protests could take place and times when people couldn't enter these areas, even if they lived in the restricted zone.

In 2003, as the controversy surrounding the rationale for the Iraq war continued, Bush announced what seemed to be a new, positive aid program for Africa. He attributed the proposal to his and Laura Bush's interest in Africa and the AIDS crisis on the continent and the advice of his secretary of state, Condoleezza Rice. He started PEPFAR—President's Emergency Plan for AIDS Relief—explaining that the program would address the HIV/AIDS pandemic that threatened to wipe out an entire generation on the continent of Africa. The program was included in the Tuberculosis and Malaria Act of 2003 (or the Global AIDS Act), a highly successful effort that has focused first on AIDS in Africa and then on tuberculosis and malaria. Progressives praised Bush's action until they discovered that it utilized abstinence-only education, forbidding the use of condoms, needle exchanges, and other harm-reduction measures. The requirement for funding abstinence-only education was found ineffective and lifted by Congress in 2008.[11]

Also in 2003, Bush acted on another antiabortion promise. He had supported banning late term, partial-birth abortion in the 2000 election campaign after President Clinton had vetoed two partial-birth abortion bans passed by a Republican-controlled Congress. Democratic presidential nominee Al Gore, maintaining his support for a woman's right to choose, had opposed the ban. Antiabortion groups had mobilized around the partial birth issue as the best way to pass some type of legislation that would undercut *Roe v. Wade*, and with Bush in office, in November 2003, Congress reenacted the ban and the president signed it into law.

The partial-birth abortion ban was immediately challenged in court, and NARAL Pro-Choice America, the Feminist Majority Foundation, the ACLU, CODEPINK, the NAACP Black Women's Health Imperative, and other groups organized a March for Women's Lives of about eight hundred thousand participants on April 25, 2004, in Washington. The march protested the partial-birth abortion ban and called for full access to contraceptive technology and sex education, all included under the rubric of women's reproductive freedom.[12]

Buses brought marchers from big cities and small towns to the usual rally on the National Mall, followed by a march through downtown Washington along Pennsylvania Avenue. On the way marchers chanted and brandished placards identifying President Bush as the leading enemy of "reproductive freedom." Speakers included past NOW president Patricia Ireland, longtime feminist activist Gloria Steinem, celebrities, and politicians, including Senator Hillary Rodham Clinton (Democrat-New York), who told the crowd, "If all we do is march today . . . that will not change the direction this country is headed under this administration."[13]

Unlike earlier marches, counter-protesters, some from anti–abortion rights activist Randall Terry's Operation Witness, marched along part of the route exchanging shouts with the marchers. Also, protesters from the

Christian Defense Coalition crossed police lines into the area set aside for the march, which led to arrests of antiabortion activists for demonstrating without a permit.

Bush was at Camp David during the protest. He returned to Washington in the late afternoon, whereupon the White House issued a statement, saying, "The president believes we should work to build a culture of life in America and regardless of where one stands on the issue of abortion, we can all work together to reduce the number of abortions through promotion of abstinence-education programs, support for parental-notification laws, and continued support for banning partial-birth abortion."[14]

After the march, reproductive justice remained the broad agenda defined by prochoicers instead of simply the right to an abortion. However, the Partial-Birth Abortion Ban Act remained intact, and the Supreme Court upheld it in Gonzales v. Carhart in 2007.[15]

As the conflict over abortion rights played out in the courts and in demonstrations, the war in Afghanistan and Iraq and constraints on civil liberties persisted and opposition grew. The Bush administration was subject to a rising wave of public criticism about the use of Guantanamo Bay Naval Base, in Cuba, as a detention facility, and about official sanctions of US-employed torture or "enhanced interrogation techniques," along with the Patriot Act and warrantless wiretapping. But the Abu Ghraib scandal led to a new crescendo of outrage. Amnesty International reports about the enhanced interrogation techniques used at Abu Ghraib prison beginning in June 2003 led to further reports, and photographs of naked, hooded, humiliated prisoners were given to the ACLU. On April 28, 2004, the pictures were aired on CBS's 60 Minutes. Thereafter, newspapers published the photographs. Although only soldiers serving at the prison were directly implicated, the whole episode tarnished the American intelligence and foreign policy communities.

Protesters against the war gathered at the 2004 presidential nominating conventions to draw attention to Bush's detention and torture policies and the Patriot Act. In August 2004, using New York and 9/11 as a backdrop for their political campaign, the Republican National Convention was held in Madison Square Garden. United for Peace and Justice, which had organized the large February 2003 protests against war in Iraq, organized the main protest rally and march of almost eight hundred thousand, according to the police count on August 29.

The next day, Still We Rise, a coalition of fifty-two New York City–based community organizations for the poor and people of color marched from Union Square to Madison Square Garden and held a rally. Then the Poor People's Economic Human Rights Campaign, a national campaign involving more than sixty organizations, held a rally at the United Nations. Thousands filled the streets, marching down Second Avenue and up Eighth Avenue to Madison Square Garden.

On Tuesday, August 31, members of the antiwar group CODEPINK and other protesters rallied at Fox News Channel headquarters and held a Fox News Shut-Up-a-Thon. About one thousand people protested the network, calling it a propaganda arm of the Republican Party. CODE-PINK got into the convention hall and disrupted prime-time addresses and Bush's acceptance speech. ACT UP activists inside the convention center chanted anti-Bush slogans, interrupting the proceedings. Some protesters from the conscientious objectors' War Resisters League, founded in 1923 as the successor to the War Anti-Enlistment League during World War I, were stopped as they walked from the World Trade Center, and 227 were arrested. Some members headed another way and got close to the convention, where they staged a "die-in." Police arrested fifty-four protesters.

On the streets, the New York Police Department carefully mapped and patrolled the protesters and jumped from hiding to make arrests as protesters marched past, corralling the arrestees with orange netting or fencing that read "Police Line Do Not Cross." These were labeled free-speech zones. The police also closed a street adjoining Union Square where protesters were marching, arresting protesters and bystanders alike.

The police detained most of the arrestees at the recently closed Hudson Pier Depot that had been converted into a temporary prison. The prisoners said the area was overcrowded, dirty, and contaminated with oil and asbestos, which left them with burns and rashes. Two months later, the New York Civil Liberties Union filed a convention lawsuit arising out of the mass arrest on a sidewalk on Fulton Street near the World Trade Center and then another suit from the mass arrest of about 400 people on East Sixteenth Street near Union Square. The ACLU argued that the mass arrest, lengthy detention, and blanket fingerprinting of protesters, journalists, and bystanders violated the First Amendment. Other plaintiffs filed their own lawsuits on the same injuries. In September, following the convention, New York Police commissioner Raymond Kelly had announced, "Most of the security aspects of the Republican National Convention played out the way we anticipated," and he congratulated police for their "fine performance" in arresting so many people. He seemed pleased that two-thirds of those arrested were not residents of New York State.[16]

Almost ten years later, on January 15, 2014, the city agreed to pay $18 million to settle the lawsuits, promising to pay $6.4 million to 430 individual plaintiffs, $6.6 million to settle a class-action lawsuit filed by 1,200 additional people, and $5 million in legal fees. The average payout to the plaintiffs was about $6,400. The city did not admit wrongdoing, claiming victory because, according to Celeste Koeleveld, executive assistant corporation counsel, "the constitutionality of key police policies used during the RNC was upheld, and an effort to restrict the NYPD's ability to police large-scale events was rejected." She conceded that "as the city and the plaintiffs acknowledged in our joint statement, it is in the best interest of those involved in this long-standing litigation to settle the remaining claims." The city could expect that interfering with peaceable protests in the future would be costly.[17]

Given the conflict over the war in Iraq and Afghanistan and his declining popularity, Bush expected a close reelection in 2004. An initiative that helped his campaign was a prescription drug benefit proposal under which Medicare beneficiaries would purchase private insurance plans from private companies. On December 8, 2003, Bush signed into law the Medicare Modernization Act of 2003, whose positive effects outweighed the negative impact. The act created new benefits, and pharmaceutical competition increased, but it was the largest expansion of Medicare benefits since the program's creation in 1965. More funds were spent on the program than the administration had anticipated, which combined with the previously passed tax cuts created a large budget deficit. But Bush's share of the over sixty-five vote increased, which helped him beat John Kerry by a thirty-five electoral-vote margin and with 50.3 percent of the popular vote. Along with the traditional election campaigning, MoveOn.org—which had started e-mail petitions against Clinton's impeachment—spent $21 million trying unsuccessfully to beat Bush.[18]

After Bush's reelection, large numbers turned out to protest at his January 20, 2005, inauguration, just as they had in 2001, this time with a litany of complaints and more evidence for outrage beyond the usurped election. Most of downtown Washington was closed to traffic. The inaugural parade route and other sites were guarded by thirteen thousand police and soldiers, some of whom penned in protesters as they held placards and chanted "Worst president ever!"; "Not my president!"; "Wanted for election fraud!" Along the parade route demonstrators bore signs such as "Guilty of War Crimes—Impeach Bush." Some protesters who had tickets to the swearing in brought large bags that had to be cleared at security checkpoints, slowing the lines. Many Bush supporters did not clear security soon enough to view the ceremonies. A pair of protesters unfurled an antiwar banner during the swearing-in ceremony, only to be removed by police and shouted down by Bush supporters chanting "USA! USA!" Moments later a heckler yelled "Boo!" as Bush delivered his speech.

Bush told the inaugural listeners, "It is the policy of the United States to seek and support the growth of democratic movements and institutions in every nation and culture, with the ultimate goal of ending tyranny in our world."[19]

Beyond Washington, protesters across the country walked out of work and school, denounced the Patriot Act, called out the names of the Iraq War dead, and held candlelight vigils to show their frustration that Bush would be entering a second term. David Williams, a forty-nine-year-old construction company owner from Oakland, California, wearing a T-shirt with Bush's photo and inscribed "International Terrorist," wanted Bush to know he didn't have a mandate. In New Orleans, about fifteen hundred people held a jazz funeral for the death of democracy. In Seattle, about one thousand people rallied, and more than two thousand in Portland, Oregon. Several thousand protesters in downtown San Francisco paraded with signs and banners with slogans such as "Not Our President," "Drop Bush Not Bombs," and "Hail to the Thief." There were a few arrests at some demonstrations when groups of Bush supporters and protesters exchanged shouts as protesters marched by. "I missed the whole thing, thank goodness," said Pat Neary, a real estate agent who joined about fifty people gathered on the snowy town common in Bridgewater, Maine, to protest Bush's reelection.[20]

In his second term, Bush had a new overall policy goal that he called an "ownership society." It involved increased home ownership, entrepreneurship, individual retirement accounts, and health insurance. Congress enacted his proposal for health savings accounts for taxpayers who had high-deductible health plans. The funds contributed to an account would not be subject to federal income tax at the time of deposit. The idea was that using funds in the accounts to pay for some health care would make individuals more aware of the need to control costs.

President Bush also tried to partially privatize Social Security payments to persons with disabilities, the unemployed, and retirees. Some projections indicated that entitlements, including Social Security, would comprise 70 percent of the federal budget by 2030. The rationale was that because people are living longer though retiring in their sixties, Social Security's revenues would not keep pace with requirements for payments. Bush argued that soon the system would be debt ridden and then bankrupt. He wanted younger workers to divert a portion of their payroll taxes, which funds Social Security, into private savings accounts. He went on a "60 Stops in 60 Days" nationwide tour to gain public support for his proposal. The proposal gained little traction, because it was difficult to explain and it appeared the revenue lost might jeopardize Social Security payments.

Despite opposition to Social Security, controversy over his health-care proposals, and his Supreme Court appointments, Bush avoided virulent criticism of his policies except for the Iraq War until August 29, 2005. Then the nation's costliest natural disaster struck along the Gulf Coast in the form of Hurricane Katrina. In the hurricane's aftermath, when the levees broke or were overtopped, lives and property were lost due to the unnatural disaster of incompetent levee building and the ineffective response to the flooding by government at all levels.

As water from Lake Pontchartrain began pouring over New Orleans's levees, flooding 80 percent of the city, tens of thousands of residents were stuck on roofs or carried away in the flood. Electrical power ceased, rescue workers and supplies were too little, too late, and the entire effort at rescue was confused. More than 1,800 people died and up to $80 billion in damage took place along the Gulf Coast in Louisiana, Mississippi, and Alabama combined.[21] Published photographs showed President Bush looking out the window of Air Force One, observing the disaster on the ground with seeming detachment and literal distance. Bush's behavior was so unlike his comforting response to 9/11, and critics mercilessly denounced his apparent ineptitude as disinterest. His early praise of Michael Brown, head of the Federal Emergency Management Agency (FEMA), "Brownie, you're doing a heckuva job," lingered in public memory after the flood. This was true despite his address to the nation from New Orleans on September 15, 2005, when Bush admitted

> The system, at every level of government, was not well coordinated and was overwhelmed in the first few days. Four years after the frightening experience of September 11th, Americans have every right to expect a more effective response in a time of emergency. When the federal government fails to meet such an obligation, I as president am responsible for the problem, and for the solution.[22]

Given the devastation and the slow response, many people agreed with performer Kanye West's conclusion: "George Bush doesn't care about black people."

During the following months, President Bush worked with Congress to secure $126 billion in funding to rebuild the battered region. The levees were rebuilt and are supposedly stronger, but the predominantly black Ninth Ward in New Orleans and other flooded areas still have not recovered. And neither did George W. Bush during his presidency. After Katrina and the floods, Bush's job-approval rating, which had already descended from the 90 percent after 9/11, went into the forties. The coming financial crisis would push his job approval into the thirties by the time he left office.[23]

The protests at Bush's second inauguration would be the last of the usual feel-good, preach-to-the-choir, mass demonstrations of his presidency. In the days leading up to the inauguration, groups that opposed him and his policies had decided they needed another set of strategies. Just being against the war or against Bush had not persuaded enough people to join the opposition. United for Peace, which organized protests on the anniversary of the Iraq War, announced they would use neighbor-to-neighbor connections, which was how Republicans turned out their base in the presidential election. Its Winter/Spring Organizing Drive would encourage smaller member groups to "make three new relationships" with organizations and communities not previously involved in antiwar work. Big city organizations could try to connect with a dozen small city groups. United for Peace told the *San Francisco Chronicle* that they had just hired the Reverend Osagyefo Sekou, a Pentecostal minister in New York, to lead efforts to reach a wider audience though churches, synagogues, and mosques. Not in Our Name, an Oakland antiwar group, said the election outcome taught them that, "surely, the goal expressed by all was the need of resistance to break outside the antiwar movement."[24] But only two of their ten chapters were in states Bush won. The antiwar groups said they would also court returning Iraq war veterans and military families who might help expand the antiwar supporters.

Organizers of a Not One Damn Dime Day protest used the Internet to urge people not to spend any money on Inauguration Day. Jesse Gordon, an activist in Cambridge, Massachusetts, who said he didn't know who started the campaign, told a reporter, "People want a way to make their voices heard." He thought the thousands of e-mails exchanged could be used to start a mailing list for future political mobilizations. In Detroit, Black-Thursday.com asked for no work on inauguration day, and in Orlando, Florida, Citizens Take Charge organized a one-day gasoline boycott.

There were protests each year on the anniversary of the Iraq War, but they grew smaller by 2007. In February of that year, Dana Priest and Anne Hull published their Pulitzer Prize–winning investigative report in the *Washington Post* on the awful medical care and physical environment for the wounded at Walter Reed Army Medical Center. For the first time, the damage done by improvised explosive devices (IEDs) in the Iraq and Afghanistan wars was brought directly to public attention. The IEDs left soldiers with severe, disabling wounds and amputations instead of increasing deaths as in earlier wars. The plight of wounded warriors became another antiwar cause, resulting in the resignation of the secretary of the army and congressional investigations.

Mass marches as protest against the war gave way to e-mail and social media, coordinating and communicating with traditional print and broadcast media. Also, more direct action took place, including demonstrations at government buildings and landmarks, at military installations, and through street blockades. E-mail was soon overtaken by Facebook and other social media, through which protesters increasingly voiced and shared their complaints.[25]

During 2007–2008, the war-weary, post-Katrina nation was battered by the economic recession. The US economy began a sharp decline in late 2007, and by the end of the Bush administration it had collapsed. Consumer spending fell, and hundreds of thousands of people lost their jobs. A housing bubble, blamed on too many unpaid mortgages, burst. Too many people, many of them working-class African Americans, were irresponsibly given mortgages at high interest rates by predatory lenders wanting to make profits and by others acting in response to the federal government's promotion of "ownership." Many Americans' homes went into foreclosure as they could not afford the monthly payments and often hidden high-interest costs. Financial institutions and markets, which Bush had wanted to use to secure Social Security monies and health-care funds, now faced collapse.

In the fall of 2008, to respond to the crisis, Bush consulted with the two presidential candidates, John McCain and Barack Obama, and on October 3, 2008, signed the bill in which Congress established the Troubled Assets Relief Program (TARP) to respond to the economic crisis. TARP included $700 billion in spending to stabilize banks, restart credit markets, support the US auto industry, and help Americans avoid foreclosure on their homes. The Obama administration maintained and grew the stimulus efforts, but the economy grew slowly for years.

The 2008 Democratic National Convention in Denver and the Republican convention in St. Paul drew protesters against the war in Iraq and other issues. Police hemmed in protesters and used other tactics similar to those used in earlier demonstrations. For the Democrats, Obama's opposition to the war, from the outset, set him clearly apart from Hillary Clinton, who, unlike the future president, had initially supported Bush's war resolution.

In both cities, the ACLU sued on behalf of plaintiffs whose First Amendment right to protest was violated and won settlements. In Denver, the settlement was agreed to in 2011, after the usual protracted litigation and delays. The lawsuit, which was filed in 2009, involved ninety-three plaintiffs, who were among those in the mass arrests undertaken by the police. The plaintiffs said police never gave an order to disperse before beginning the arrests and had no probable cause to arrest everyone. The agreement required reform in police procedures and warnings. The agreement required a $200,000 payout to the plaintiffs, with most going to the original eight who sued first and twenty dollars each going to another eight-four people made part of the suit when it was granted class-action status. Noting problems other cities had experienced, Denver arranged payment from an insurance policy the city bought before the convention.[26]

In St. Paul, before the 2008 Republican Convention, the police raided homes of suspected demonstration organizers, reminiscent of the raids in

Washington before the 2000 IMF-World Bank protests. Police also seized several laptop computers, digital cameras, schedules, and seven thousand welcoming guides that organizers planned to distribute to protesters.

These raids did not stop about ten thousand activists, who had obtained a permit, from marching from the capitol to the Xcel Energy Center, the location of the convention. They passed more than two thousand police in riot gear along their route. More police patrolled the area, others flew over in a helicopter, and still others looked down from sniper positions atop business buildings. Most of the marchers were local families and college students spending their Labor Day holiday protesting the GOP and the Iraq War.

But soon black bloc protesters attracted the media's attention as they left the march and began vandalizing property, setting a fire in a garbage dumpster, damaging five police squad cars, and smashing three giant display windows at a Macy's department store. They used the flaming garbage dumpsters to block traffic, while others linked arms and cornered members of the Connecticut Republican delegation as they were walking to a security checkpoint to enter the Xcel Energy Center. Some protesters threw rocks and bottles full of water and bleach; others spit on delegates. Police indiscriminately used pepper spray, rubber bullets, concussion grenades, and excessive force. The riots continued into the night and into the next day. In the end, more than 250 individuals were arrested.

Media coverage of the 2008 Republican convention focused on vice presidential nominee Sarah Palin and presidential nominee John McCain, hardly mentioning any of the nonviolent protests, though there were reports on the anarchists. However, the protests continued, because the war continued, and is continuing.

By January 2009, George W. Bush ended his two terms as an unpopular president, with a 34 percent Gallup disapproval rating, after the ups and downs of his ratings over the eight years of his presidency. His biggest success in the minds of the American people as he left office was that the country wasn't attacked again after September 11, 2001. But the fault lines in the US electoral system that put him in office in the first place, via a 2000 Supreme Court decision, remained significantly unremedied.

Our Civil Rights Commission report on disenfranchisement as a result of the Bush-Gore contested election got some attention. Congress used it in enacting the Help America Vote Act of 2002. The legislation required provisional ballots when an individual's registration could not be validated at the polls on Election Day and made funding available for training and voter education. It established an Election Assistance Commission, but Congress rejected the commission's recommendation that the Assistance Commission require states to meet standards for voting machines and procedures as a condition of receiving federal funds. Since Congress did not accept the Civil Rights Commission recommendation to require compliance with honest practices in compiling and purging lists and standardizing counting and equipment procedures, the Assistance Commission essentially gave each state its financial allocation without any substantive improvement or protection for voters.

After 9/11, energy toward election reform dissipated, not to reemerge until organized opposition to voter ID laws and other methods of voter suppression surfaced with the 2013 Supreme Court decision in *Shelby v. Holder*. By the time Bush was reelected, in 2004, attention to how the United States elects presidents was removed from the forefront of the national dialogue. But, certainly, with the presidential election of 2016, it has resurfaced.

The communications revolution that made organizing resistance faster was also crucial to Barack Obama's 2008 winning presidential campaign. Using fewer paid organizers, his campaign used the Internet to advantage for advertising on YouTube, communication with voters, fund-raising, opposition research, and defending against attacks. The result was the election of an avowedly antiwar, pro–civil rights, pro–women's rights, and prochoice president, who seemed to be what progressive voters and protesters had been seeking. Once he was in office, if they disagreed with some of his policies, they would find themselves trying to influence a "friendly president." Whether influencing either "bad" or "friendly" presidents, protest is an essential ingredient of politics in a democracy.

Lessons Learned

AFTER DONALD TRUMP'S SURPRISING ELECTION, opponents gradually overcame their shock and began thinking of how to oppose his policies and undermine his validity. By December 14, 2016, former congressional staffers had organized a nonprofit and put online a guide to influencing individual members of Congress. *Indivisible* is based in part on Tea Party success in the Republican takeover of Congress in 2010 and immediately went viral. Trump's inauguration stimulated a gigantic Women's March on Washington and in other cities and countries in January 2017 to show discontent and repudiation of any idea that he had received a mandate. There have been other marches on Washington since then—for science, for slowing climate change—and they are becoming a regular part of the anti-Trump landscape.

Though he lost the popular vote by a wide margin, Trump, like previous minority presidents, seems bent on implementing his campaign promises on health care, immigration, military buildup, and other issues. Indigenous people had mounted strong protests, which wrung a concession from President Obama to stop the Keystone pipeline through the Dakotas that would ruin their water, but Trump approved the project in only a matter of days after taking office. The Republicans' proposals for repealing and replacing the Affordable Care Act by cutting coverage, ignited protests at town hall meetings and elsewhere in the early months of his presidency. His executive order calling for a moratorium on refugees and entry of immigrants from certain Muslim-majority countries generated litigation and protests at airports and other places. Negative lower-court decisions followed, as did a modified executive order, which has also been attacked.

None of these battles is over. In addition to the issues mentioned above, Trump's budget proposals making large cuts in social programs, increasing military spending, and promising tax cuts to the wealthy threaten to increase inequality. Much resistance work still needs to be done.

Today, social media and advanced technological communication make it easier to organize than it was back in the 1960s and beyond. The protests and demonstrations described in this book occurred through the use of telephone trees, word of mouth, posters and placards, radio interviews, and snail mail. The Seattle International Monetary Fund and World Trade Organization protests in 1999 were the first international protests coordinated over the Internet using streaming devices, including a virtual sit-in on the WTO website. Communication has become considerably easier over time. Mimeographs in the 1950s, 1960s, and 1970s, and then fax machines and copiers in the 1980s made it easier to get the word out. Telecommunications, cable television, and the Internet became generally available between 1993 and 1995 and radically transformed the way protests were conducted by the end of the 1990s. Chat lines, online bulletin boards, and e-mail also came into vogue in the 1990s, followed in the 2000s by social-networking services such as Facebook (2004) and Twitter (2006). Today, protests organized by movements such as Black Lives Matter and the Women's March rely heavily on social media to inform and mobilize protesters.

But the advances in communication technology also make it easier for authorities to conduct surveillance and spread disinformation to disrupt protest. In addition, the easy use of social media makes it more difficult to sustain protest through disruption, which, along with strategic organizing and education about the issues, produces change. Some people still mistake using Twitter or Facebook as the sum and total of their protest.

Social media is effective for informing potential protesters and disseminating information and photographs of protests. It is also effective for countering media narratives that may focus on individuals—sometimes undercover officers—who decide to foment violence or on police actions against reporters rather than the message of the protests. It is also the case that, in addition to marches, sit-ins, hunger strikes, and acts of guerrilla theater are important demonstrations. But resisters must understand that media cannot cover them unless they *do* something, which is why showing up is still required. Also, the media requires newness, change in tactics, and nimbleness to keep the story alive.

National organizations are at times supportive of mass protest, and at other times they would rather operate by lobbying, litigation, and campaign contributions. Working in coalitions means that they can focus on legislation or policy changes that achieve the movement's goals. Ending US support of apartheid involved a simple slogan that required legislation. Black Lives Matter engaged civil rights organizations such as the NAACP and its Legal Defense Fund in persuading the Obama administration to push consent decrees to reform police departments.

A successful movement insists on a connection between policy and changes in faces or parties. I'll never forget going to Texas in the early 1980s for Jim Wright when he was majority leader of the House of Representatives. At an NAACP dinner, everyone kept walking up and interrupting him, yelling, "Jim, let me tell you this or that." I said to my local host, "Wow, they don't show much respect for the House majority leader" and she replied, "Well, he wouldn't even be in Congress if we hadn't elected him, and if he doesn't do what we want, we won't reelect him."

ACKNOWLEDGMENTS

Sylvia Hill, Cecelie Counts, Roger Wilkins, William Lucy, Adwoa Dunn-Mouton, Cruz Reynoso, Elaine Jones, Ralph Neas, Dom Ruscio, and others shared their recollections of our persistent efforts in the cause of progressive social and political change. Julius Coles, as an Agency for International Development officer in Vietnam, let me stay with him and other Foreign Service officers each time I came in from the field to Ho Chi Minh City (Saigon). Longtime black Republican human rights advocates Samuel Jackson from Kansas and Francis Guess of Tennessee taught me how to negotiate my way in Washington when their party was in control. My high school history teacher, Minerva Hawkins, first taught me about the pains and rewards of resistance.

Mark Boss, Alan Abramson, Alexander Wilson, Bevan Dufty, and Larry Barat, over many dinner discussions, kept me focused. Longtime political communication strategists Emily Tynes and Gwen McKinney helped clarify the narrative.

Melinda Chateauvert provided essential material on the March on Washington movement. Todd Gitlin was kind enough to share a profound essay on the anti–Vietnam War protest before its publication. Maida Odom and Melinda Chateauvert read all or portions of the manuscript at different stages of development and provided insightful commentary. As usual, my graduate students Anthony Pratcher, Rasul Miller, and Camille Suarez, and other students in my seminar and Thursday afternoon drop-in sessions, debated the interpretations.

Working with staff at Beacon, and in particular my editor, Gayatri Patnaik, who persuaded me to write this book, was a great pleasure.

NOTES

INTRODUCTION: HISTORY LESSONS

1. Zeynep Tufekci, *Twitter and Tear Gas: The Power and Fragility of Networked Protest* (New Haven, CT: Yale University Press, 2017).

2. Lorraine Boissoneault, "The Original Women's March on Washington and the Suffragists Who Paved the Way," Smithsonian.com, January 21, 2017; "Bonus Bill Becomes Law," *New York Times*, January 28, 1936; "House Swiftly Overrides Bonus Veto by Roosevelt," *New York Times*, January 25, 1936.

CHAPTER 1: FRANKLIN D. ROOSEVELT AND THE MARCH
ON WASHINGTON MOVEMENT

1. Jervis Anderson, *A. Philip Randolph: A Biographical Portrait* (New York: Harcourt Brace Jovanovich, 1972), vii.

2. Unless otherwise noted, the material in this chapter is taken from David Lucander, "It Is a New Kind of Militancy: March on Washington Movement, 1941–46," PhD diss., University of Massachusetts, Amherst, 2010; the book *Winning the War for Democracy: The March on Washington Movement, 1941–1946* (Champaign: University of Illinois Press, 2014), which is based on Lucander's dissertation; or my own recollections. Melinda Chateauvert characterized this moment as "the first national nonviolent action to demand an end to job discrimination and race segregation" in *Marching Together: Women of the Brotherhood of Sleeping Car Porters* (Urbana: University of Illinois Press, 1998). See also Patricia Sullivan, *Days of Hope: Race and Democracy in the New Deal Era* (Chapel Hill: University of North Carolina Press, 2006), 135; Paula F. Pfeffer, *A. Philip Randolph: Pioneer of the Civil Rights Movement* (Baton Rouge: Louisiana State University Press, 1990).

3. Brooks Jackson, "Blacks and the Democratic Party," FactCheck.org, posted April 18, 2008, http://www.factcheck.org/2008/04/blacks-and-the-democratic-party/.

4. Gerhard Peters and John T. Woolley, "A. Philip Randolph Statement on the Death of the Civil Rights Leader," *American Presidency Project*, May 17, 1979, http://www.presidency.ucsb.edu/ws/?pid=32354. When the president began with "I didn't want

to discriminate against Andy Young by interrupting his remarks," laughter ensued because when I [Mary Frances Berry] introduced the president, I slipped and said, "The President intends to discriminate," instead of "the president intends to demonstrate his commitment, etc.," eliciting howls from my political and civil rights friends in the audience, who laughed even more when I nervously said I had made a Freudian slip.

5. Lucander, "It Is a New Kind of Militancy," 367n5; St. Clair Drake and Horace Cayton, *Black Metropolis: A Study of Negro Life in a Northern City* (New York: Harper, 1962), 84–85; Gary Jerome Hunt, "Don't Buy Where You Can't Work: Urban Boycotts Movements During the Depression," PhD diss., University of Michigan, 1977. See also John Dittmer, *Local People: The Struggle for Civil Rights in Mississippi* (Urbana: University of Illinois Press, 1994).

6. Barbara Ransby, *Ella Baker & the Black Freedom Movement: A Radical Democratic Vision* (Chapel Hill: University of North Carolina Press, 2003), 188.

7. William Doyle, *Inside the Oval Office: The White House Tapes from FDR to Clinton* (New York: Kodansha Press, 1999), chap. 1; Herbert Garfinkel, *When Negroes March: The March on Washington Movement in the Organizational Politics for FEPC* (New York: Macmillan, 1969), 34.

8. David Welky, *Marching Across the Color Line: A. Philip Randolph and Civil Rights in the World War II Era* (New York: Oxford University Press, 2013), 47.

9. William P. Jones, The March on Washington: *Jobs, Freedom, and the Forgotten History of Civil Rights* (New York: W. W. Norton, 2014).

10. David Lucander, *Winning the War for Democracy: The March on Washington Movement, 1941–1946* (Urbana: University of Illinois Press, 2014), 25.

11. Lucander, "It Is a New Kind of Militancy," 37 and notes there cited. I knew Rauh later, in the 1980s, in the Leadership Conference on Civil Rights.

12. David Lucander, "Beyond A. Philip Randolph: Grassroots Protest and the March on Washington Movement," in *Reframing Randolph: Labor, Black Freedom, and the Legacies of A. Philip Randolph*, ed. Andrew E. Kersten and Clarence Lang (New York: New York University Press, 2015), 196.

13. Melinda Chateauvert, *Marching Together: Women of the Brotherhood of Sleeping Car Porters* (Urbana: University of Illinois Press, 1997), 165.

14. Much of this chapter relies on essays in Kersten and Lang, *Reframing Randolph*, and Lucander, "It Is a New Kind of Militancy." See also Cynthia Taylor, "Keeping His Faith: A. Philip Randolph's Working Class Religion," in Kersten and Lang, *Reframing Randolph* and notes there cited; Garfinkel, *When Negroes March*, 92; Pfeffer, *A. Philip Randolph*, 52–53; "2000 Attend Mass Meeting," *Pittsburgh Courier*, October 3, 1942.

15. Enoc P. Waters, "Two Lynched Boys Were Ace Scrap Iron Collectors in Mississippi Town—Part 1," *Chicago Defender*, March 6, 1943; and Enoc P. Waters, "Ignorance and War Hysteria Found Underlying Causes of 2 Lynchings—Part 2," *Chicago Defender*, March 13, 1943.

16. "Randolph Tells Philosophy Behind 'March' Movement," *Chicago Defender*, June 19, 1943; "Randolph to Adopt Gandhi Technique," *Chicago Defender*, January 9, 1943; and "Randolph Blasts Courier as 'Bitter Voice of Defeatism,'" *Chicago Defender*, June 12, 1943, 13.

17. Melinda Chateauvert, "Randolph and Women," in Kersten and Lang, *Reframing Randolph*.

18. "Truman, A. Philip Randolph and the Desegregation of the Armed Forces," *White House Historical Association*, lesson plan, https://www.whitehousehistory.org/teacher-resources/truman-a-philip-randolph-and-the-desegregation-of-the-armed-forces.

19. Ibid.

20. Pfeffer, A. *Philip Randolph*, 137.

21. Doris Kearns Goodwin, *No Ordinary Time: Franklin and Eleanor Roosevelt; the Home Front in World War II* (New York: Simon & Schuster, 2013), 250.

22. Grant Reynolds and A. Philip Randolph letter of June 29, 1948.

23. "Executive Order 9981," July 26, 1948, https://www.trumanlibrary.org/9981a.htm.

24. The Leadership Conference on Civil Rights (LCCR) was founded in 1952. In 1969, the Leadership Conference Education Fund was founded as the education and research arm of the Leadership Conference. The Education Fund's initiatives are grounded in the belief that an informed public is more likely to support effective federal civil rights and social justice policies. In January 2010, the LCCR changed its name to the Leadership Conference on Civil and Human Rights, a move designed to reflect the founding principles of the LCCR and recognize the central importance of both civil rights and human rights in the work of the coalition. The Leadership Conference Education Fund, having been known as the Leadership Conference on Civil Rights Education Fund for many years, revived its original name, the Leadership Conference Education Fund.

25. Ransby, *Ella Baker & the Black Freedom Movement*, 177.

26. Jennifer Scanlon, *Until There Is Justice: The Life of Anna Arnold Hedgeman* (New York: Oxford University Press, 2016); Anna Arnold Hedgeman, *The Trumpet Sounds: A Memoir of Negro Leadership* (New York: Holt, Rinehart, 1964); and *The Gift of Chaos: Decades of American Discontent* (New York: Oxford University Press, 1977).

27. "Civil Rights Pioneer Gloria Richardson, 91, on How Women Were Silenced at 1963 March on Washington," *Democracy Now!*, August 27, 2013, http://www.democracynow.org/2013/8/27/civil_rights_pioneer_gloria_richardson_91.

CHAPTER 2: THE MOVEMENT AGAINST THE VIETNAM WAR

1. In Joyce Hoffman, *On Their Own: Women Journalists and the American Experience in Vietnam* (New York: Da Capo Press, 2008), the introduction explains the accreditation process and includes stories of some of the women journalists, but the author explains that the study is not comprehensive.

2. Todd Gitlin, *The Vietnam War: An Intimate History* (forthcoming) to accompany Ken Burns's documentary series on Vietnam.

3. John A. Farrell, "Nixon's Vietnam Treachery," *New York Times*, December 31, 2016; Robert Dallek, *Nixon and Kissinger: Partners in Power* (New York: HarperCollins, 2007), 73–75. In 1997, Anna Chennault admitted, "I was constantly in touch with Nixon and Mitchell"; see David Taylor, "The Lyndon Johnson Tapes: Richard Nixon's Treason," *BBC News Magazine*, March 22, 2013; Colin Schultz, "Nixon Prolonged Vietnam War for Political Gain—and Johnson Knew About It, Newly Unclassified Tapes Suggest," Smithsonian.com, March 18,2013, http://www.smithsonianmag.com /smart-news/nixon-prolonged-vietnam-war-for-political-gainand-johnson-knew-about -it-newly-unclassified-tapes-suggest-3595441.

4. Todd Gitlin, *The Whole World Is Watching: Mass Media in the Making and Un-making of the New Left* (Berkeley: University of California Press, 1980), 206–8.

5. George C. Herring, *America's Longest War: The United States and Vietnam, 1950–1975*, 4th ed. (Boston: McGraw-Hill, 2002); David Kaiser, *American Tragedy: Kennedy, Johnson and the Origins of the Vietnam War* (Cambridge, MA: Belknap Press of Harvard University Press, 2000); Stanley Karnow, *Vietnam: A History* (London: Penguin, 1997).

6. Tity de Vries, "The 1967 Central Intelligence Agency Scandal: Catalyst in a Transforming Relationship Between State and People," *Journal of American History* 98, no. 4 (2012): 1075–92.

7. Jim Miller, *Democracy Is in the Streets: From Port Huron to the Siege of Chicago* (New York: Simon and Schuster, 1987); Tom Hayden, *Reunion: A Memoir* (New York: Collier, 1989); Jennifer Frost, *An Interracial Movement of the Poor: Community Organizing and the New Left in the 1960s* (New York: New York University Press, 2001); Gitlin, *The Whole World Is Watching*; Francesca Polletta, *Freedom Is an Endless Meeting: Democracy in American Social Movements* (Chicago: University of Chicago Press, 2002).

8. This document represents several months of writing and discussion among the Students for a Democratic Society membership, a draft paper, and revision by its June 11–15, 1962, national convention in Port Huron, Michigan.

9. Seth Rosenfeld, *Subversives: The FBI's War on Student Radicals and Reagan's Rise to Power* (New York: Picador, 2013); Jo Freeman, *At Berkeley in the Sixties: The Making of an Activist* (Bloomington: Indiana University Press, 2003).

10. August 4 is also the day the bodies of three civil rights workers, Michael Schwerner, James Chaney, and Andrew Goodman, were found in Philadelphia, Mississippi, forty-four days after they were murdered.

11. Farrell, "Nixon's Vietnam Treachery"; Dallek, *Nixon and Kissinger*, 73–75.

12. Todd Gitlin, *The Sixties: Years of Hope, Days of Rage* (1987; New York: Bantam Books, 1993); "March on Washington April 17, 1965"; *Resistance and Revolution: The Anti–Vietnam War Movement at the University of Michigan 1965–72*, online art exhibit,

http://michiganintheworld.history.lsa.umich.edu/antivietnamwar/. "We were outraged" at the president's betrayal and by Cold War liberalism more generally, SDS president Todd Gitlin, a graduate student in political science at the University of Michigan, recalled in his 1987 memoir. Gitlin and Paul Booth, coleaders of SDS's Peace Research and Education Project, considered launching a campaign of resistance against the military draft. Ultimately, they decided on a resolution demanding American withdrawal from Vietnam.

13. "March on Washington April 17, 1965," and notes there cited.

14. Ibid.

15. Ibid.; "Protest on Vietnam in Capital Today," *New York Times*, April 17, 1965; "15,000 White House Pickets Denounce Vietnam War," *New York Times*, April 18, 1965.

16. "March on Washington April 17, 1965," and notes there cited; "Protest on Vietnam in Capital Today," *New York Times*, April 17, 1965; and "15,000 White House Pickets Denounce Vietnam War," *New York Times*, April 18, 1965.

17. Lyndon B. Johnson, "Address at Johns Hopkins University: 'Peace Without Conquest,'" April 7, 1965, *American Presidency Project*, http://www.presidency.ucsb.edu /ws/?pid=26877.

18. *Public Papers of the Presidents of the United States: Lyndon B. Johnson, 1965, Book 1* (Ann Arbor: University of Michigan Library, 2005), 394–99; Dror Yuravlivker, "'Peace Without Conquest': Lyndon Johnson's Speech of April 7, 1965," *Presidential Studies Quarterly* 36 (2006): 457–81.

19. Gitlin, *The Whole World Is Watching*, 25.

20. "The Vietnam War: The Jungle War, 1965–1968," *The History Place*, http://www .historyplace.com/unitedstates/vietnam/index-1965.html, accessed August 15, 2017.

21. "March on Washington April 17, 1965."

22. 50 U.S.C. § 462(b)(3).

23. "1965," The Pacifica Radio/UC Berkeley Social Activism Sound Recording Project: Anti-Vietnam War Protests in the San Francisco Bay Area & Beyond, last update May 10, 2012, http://www.lib.berkeley.edu/MRC/pacificaviet.html#1965.

24. "August 30, 1965: LBJ Signs Draft Card-Burning Law," *Today in Civil Liberties History*, http://todayinclh.com/?event=lbj-signs-draft-car-burning-law, accessed August 15, 2017.

25. "300 Pacifists Fail to Stop Troop Train," *Chicago Tribune*, August 13, 1965.

26. See, for example, October 13, 1965, letter to the faculty of the University of Michigan.

27. Alan Rohn, "Napalm in Vietnam War," *The Vietnam War*, last updated April 3, 2017, http://thevietnamwar.info/napalm-vietnam-war/.

28. Beth Bailey, *America's Army: Making the All-Volunteer Force* (Cambridge, MA: Harvard University Press, 2009), 20.

29. United States v. Miller, 367 F.2d 72 (2nd Cir. 1966). Miller served twenty-two months in federal prison.

30. Austin C. Wehrwein, "US Investigates Anti-Draft Groups: Katzenbach Says Reds Are Involved in Youth Drive," *New York Times*, October 18, 1965, cited in Gitlin, *The Sixties*, 95.

31. Paul Montgomery, "Diverse Groups Join in Protest," *New York Times*, November 28, 1965; John Herbers, "Typical Marcher: Middle-Class Adult," *New York Times*, November 28, 1965.

32. Herbers, "Typical Marcher."

33. Ibid.

34. Ibid.

35. Tinker v. Des Moines Sch. Dist., 393 U.S. 503 (1969).

36. Christian G. Appy, *Patriots: The Vietnam War Remembered from All Sides* (London: Ebury, 2003), an oral history of a Senator Fulbright staffer.

37. James Peck, *Underdogs vs. Upperdogs* (Canterbury, NH: Greenleaf Books, 1969); Fred Halstead, *Out Now: A Participant's Account of the Movement in the United States Against the Vietnam War* (New York: Monad Press, 1978).

38. John H. Fenton, "7 War Protesters Beaten in Boston: Draft Card Burning Sparks Attack by 50 School Boys," *New York Times*, April 1, 1966.

39. United States v. O'Brien, 391 U.S. 367 (1968).

40. Ratification, however, was subject to a reservation that napalm can be used if doing so would save civilian lives.

41. John Herbers, "War Foes Clash with House Unit; 17 Are Arrested," *New York Times*, August 17, 1966.

42. Noam Chomsky, "The Responsibility of Intellectuals," *New York Review of Books*, Special Supplement, February 23, 1967, http://www.nybooks.com/articles/1967/02/23/a-special-supplement-the-responsibility-of-intelle/.

43. Douglas Robinson, "Dr. King Proposes a Boycott of War," *New York Times*, April 5, 1967.

44. Douglas Robinson, "Throngs to Parade to UN Today," *New York Times*, April 15, 1967; "Peace Group to Try to See Johnson," *New York Times*, April 19, 1967.

45. Bob Orkand, "'I Ain't Got No Quarrel with Them Vietcong,'" op-ed, *New York Times*, June 27, 2017, https://www.nytimes.com/2017/06/27/opinion/muhammad-ali-vietnam-war.html.

46. Martin Waldron, "Clay Guilty in Draft Case; Gets Five Years in Prison," *New York Times*, July 20, 1967.

47. Patrick E. Jamieson, "Seeing the Lyndon Johnson Presidency Through the March 31, 1968, Withdrawal Speech," *Presidential Studies Quarterly* 29 (March 1999): 134–49.

48. "Continuing Operations Against the 2d NVA Division," Operation COCHISE, August 9–18, 1967, http://www.combatwife.net/cochise.htm, accessed June 19, 2017. The operations forced a major portion of the North Vietnam Army's Second

Division to withdraw temporarily. The US forces Third Battalion command did not delude itself into believing the North Vietnamese would leave the densely populated, rice-bearing lands of the region.

49. "Tragic Valor of Marines at Con Thien," ConsortiumNews.com, May 29, 2016, https://consortiumnews.com/2016/05/29/tragic-valor-of-marines-at-con-thien/. Don North and other journalists who were there after I left wrote graphic descriptions of some of the dangers at Con Thien, including calling it "Hill of Angels" or "a little piece of hell." What I've written is based on my experiences.

50. "October 21, 1967, March," *Resistance and Revolution: The Anti-Vietnam War Movement at the University of Michigan 1965–72*, and notes there cited.

51. Tim Weiner, "Robert S. McNamara, Architect of a Futile War, Dies at 93," obituary, *New York Times*, July 6, 2009.

52. Thomas W. Lippman, "Defense Secretary, Architect of US Involvement in Vietnam Robert McNamara Dies," obituary, *Washington Post*, July 7, 2009, http://www.washingtonpost.com/wp-dyn/content/article/2009/07/06/AR2009070601197.html.

53. Weiner, "Robert S. McNamara."

54. M. A. Farber, "General Disputes Quote in CBS Trial," *New York Times*, November 30, 1984, http://www.nytimes.com/1984/11/30/arts/general-disputes-quote-in-cbs-trial.html.

55. Milton J. Bates et al., eds., *Reporting Vietnam, Part 1: American Journalism, 1959–1969* (New York: Library of America, 1998).

56. James Jones, "Behind LBJ's Decision Not to Run in '68," op-ed, *New York Times*, April 16, 1988, http://www.nytimes.com/1988/04/16/opinion/behind-lbj-s-decision-not-to-run-in-68.html.

57. "Bernard S. Redmont, 98, Broke Story on Vietnam War," obituary, *New York Times*, February 6, 2017.

58. Jones, "Behind LBJ's Decision Not to Run in '68."

59. "H. R. Haldeman's Notes from Oct. 22, 1968," *New York Times*, December 31, 2016, https://www.nytimes.com/interactive/2016/12/31/opinion/sunday/haldeman-notes.html.

60. Farrell, "Nixon's Vietnam Treachery"; Dallek, *Nixon and Kissinger*, 73–75.

61. "The Universities and the War in Vietnam," *Minerva* 7 (Autumn–Winter 1968–69): 325–28; Robert M. Neer, *Napalm: An American Biography* (Cambridge, MA: Harvard University Press, 2015); Mark Rudd, *My Life with SDS and the Weathermen* (New York: Harper Collins, 2014); George Keller, "Six Weeks That Shook Morningside Heights: A Special Report," *Columbia College Today*, Spring 1968, http://www.college.columbia.edu/cct_archive/cct_spring_1968.pdf.

62. T. J. Davis, conversation with the author, March 2017; Roger Kahn, *The Battle for Morningside Heights: Why Students Rebel* (New York: William Morrow, 1970).

63. Bradley Stefan, *Harlem vs. Columbia University: Black Student Power in the Late 1960s* (Champaign-Urbana: University of Illinois, 2009), 5–19, 164–91.

64. Gerald McKnight, *The Last Crusade: Martin Luther King Jr., the FBI, and the Poor People's Campaign* (Boulder, CO: Westview, 1998).

65. Adria Battaglia, "The Rhetoric of Free Speech: Regulating Dissent Since 9/11," PhD diss., University of Texas Austin, 2010, chap. 5 and notes there cited.

66. The National Mobilization Committee to End the War in Vietnam (Mobe) and the Black Panther Party held demonstrations every day during the trials. Judge Julius Hoffman sentenced the defendants and their attorneys to unprecedented prison terms ranging from two-and-a-half months to four years for contempt of court. The convictions were eventually reversed on appeal, and the government declined to bring the case to trial again. In February 1970, five of the remaining seven Chicago Conspiracy defendants were convicted on the charge of intent to incite a riot while crossing state lines, but none was found guilty of conspiracy.

67. Gitlin, *The Whole World Is Watching*, 5. "In 1968, 1969, and 1970, the New Left was like the character in the Roadrunner cartoons who in his fervor and ignorance . . . keeps running and running until he looks down and sees he is running on air. Then he crashes." (ibid., 236). Gitlin also notes that student movements are vulnerable because their members are young, hubristic, and only available for a short time (ibid., 239).

68. Ron Jacobs, *The Way the Wind Blew: A History of the Weather Underground* (London: Verso, 1997).

69. Ibid.

70. Godfrey Sperling, "Nixon's 'Secret Plan' That Never Was," *Christian Science Monitor*, December 9, 1997, https://www.csmonitor.com/1997/1209/120997.opin.column.1.html.

71. Seymour Hersh, "The Scene of the Crime: A Reporter's Journey to My Lai and the Secrets of the Past," *New Yorker*, March 30, 2015: "In November, 1969, I wrote five articles about Calley, Meadlo, and the massacre. I had gone to *Life* and *Look* with no success, so I turned instead to a small antiwar news agency in Washington, the Dispatch News Service."

72. Richard Nixon, "President's News Conference," September 26, 1969, *American Presidency Project*, http://www.presidency.ucsb.edu/ws/?pid=2246.

73. "War Protests," *UPI 1969 Year in Review*, audio recording (1969), http://www.upi.com/Archives/Audio/Events-of-1969/War-Protests.

74. Gitlin, *The Whole World Is Watching*, 223–32 et seq details documents the use of media and the involvement of cabinet officers and the like to discredit the movement in advance of the November 15 march. There were militants who engaged in radical activities and wanted to be seen as different from the moderates, but that was not most people in the march.

75. Howard B. Means, *67 Shots: Kent State and the End of American Innocence* (Boston: Da Capo Press, 2016); Rachel Krantz, *The Biographical Dictionary of Black Americans* (New York: Facts on File, 1992). On May 14, in Jackson, Mississippi, city and state police killed a student at historically black Jackson State College and injured twelve others in a protest stimulated by incorrect news of a murdered black political official, not about the Vietnam War.

76. Mario T. Garcia, *Blowout: Sal Castro and the Struggle for Educational Justice* (Chapel Hill: University of North Carolina Press, 2011).

77. Yvonne Villarreal, "Review: 'Man in the Middle Separates Ruben Salazar from His Myth," *Los Angeles Times*, August 26, 2014.

78. Joan Hoff, *Nixon Reconsidered* (New York: Basic Books, 1995).

79. Mike Gravel, Noam Chomsky, and Howard Zinn, *The Pentagon Papers, 1–4: The Senator Gravel Edition; The Defense Department History of United States Decision Making on Vietnam* (Boston: Beacon Press, 1971). "TV Guide was announcing on September 27, 1969 . . . the networks were going to be shifting toward 'exploring middle and lower-middle-class Americans.'" (Gitlin, *The Whole World Is Watching*, 279.)

CHAPTER 3: WINNING WHILE LOSING

1. "Gubernatorial Candidate Reagan's Speech to Western Wood Products Association," *San Francisco Chronicle*, March 12, 1966.

2. For a complete examination of the controversy over the Civil Rights Commission, see my history of the commission, Mary Frances Berry, *And Justice for All: The United States Commission on Civil Rights and the Continuing Struggle for Freedom in America* (New York: Alfred A. Knopf, 2009), 182–215. Reporter Alfreda Madison told me of Reagan's comment. See p. 184 and notes there cited.

3. Lou Cannon, *President Reagan: The Role of a Lifetime* (New York: Simon & Schuster, 1991), 295; "The Little Strike That Grew to *La Causa*," *Time*, July 4, 1969; Tim Mak and Vivyan Tran, "7 Famous Food Moments," *Politico Photo Gallery* and *AP Photos* (1969), http://www.politico.com/gallery/2012/07/7-famous-food-moments/000254–003180.html.

4. Nathaniel Sheppard Jr., "Protesters Against Reagan March to Capitol," *New York Times*, May 2, 1982.

5. Eric Pianin et al., "250,000 March to Protest Reagan Policies," *Washington Post*, September 20, 1981.

6. Richard C. Auxier, "Reagan's Recession," Pew Research Center, December 14, 2010, http://www.pewresearch.org/2010/12/14/reagans-recession/.

7. Martha R. Burt, *Over the Edge: The Growth of Homelessness in the 1980s* (New York: Russell Sage Foundation, 1992).

8. Jason DeParle, "Mitch Snyder, 46, Advocate of Homeless," *New York Times*, July 6, 1990, http://www.nytimes.com/1990/07/06/obituaries/mitch-snyder-46-advocate-of-homeless.html.

9. Peter Dreier, "Reagan's Real Legacy," *Nation*, February 4, 2011.

10. Sheppard, "Protesters Against Reagan March to Capitol."

11. Larry Green, "15,000 Farmers Angrily Protest Reagan Policies," *Los Angeles Times*, February 28, 1985; George de Lama and Lea Donosky, "Reagan Kills Farm Bill, No Bailout for Farmers in Deep Debt," *Chicago Tribune*, March 7, 1985; Sonja Hillgren, "A Protesting Farmer Told Congress Today," UPI, March 5, 1985.

12. Lawrence K. Altman, "Fewer Aids Cases Filed at End of 1983," *New York Times*, January 6, 1984. But see Allen White, "Reagan's AIDS Legacy/Silence Equals Death," *SFGate*, June 8, 2004, citing the CDC report that there were 4,177 reported cases and 1,807 deaths in the US by April 23, 1984.

13. "Gubernatorial Candidate Reagan's Speech to Western Wood Products Association," March 12, 1966, Ronald Reagan Gubernatorial Audiotape Collection, Reagan Library, https://reaganlibrary.gov/48-governor-s-office/8990-ronald-reagan-gubernatorial-audiotape-collection.

14. Marco Giugni, *Social Protest and Policy Change: Ecology, Antinuclear, and Peace Movements in Comparative Perspective* (Lanham, MD: Rowman & Littlefield, 2004). Later such actions led to an environmental justice executive order in the Clinton administration.

15. Philip Shabecoff, "Bush Cuts Back Areas off Coasts Open for Drilling," *New York Times*, June 27, 1990, http://www.nytimes.com/1990/06/27/us/bush-cuts-back-areas-off-coasts-open-for-drilling.html.

16. Francis X. Clines, "Watt Asks That Reagan Forgive 'Offensive' Remark About Panel," *New York Times*, September 23, 1983, http://www.nytimes.com/1983/09/23/us/watt-asks-that-reagan-forgive-offensive-remark-about-panel.html.

17. Berry, *And Justice for All*, 190–92.

18. Ibid., 182–215.

19. Kiron K. Skinner, Annelies Anderson, and Martin Anderson, eds., *Reagan: A Life in Letters* (New York: Free Press, 2003), 330–40; Lou Cannon, *Reagan* (New York: G. P. Putnam & Sons, 1982), 381–86; William Johnson, "The Push to the Right: Reagan's Alter Ego Meese Stands at Pinnacle of US Law Enforcement," *Globe and Mail*, August 29, 1985.

20. Shelby v. Holder, 570 US (2013) 133 SCT 2612; Charles S. Bullock III and Katharine Ingles Butler, "Voting Rights," in *The Reagan Administration and Human Rights*, ed. Tinsley E. Yarbrough (New York: Praeger, 1985), 29–31; Michael Pertschuk, *Giant Killers* (New York: W. W. Norton, 1986), 148.

21. 446 U.S. 55 (1980).

22. 79 Stat. 437, as amended, 42 U.S.C. § 1937.

23. Frank R. Parker, "The 'Results' Test of Section 2 of the Voting Rights Act: Abandoning the Intent Standard," *Virginia Law Review* 69 (1983): 715, 726–29.

24. 446 U.S. at 60–61, 65.

25. Bolden v. City of Mobile, 542 F. Supp. 1050 (1982). Judge Pittman offered several suggestions for a new system, but perhaps because of Justice Blackmun's chastisement, he withheld imposing a remedy to give the Alabama legislature and Mobile voters a chance to devise a new system.

26. Parker, "The 'Results' Test of Section 2 of the Voting Rights Act," 735–37.

27. "Should the Supreme Court Strike Down the 'Preclearance' Provision of the Voting Rights Act?," *US News & World Report, Debate Club*, February 27, 2013, https://www.usnews.com/debate-club/should-the-supreme-court-strike-down-the-preclearance-provision-of-the-voting-rights-act.

28. Keith Nicholls, "Politics and Civil Rights in Post–World War II Mobile," in *Mobile: The New History of an Old City*, ed. Michael V. R. Thomason (Tuscaloosa: University of Alabama Press, 2001), 271–72.

29. The legislation included the Civil Rights Act of 1957, the Civil Rights Act of 1960, the Civil Rights Act of 1964, the Voting Rights Act of 1965, and the Fair Housing Act of 1968. It helped to organize the 1963 March on Washington and promoted the establishment of a Civil Rights Division in the Justice Department. LCCR also led the fight for Title IX of the Education Amendments of 1972, which prohibits sex discrimination in educational programs or activities receiving federal funding; for Section 504 of the Rehabilitation Act of 1973, which prohibits discrimination against people with disabilities in federally assisted programs; and for the Age Discrimination Act of 1975, which prohibits age discrimination in programs or activities receiving federal funds.

30. Leadership Conference on Civil and Human Rights and Leadership Conference Education Fund, http://www.civilrights.org/about/history.html; Steven F. Lawson, *Black Ballots: Voting Rights in the South, 1944–1969* (New York: Columbia University Press, 1976), 144–45, 385n22; Robert Frederick Burk, *The Eisenhower Administration and Black Civil Rights* (Knoxville: University of Tennessee Press, 1984), 206–7; Pfeffer, *A. Philip Randolph*, 108; Pertschuk, *Giant Killers*, 149–50. LCCR membership has since grown to 180 organizations. The Sears quotation is from Ralph Neas's notes, copy in my possession.

31. Bullock and Butler, "Voting Rights," 31, quoting *Congressional Quarterly Weekly Report*, December 26, 1981, p. 2605.

32. Ibid., 32; Pertschuk, *Giant Killers*, 157–59, 176; Robert Pear, "Accord Reported on Extending Voting Rights Act," *New York Times*, July 30, 1981; Robert Pear, "New Split Looms on Voting Rights," *New York Times*, August 1, 1981.

33. Herbert H. Denton, "Black Social Club Donates $600,000 to Activist Groups," *Washington Post*, August 3, 1981.

34. Dianne Pinderhughes, "Interest Groups and the Extension of the Voting Rights Act in 1982," paper delivered at the American Political Science Association meeting, 1983; Henry Hyde, "The Voting Rights: To What Are Minorities Entitled?,"

op-ed, *Washington Post*, August 4, 1981; Birmingham march, WashingtonPost.com, August 10, 1981.

35. Olatunde Johnson, "The Story of Bob Jones University v. United States: Race, Religion, and Congress' Extraordinary Acquiescence," in *Statutory Interpretation Stories*, ed. William N. Eskridge Jr., Philip P. Frickey, and Elizabeth Garrett (New York: Foundation Press, 2011), 128–43; Philip B. Heymann and Lance Liebman, eds., *The Social Responsibilities of Lawyers: Case Studies* (New York: Foundation Press, 1988), 132–40 (copies of relevant documents are reprinted at 154–75); Norman C. Amaker, *Civil Rights and the Reagan Administration* (Washington, DC: Urban Institute Press, 1988), 52–53. Bob Jones University was not the only segregated school that maintained tax exempt status for years after the IRS issued the rule denying it. In May 1978, the United States Commission on Civil Rights called attention to the existence of at least seven segregated schools in Mississippi that were still tax exempt. Tinsley E. Yarbrough, "Tax Exemptions and Private Discriminatory Schools," in Yarbrough, *The Reagan Administration and Human Rights*, 110–11.

36. Johnson, "The Story of Bob Jones University v. United States," 142–44; Amaker, *Civil Rights and the Reagan Administration*, 53.

37. Johnson, "The Story of Bob Jones University v. United States," 130–32, 144.

38. Edwards, quoted in John Herbert Roper, "The Voting Rights Extension Act of 1982," *Phylon* 45, no. 3 (1984): 193.

39. Johnson, "The Story of Bob Jones University v. United States," 145–46; Heymann and Liebman, *Social Responsibilities of Lawyers*, 140–47; Amaker, *Civil Rights and the Reagan Administration*, 5–54.

40. Johnson, "The Story of Bob Jones University v. United States," 146; Heymann and Liebman, *Social Responsibilities of Lawyers*, 149.

41. Johnson, "The Story of Bob Jones University v. United States," 147; Heymann and Liebman, *Social Responsibilities of Lawyers*, 149–50.

42. Edwards, quoted in Roper, "The Voting Rights Extension Act of 1982," 193.

43. Voting Rights Act Amendments of 1982, Pub. L. 97–205, June 29, 1982, 96 Stat. 131, § 2.

44. Steven Roberts, "President Backs Bipartisan Plan on Voting Law," *New York Times*, May 4, 1982; Remarks on Signing H.R. 3112 into Law, 18 Weekly Comp. Pres. Doc. 846 (June 29, 1982); Howell Raines, "Voting Rights Act Signed by Reagan," *New York Times*, June 30, 1982; Bullock and Butler, "Voting Rights," 32, citing Nadine Cohodas, "Administration Defends Civil Rights Record," *Congressional Quarterly Weekly Report*, February 4, 1983, 266.

45. Through alumni and friends, the college maintains extensive ties to conservative think tanks and Republican politicians. Lee Edwards, *Freedom's College: The History of Grove City College* (Washington, DC: Regnery, 2000), 274–75. In its official materials, the college highlights its consistent ranking by the Young America's

Foundation and Free Congress Foundation as one of the most conservative schools in the country and also its teaching and advocacy of free market economic theory.

46. Grove City College v. Bell, 465 U.S. 555, 557–76 (1984).

47. Bob Packwood, "Discrimination Aided," *New York Times*, April 20, 1984 (Packwood was a Republican senator from Oregon); Robert Pear, "Justice Dept. Open to New Rights Bill," *New York Times*, March 3, 1984 (civil rights advocates concerns); Amaker, *Civil Rights and the Reagan Administration*, 59.

48. Smith, quoted in Linda Greenhouse, "High Court Backs Reagan's Position on a Sex Bias Law," *New York Times*, February 29, 1984; Pear, "Justice Dept. Open to New Rights Bill," (quoting William Bradford Reynolds on Reagan administration position); Robert Pear, "23 Cases on Civil Rights Closed After Court Rules," *New York Times*, June 3, 1984; Hugh Davis Graham, "The Storm over Grove City College: Civil Rights Regulation, Higher Education, and the Reagan Administration," *History of Education Quarterly* 18, no. 4 (Winter 1998): 418 (DOJ action, citing "Injustice Under the Law: The Impact of the *Grove City College* Decision on Civil Rights in America," n.d., Leadership Conference on Civil Rights Papers, Manuscript Division, Library of Congress). Within three months, it shut down twenty-three enforcement investigations, narrowed eighteen others, and was reviewing thirty-one more.

49. Robert Pear, "Bill to Extend Rights Coverage Sets Off Dispute," *New York Times*, March 7, 1984; Robert Pear, "Trying to Tie Strings to Federal Aid," *New York Times*, March 11, 1984 (bills introduced); Martin Tolchin, "Senate Crushes a Move to Block Civil Rights Bill," *New York Times*, September 30, 1984 (for the Goldwater and Wallop quotations); "House Approves Civil Rights Bill," Associated Press, June 27, 1984 (regarding House approval and Hatch quotation); Martin Tolchin, "Civil Rights Plan Shelved as Senate Moves on Spending," *New York Times*, October 3, 1984.

50. Larry Margasak, "Bill to Restore Civil Rights Protections Advances, but Abortion Fight Looms," Associated Press, May 23, 1985; "Abortion Limits Rejected in Bill," *New York Times*, May 23, 1985.

51. Stuart Taylor, "Ad Against Bork Still Hotly Contested," *New York Times*, October 21, 1987. The ad is available for viewing on YouTube, https://www.youtube.com/watch?v=NpFe1olkF3Y.

52. Elena Kagan, "Review: Confirmation Messes, Old and New," *University of Chicago Law Review* 62, no. 2 (Spring 1995): 919–42.

53. Irvin Molotsky, "Senate to Override Court, Votes a Bill Extending Anti-Bias Laws," *New York Times*, January 29, 1988; Irvin Molotsky, "House Passes Bill to Upset a Limit on US Rights Law," *New York Times*, March 3, 1988; Helen Dewar, "Religious Leaders Assail Moral Majority's 'Scare Tactics' Over Civil Rights Bill," *Washington Post*, March 19, 1988; David Anderson, "Civil Rights Leaders, Abortion Foes Clash Over Legislation," United Press International, March 26, 1987.

54. Charlotte Saikowski, "Will Civil Rights Stand Come Back to Haunt Bush Campaign?" *Christian Science Monitor*, March 23, 1988; Civil Rights Restoration Act, Pub. L. No. 100–259, 102 Stat. 28 (1988). Soon after the statute was enacted, Grove City College prohibited students from accepting federal grants. In 1996, it prohibited their accepting Stafford and Plus loans, and it has continued those policies and accepted no other federal funding, enabling it to avoid complying with Title IX. As of May 2011, the full-time faculty of 148 included only 44 women, nearly half of whom were concentrated in three academic departments: modern languages (7), education (6), and physical education (6). Men chaired twenty of the twenty-three departments. Among eleven top-level administrators listed in the 2010–2011 college catalogue— president, provost, vice presidents, deans, and assistant deans—there was one woman.

55. Pub. L. No. 100–430, 102 Stat. 1619 (1988) (amending 42 U.S.C. §§ 3601–19 (1982)) (Fair Housing Act Amendments); Pub. L. No. 98–399, 98 Stat.1473 (1983) (King holiday); Pub L. No. 100–383, 102 Stat. 903 (1988) (redress for Japanese internment); Ralph Neas interview with author, March 2009.

56. Details on all federal judges can be found on the website of the Federal Judicial Center, Biographical Directory of Federal Judges, http://www.fjc.gov, the information can be sorted by appointing president, among other ways; Sheldon Goldman, *Picking Federal Judges: Lower Court Selection from Roosevelt Through Reagan* (New Haven, CT: Yale University Press, 1997), 308–9; Herman Schwartz, *Packing the Courts: The Conservative Campaign to Rewrite the Constitution* (New York: Charles Scribner's Sons, 1988), 58; Donald R. Songer, Sue Davis, and Susan Haire, "A Reappraisal of Diversification in the Federal Courts: Gender Effects in the Courts of Appeals," *Journal of Politics* 56, no. 2 (May 1994): 425–39, 425n2.

57. Gerhard Peters and John T. Woolley, "Republican Party Platform of 1980," American Presidency Project, July 15, 1980, 297, http://www.presidency.ucsb.edu/ws /index.php?pid=25844#axzz1KwNtLc1O; Goldman, *Picking Federal Judges*.

58. During his 1966 gubernatorial campaign, Reagan criticized the outgoing governor, Pat Brown, for appointing political cronies and promised to take politics out of judicial appointments. In public statements, personal correspondence, and his 1990 autobiography *An American Life* (New York: Simon & Schuster), Reagan characterized the process as apolitical. In *An American Life*, for example, he wrote, "In a country ruled by laws, it seemed to me that nothing was more important than removing politics from the process of choosing judges. . . . So I sent out an order to set up a new system to take politics out of the selection of judges." The system, as he described it, involved getting input from lawyers in the community, a citizen's group in the same community, and judges sitting in the district. Their recommendations, he continued, were sent to him and ranked. "Without exception," he wrote, "I chose the person at the top of the rating. Politics or party membership played no part in the selection" (174–75); Kiron K. Skinner, Annelise Graebner Anderson, and Martin Anderson, eds., *Reagan: A Life*

in Letters (New York: Free Press, 2003), 208 (letter to "Bob Circa 1974"); "Transcript of Ronald Reagan's Remarks at News Conference in Los Angeles," *New York Times,* October 15, 1980.

59. Lou Cannon, *Governor Reagan: His Rise to Power* (New York: Public Affairs, 2003), 219–22.

60. Peters and Woolley, "Republican Party Platform of 1980," 287–91; Goldman, *Picking Federal Judges,* 287–91; Schwartz, *Packing the Courts,* 53–54, 61–62; Nancy Scherer, *Scoring Points: Politicians, Activists, and the Lower Federal Court Appointment Process* (Stanford, CA: Stanford University Press, 2005), 18–19. Scherer argues that diminished senatorial and American Bar Association influence in appellate court nominations has continued under succeeding administrations of both parties. All agree that Senate leaders successfully resisted administration efforts to weaken senatorial privilege with respect to district court nominations.

61. Goldman, *Picking Federal Judges,* 291–96; Schwartz, *Packing the Courts,* 60–61; David Alistair Yalof, *Pursuit of Justices: Presidential Politics and the Selection of Supreme Court Justices* (Chicago: University of Chicago Press, 1999), 142–44.

62. Adam Meyerson, "One Hundred Conservative Victories: The Reagan Years," *Policy Review* (Spring 1989) ("Confirmation of Stephen Williams as judge on US Appeals Court for D.C. Circuit added to earlier confirmations of Robert Bork, Kenneth Starr, Laurence Silberman, James Buckley, and Antonin Scalia [later replaced by Douglas Ginsburg], gives conservatives a majority on nation's second most important court, formerly the bastion of liberal judicial activism."); Schwartz, *Packing the Courts,* 152.

63. Nominees' ages when they joined the court, by nominating president: Reagan—O'Connor (51), Scalia (46), Kennedy (51); George H. W. Bush—Thomas (43); Clinton—Souter (50), Ginsburg (66), Breyer (56); George W. Bush—Alito (55), Roberts (50); Obama—Sotomayor (55), Kagan (50); Trump—Gorsuch (49).

64. Schwartz, *Packing the Courts,* 59–60, 133–34, 142–44. Notable examples of the Reagan youth movement were Richard A. Posner, Seventh Circuit, age forty-two; Frank Easterbrook, Seventh Circuit, age thirty-five; Kenneth Starr, DC Circuit, age thirty-six; J. Harvey Wilkinson, Fourth Circuit, age thirty-nine; Alex Kozinski, Ninth Circuit, age thirty-four; and Edith Jones, Fifth Circuit, age thirty-six.

65. Joan Biskupic, *Sandra Day O'Connor: How The First Woman on the Supreme Court Became Its Most Influential Justice* (New York: ECCO, 2005), 70–80; Adam Liptak, "Court Under Roberts Is Most Conservative in Decades," *New York Times,* July 24, 2010.

66. Analysis of their jurisprudence is beyond the scope of this book, but a quantitative study of the appellate courts by the political scientist Nancy Scherer suggests the degree to which politicized judicial selection affects outcomes. Scherer compares the voting behavior of judges appointed by Presidents Nixon through Clinton in cases decided by the courts of appeals between January 1, 1994, and December 31, 2001,

involving four types of issues: claims of race discrimination; federalism issues under the Ninth and Tenth Amendments; abortion; and the legality of searches and seizures under the Fourth Amendment. In cases involving claims of race discrimination, Scherer found that, using Clinton appointees as a baseline and holding a host of other variables constant, the probability of a vote against a minority plaintiff increases by 28 percentage points with a Reagan or Bush appointee, and increases to a lesser extent with a Nixon appointee. Carter appointees vote about the same as Clinton appointees. In the cases involving federalism issues, again using Clinton appointees as a baseline and holding other variables constant, the likelihood of a vote against the federal government increases by 21 percentage points with a Reagan appointee and by 27 percentage points with a Bush appointee. Nixon appointees are more likely to vote against the federal government by 16 percentage points, and Carter appointees less likely by 7 percentage points. Scherer, *Scoring Points: Politicians, Activists, and the Lower Federal Court Appointment Process* (Palo Alto, CA: Stanford University Press, 2005).

67. Steve Roberts, "Reagan's Social Issues: Gone but Not Forgotten," *New York Times*, September 11, 1988.

CHAPTER 4: THE FREE SOUTH AFRICA MOVEMENT

1. Mary Frances Berry, "The Wait for Mandela Is Over," *Philadelphia Inquirer*, February 22, 1990.

2. Unless otherwise noted, this chapter is based on conversations with other members of the FSAM steering committee, my own recollections, and Randall Robinson's recollections in Randall Robinson, *Defending the Spirit: A Black Life in America* (New York: Dutton, 1998).

3. Leo Robinson, "From Local to National: Bay Area Connections," in *No Easy Victories: African Liberation and American Activists over a Half Century, 1950–2000*, ed. William Minter, Gail Hovey, and Charles Cobb Jr. (Trenton, NJ: Africa World Press, 2008).

4. "Sharpeville Massacre, 21 March 1960," *South African History Online*, http://www.sahistory.org.za/topic/sharpeville-massacre-21-march-1960, accessed August 15, 2017.

5. Gitlin, *The Whole World Is Watching*, 34–43.

6. "Nelson Mandela Death: In His Own Words," *BBC News*, December 6, 2013, http://www.bbc.com/news/world-africa-10743920.

7. National Security memorandum #39 NSSM, Office of the Historian, US State Department, https://history.state.gov/historicaldocuments/frus1969-76v28/d17.

8. Eric J. Morgan, "His Voice Must Be Heard: Dennis Brutus, the Anti-Apartheid Movement, and the Struggle for Political Asylum in the United States," *Peace and Change: A Journal of Peace Research* (2015), http://www.academia.edu/24814099/His _Voice_Must_Be_Heard_Dennis_Brutus_the_Anti-Apartheid_Movement_and_the _Struggle_for_Political_Asylum_in_the_United_States. Activists began a campaign

to boycott Gulf to protest the oil company's support of Portuguese colonial rule. Union workers around the country began refusing to unload ships carrying Rhodesian chrome.

9. Maida Odom and Gerald B. Jordan, "Sullivan Calls for Embargo," *Philadelphia Inquirer*, June 4, 1987.

10. Article 19, chapter 10.210–10–220, San Francisco Administrative Code (1978).

11. Robert K. Massie, *Loosing the Bonds: The United States and South Africa in the Apartheid Years* (New York: Nan Talese, 1997).

12. His later opposition to LGBT rights on religious grounds did not come up at the time.

13. David Lawrence Horne, "The Pan-African Congress: A Positive Assessment," *Black Scholar* 5 (July–August 1974): 2–11; Earl Ofari, "A Critical Review of the Pan-African Congress," *Black Scholar* 5 (July–August 1974): 12–15.

14. They included Democratic senators Paul Sarbanes of Maryland, Alan Cranston from California, Christopher Dodd from Connecticut, and Carl Levin of Michigan. Republican senator Lowell Weicker from Connecticut was there and kept Senators Richard Lugar and Nancy Kassebaum informed. From the House were Fauntroy and Democratic members Mickey Leland from Texas, Steve Solarz from New York, Mervyn Dymally from California, George Crockett from Michigan, William Gray from Pennsylvania, and Howard Wolpe, chair of the subcommittee, from Michigan.

15. Odom and Jordan, "Sullivan Calls for Embargo."

16. Berry, "The Wait for Mandela Is Over"; Christopher Wren, "South Africa's New Era: Mandela Freed Urges Step-Up in Pressure to End White Rule," *New York Times*, February 12, 1990.

17. Sylvia Hill, "Progress Report on Congress Organizing," *Black Scholar* 5 (April 1974): 35–39.

CHAPTER 5: A "KINDER AND GENTLER" PRESIDENCY

1. Spencer Rich, "HHS Secretary Still Struggling for Influence," *Washington Post*, January 17, 1990. Those suggested by antiabortion groups ended up being named to top jobs, including Constance Horner as undersecretary; Sullivan said she was already on his short list.

2. "Wholesale Price of AIDS Drug Reduced 20%," *Chicago Tribune*, September 19, 1989.

3. Lyndsay Griffiths, "AIDS Protestors Taunt Bush at White House," *Chicago Sun-Times*, October 13, 1992.

4. Edwin Chen, "Thousands Join War Protests Across US," *Los Angeles Times*, October 21, 1990.

5. *Annual Report of the Attorney General of the United States* (Washington, DC: Dept. of Justice, 1989), 15, 14.

6. Richard Bryant Treanor, *We Overcame: The Story of Civil Rights for Disabled People* (Falls Church, VA: Regal Direct, 1993); Joseph A. Califano Jr., *Governing America: An Insider's Report from the White House and the Cabinet* (New York: Simon and Schuster, 1981), 60–61; Annie Nakao, "A Big Day for Disabled: Occupation of Federal HEW Offices in 9 Cities Ignited Movement 20 Years Ago," *San Francisco Examiner*, April 4, 1997; Susan Schweik, "Lomax's Matrix: Disability Black Power and the Black Power of 504," *Disability Studies Quarterly* 31 (2011), http://dsq-sds.org/article/view/1371/1539.

7. "Handicapped Win Demands: End HEW Occupation," *Black Panther*, May 7, 1977.

8. Schweik, "Lomax's Matrix"; Joseph D. Whitaker, "Handicapped Gather at HEW to Agitate for Rights," *Washington Post*, April 6, 1977; Rev. Cecil Williams, Glide Memorial Church, April 1977, "Day by Day, You Educated America," http://longmoreinstitute.sfsu.edu/patient-no-more/april-1977-day-day; Roberta Ann Johnson, "Mobilizing the Disabled," in *Waves of Protest: Social Movements Since the Sixties*, ed. Jo Freeman and Victoria Johnson (Lanham, MD: Rowman and Littlefield, 1999), 25.

9. See the discussion in Arlene Mayerson, "The History of the Americans with Disabilities Act: A Movement Perspective," Disability Rights Education & Defense Fund (July 1992), https://dredf.org/news/publications/the-history-of-the-ada/.

10. Eaton Williams Jr., "Disabled Persons Rally, Crawl Up Capitol Steps; Scores Protest Delays in Passage of Rights Legislation: The Logjam in the House Is Expected to Break Soon," *Los Angeles Times*, March 13, 1990.

11. Berry, *And Justice for All*, 256.

12. Ibid.

13. Ibid., 257.

14. Dorothy Gilliam, "Bush Risking Racial Firestorm," *Washington Post*, May 28, 1990, https://www.washingtonpost.com/archive/local/1990/05/28/bush-risking-racial-firestorm/a1ead784-2110-4e1a-ac35-86bb764d37c9/.

15. The White House and Justice Department stalled, but Congress passed the Kennedy-Hawkins bill. A filibuster failed. In the November 1990 elections, Jesse Helms, in his reelection race, used a "quota" ad to defeat Harvey Gantt. So did Pete Wilson in his attempt to defeat Dianne Feinstein. Leaders of major civil rights organizations urged Bush not to veto the Civil Rights Act, but he said he couldn't go along with a measure that could lead to hiring quotas. Associated Press online, May 19, 1990.

16. Berry, *And Justice for All*, 258–59; Derrick Z. Jackson, "Focus: Chamber Speaks, Bush Listens," *Boston Globe*, October 18, 1990.

17. Terence Hunt, "President Vetoed a Major Civil Rights Bill Monday," *Boston Globe*, October 28, 1990; Steven Holmes, "President Vetoes Civil Rights Act, Says Law Would Mean Job Quotas," *New York Times*, October 23, 1990.

18. Steven Holmes, "On Job Rights Bill, a Vow to Try Again in January," *New York Times*, October 26, 1990, http://www.nytimes.com/1990/10/26/us/on-job-rights-bill-a-vow-to-try-again-in-january.html?pagewanted=all.

19. Berry, *And Justice for All*, 265; Ann Devroy, "President Signs Civil Rights Bill," *Washington Post*, November 22, 1991.

20. C. Boyden Gray, "Civil Rights: We Won, They Capitulated," op-ed, *Washington Post*, November 14, 1999.

21. Berry, *And Justice for All*, 267; William T. Coleman and Vernon E. Jordan Jr. "How the Civil Rights Bill Was Really Passed," *Washington Post*, November 18, 1991.

22. Berry, *And Justice for All*, 268; House Subcommittee on Civil and Constitutional Rights, Hearings on Police Brutality, 102d Congress, 1st sess. March 20 and April 17, 1991, 320.

23. Ann Devroy, "Bush Reaches Out to Activists for Advice, Presidential Leadership, Huge Federal Effort Are Urged," *Washington Post*, May 2, 1992; "Bush Links Rioting to 60's Policy," *Washington Post*, May 7, 1992; Berry, *And Justice For All*, 368–69.

24. Darrell Holland, "Church Leader Who Visited LA Said Violence Must End," *Cleveland Plain Dealer*, May 5, 1992.

25. "History of Marches and Mass Actions," National Organzation for Women, http://now.org/about/history/history-of-marches-and-mass-actions/, accessed August 30, 2017.

26. *Capital Times* (Madison, Wisconsin), April 6, 1992.

27. James H. Rubin, "Opposing Sides Dispute Impact of Abortion Ruling," *New York Times*, July 1, 1992.

28. Phillip Dine, "Women Leaders Arrested in Protest at White House," *St. Louis Post Dispatch*, July 1, 1992.

29. "Abortion Foes List Wanted Doctors," *Palm Beach Post*, April 4, 1992; "AntiAbortion Activists Print Posters on Doctors," Seattle Times News Service, April 10, 1992.

30. "Abortion Foes Post 'Wanted' Doctors," Associated Press, April 5, 1992.

31. Harry Stainer, "Abortion Issue Divides 2 Rallying Feminist Groups," *Cleveland Plain Dealer*, August 23, 1992.

CHAPTER 6: THE ADAPTABLE PRESIDENT

1. Holly Morris, "Civil Rights Leaders Back End to Military Ban, Coretta King, Joseph Lowery at Forefront," *Atlanta Journal Constitution*, July 1, 1993.

2. Richard Berke, "Democrats Woo Black Lawmakers," *New York Times*, September 9, 1993.

3. "Oklahoma City Bombing," History.com, http://www.history.com/topics/oklahoma-city-bombing, accessed August 15, 2017.

4. Barbara Vobejda and Judith Havemann, "2 HHS Officials Quit Over Welfare Changes," *Washington Post*, September 12, 1996; Peter Edelman, "The Worst Thing Clinton Has Done," *Atlantic*, March 1997; Cathy Cohen, *The Boundaries of Blackness: AIDS and the Breakdown of Black Politics* (Chicago: University of Chicago Press, 1999), chap. 1.

5. Michelle Alexander, *The New Jim Crow: Mass Incarceration in the Age of Color-blindness* (New York: New Press, 2010).

6. Violent Crime Control and Law Enforcement Act of 1994, 108 Stat. 1796 (1994); Anne Gearan and Abby Phillip, "Clinton Regrets 1996 Remark on 'Super-predators' After Encounter with Activist," *Washington Post*, February 25, 2016; James Forman Jr., *Locking Up Our Own: Crime and Punishment in Black America* (New York: Farrar, Straus & Giroux, 2017).

7. Brooke A. Masters, "Gays Hope for Higher Profile During Inaugural Week and Beyond," *Washington Post*, December 19, 1992.

8. Eric Schmitt, "Pentagon Chief Warns Clinton on Gay Policy," *New York Times*, January 25, 1993.

9. Urvashi Vaid, preface *to Virtual Equality: The Mainstreaming of Gay and Lesbian Liberation* (New York: Anchor, 1995).

10. Morris, "Civil Rights Leaders Back End to Military Ban"; "Arena: Gays in the Military—Should Don't Ask, Don't Tell Be Scrapped?," discussion, *Politico*, February 2, 2010.

11. Joshua Gamson, "Whose Millennium March?," *Nation*, March 30, 2000; Robin Toner, "A Gay Rights Rally over Gains and Goals," *New York Times*, May 1, 2000.

12. Carey Goldberg, "Hispanic Groups Prepare to March to Washington," *New York Times*, October 9, 1996; Pamela Constable, "Immigrants Demand Rights, Respect at DC March," *Washington Post*, October 13, 1996.

13. *Migration News* 3, no. 11 (December 1996); David Johnston, "Government Quickly Using Power of New Immigration Law," *New York Times*, October 22, 1996; George Ramos, "Thousands of Latinos March in Washington," *Los Angeles Times*, October 13, 1996.

14. Randy Shaw, *Reclaiming America: Nike, Clean Air, and the New National Activism* (Berkeley: University of California Press, 1999), 6–7.

15. *Federal Register* 64, Presidential Documents 63169, 63170 (Washington, DC: Government Printing Office, November 18, 1999).

16. Mike Moore, "Seattle Conference Doomed to Succeed," *WTO News*, November 30, 1999.

17. Battaglia, "The Rhetoric of Free Speech"; Bob Young and Jim Brunner, "City to Pay Protesters $250,000 to Settle WTO Suit," *Seattle Times*, January 17, 2004; Colin McDonald, "Jury Says Seattle Violated WTO Protesters' Rights," *Seattle Post-Intelligencer*, January 30, 2007.

18. United States District Court for the District of Columbia Notice of Class Action, Proposed Class Settlement and Hearing, Becker, et al., v. District of Columbia, et al., Case No. 01- CV-0811 (PLF)(JMF), http://www.classactionlitigation.com/beckrnot.pdf; "Reporters Arrested Covering Violence in DC, Miami, War in Chechnya," Reporters Committee on Freedom of the Press, October 31, 2011; Becker, et al. v. District of Columbia, et al. No. 1:2001cv00811—Document 345 (D.D.C. 2009).

19. Adam Nagourney, "Mrs. Clinton Backs Gun-Control Initiative," *New York Times*, May 10, 2000; Robin Toner, "Mothers Rally to Assail Gun Violence," *New York Times*, May 1, 2000; "Million Mom Full Fifteen Year Timeline," Brady Campaign to Prevent Gun Violence, http://www.bradycampaign.org/million-mom-full-15-year-timeline.

20. Robinson, *Defending the Spirit*, 240–41.

21. Howard Kurtz, "A Striking Success," *Washington Post*, June 23, 1994.

22. Ibid.

23. Robinson, *Defending the Spirit*, 193–205, 215; Karen De Witt, "Hunger Strike on Haiti: Partial Victory at Least," *New York Times*, May 9, 1994.

24. "How Rape Was Declared a War Crime," *Sound Vision*, April 7, 2017; Jill Bendery, "No Place to Run No Place to Hide: The Balkanization of Women's Bodies," *On the Issues* (Summer 1993); Alan Riding, "European Inquiry Says Serbs' Forces Have Raped 20,000," *New York Times*, January 9, 1993.

25. Beverly Allen, *Rape Warfare: Hidden Genocide in Bosnia-Herzegovina and Croatia* (Minneapolis: University of Minnesota Press, 1996).

26. "The Perils of Indifference: Lessons Learned from a Violent Century," official White House transcript, April 12, 1999.

27. "Text of Clinton's Rwanda Speech," *CBS News*, March 25, 1998, http://www.cbsnews.com/news/text-of-clintons-rwanda-speech/; "Text of Clinton's Rwanda Speech March 25, 1998," Associated Press, 1998.

28. Kenneth J. Cooper, "House Approves US Canada-Mexico Trade Pact on Vote of 234–200, Giving Clinton Big Victory," *Washington Post*, November 18, 1993.

29. Alison Mitchell, "Impeachment the Overview: Clinton Impeached; He Faces Senate Trial, 2d in History; Vows to Do Job Till Term's Last Hour," *New York Times*, December 20, 1998; http://www.carolmoore.net/photos/impeach-demo-photos.html.

30. Dexter Scott King and Ralph Wiley, *Growing Up King: An Intimate Memoir* (New York: Grand Central, 2003).

31. Berry to Reno, February 1999, copy in my possession; Berry, *And Justice for All*, 291.

32. Steven A. Holmes, "Clinton Orders Investigation on Possible Racial Profiling," *New York Times*, June 10, 1999.

CHAPTER 7: UNNATURAL DISASTERS

1. NBC Universal's Concert for Hurricane Relief, September 2, 2005.

2. US Commission on Civil Rights, "Voting Irregularities in Florida During the 2000 Presidential Election: Executive Summary," http://www.usccr.gov/pubs/vote2000/report/exesum.htm.

3. Bush v. Gore, 531 U.S. 98 (2000).

4. David Montgomery and Arthur Santana, "After Seattle, Protest Reborn," *Washington Post*, April 2, 2000; Alex S. Vitale and Brian Jordan Jefferson, "The Emergence

of Command and Control Policing in Neoliberal New York," in *Policing the Planet: Why the Policing Crisis Led to Black Lives Matter*, ed. Jordan T. Camp and Christina Heatherton (New York: Verso, 2016).

5. "Restoration of the Mexico City Policy," *Memorandum for the Administrator of the United States Agency for International Development Federal Register*, March 28, 2001; Unborn Victims of Violence Act of 2004 (Public Law 108–212).

6. Dan Rather, *Late Night with David Letterman*, September 17, 2001; Victor Navasky, foreword to Barbie Zelizer and Stuart Allen, eds., *Journalism After September 11* (London: Routledge, 2002), xiii–xviii, xv; Howard Kurtz, "CNN Chief Orders 'Balance' in War News: Reporters Are Told to Remind Viewers Why US Is Bombing," *Washington Post*, October 31, 2001.

7. Congress passed a law in 2008 after the fact, authorizing his actions. James Risen and Eric Lichtblau, "Bush Lets US Spy on Callers Without Courts," *New York Times*, December 16, 2005; Robert Swansbrough, *Test by Fire: The War Presidency of George W. Bush* (New York: Palgrave Macmillan, 2008), 105–22.

8. Del Quentin Wilber, "DC to Pay $8.25 Million to Settle Mass Arrest Suit," *Washington Post*, December 16, 2009.

9. "Cities Jammed in Worldwide Protest of War in Iraq," CNN.com, February 16, 2003.

10. Ibid.

11. Michaeleen Doucleff, "US Spent $1.4 Billion to Stop HIV by Promoting Abstinence. Did It Work?," NPR, May 3, 2016, http://www.npr.org/sections/goatsandsoda/2016/05/03/476601108/u-s-spent-1-4-billion-to-stop-hiv-by-promoting-abstinence-did-it-work.

12. Robin Toner, "Huge Crowds in Washington for Abortion-Rights Rally," *New York Times*, April 25, 2004.

13. Cameron W. Barr and Elizabeth Williamson, "Women's Rally Draws Vast Crowd," *Washington Post*, April 26, 2004.

14. Barr and Williamson, "Women's Rally Draws Vast Crowd."

15. Gonzales v. Carhart, 550 US 124 (2007).

16. Schiller v. City of New York, 245 F.R.D. 112 (S.D.N.Y. 2007; 2007 WL 735010).

17. In Re city of New York, 607 F.3d 923 (2010); "City and Plaintiffs Agree to Settle Republican National Convention Litigation," press release, New York City Law Department Office of the Corporation Counsel, January 15, 2014.

18. "Poll: Support for Bush, Iraq War Dropping," CNN.com, May 22, 2004; Bruce Bartlett, "Medicare Part D: Republican Budget Busting," *New York Times*, November 9, 2013.

19. Peter Baker and Michael Fletcher, "Bush Pledges to Spread Freedom," *Washington Post*, January 21, 2005.

20. "Bush Second Inaugural," *NBC Nightly News*, January 21, 2005.

21. "Katrina Impacts," *Hurricanes: Science and Society,* http://hurricanescience.org/history/studies/katrinacase/impacts/, accessed August 15, 2017.

22. "President Discusses Hurricane Relief in Address to Nation," September 15, 2005, White House Archives, https://georgewbush-whitehouse.archives.gov/news/releases/2005/09/20050915-8.html.

23. Bruce Alpert, "George W. Bush Never Recovered Politically from Katrina," *New Orleans Times Picayune,* August 28, 2015; "George W. Bush Presidential Job Approval," Gallup, http://www.gallup.com/poll/116500/presidential-approval-ratings-george-bush.aspx, accessed June 19, 2017.

24. Joe Garofoli, "Bush Protesters Rethink Tactics: Critics Hope to Move Beyond Self-Satisfaction of Anti-War Protests, Gain Wider Voting Base," *San Francisco Chronicle,* January 16, 2005, http://www.sfgate.com/politics/joegarofoli/article/Bush-protesters-rethink-tactics-Critics-hope-to-2738286.php.

25. Kristen M. Daum and Tami Abdollah, "Protests Mark Iraq's War 5th Anniversary," *Los Angeles Times,* March 20, 2008.

26. John Ingold, "Finally Denver Settles Over Mass Arrests During 2008 Democratic Convention," *Denver Post,* October 12, 2011.

INDEX